PRAISE FOR NICARAGUA

"Professor Kovalik sweeps away fake news and fake history disseminated by the mainstream media concerning Nicaragua, documenting a gruesome history of US interventionism and crimes in Nicaragua. Highlighting the achievements of the Sandinistas in the field of human rights and social justice, he refutes US caricatures and denounces CIA attempts to destabilize Nicaragua to facilitate undemocratic 'regime change.'"

—ALFRED DE ZAYAS, UN Independent Expert for the promotion of an international democratic and equitable order

"Dan Kovalik courageously and clinically exposes the chaos that plagued Nicaragua in 2018 as a deadly U.S.-backed coup aimed at unraveling a popular revolutionary worker's movement—not the popular uprising Western media portrayed it as. His book is an essential corrective."

—MAX BLUMENTHAL, *The Gray Zone*

"Virtually every news item in print or on TV about Nicaragua, from its past to the present, demonizes Nicaragua, ignoring its uplifting public programs while describing it as a repressive dictatorship. Nicaragua is a perfect example of being the object of nearly universal, orchestrated fake news and false information. In fact, the reporting is so horrible, one can substitute the exact opposite of whatever is being said about its government and democratically elected President, Daniel Ortega, and Vice President, Rosario Murillo. Repressive? Just the opposite, very free and open. Dictatorship? Nicaragua operates with free and fair elections, observed, far more open than those in the United States, for example.

"Now Daniel Kovalik, international human rights attorney who has been visiting Nicaragua since 1987, has provided a clearly written and well-documented (453 endnotes), factual account—an honest history of Nicaragua from the 1850s to the present—in less than 180 pages. Readers will be well versed to contradict the constant lies presented to the public by the incredibly corporate-controlled news and Silicon Valley media. Hats off to Mr. Kovalik for setting the record straight and producing this handy guide for rebutting all the news media bullshit."

—S. BRIAN WILLSON, lawyer, author of *Don't Thank Me for My Service*, resident of Nicaragua

MORE PRAISE

"Retracing US-Nicaraguan history from Grant through the present, Kovalik distinguishes between rhetoric and truth, quislings and Sandinistas, imperialists and revolutionaries. The wannabe American Left should read this book. Kovalik demolishes the dominant Western narrative. He shares the hard-won gains of today's Nicaragua, explains Daniel Ortega's enduring popularity and powerfully defends why the Sandinistas are deserving of our continued solidarity. This book is must-read to understand Nicaragua in the 21st century and fills a stark gap in contemporary Latin American Studies. May it lead to further study in situ and less arm-chair pontificating by politicians and intellectuals."

—SOFIA M. CLARK, Professor of Political Science, UNAN-Managua

"Dan Kovalick's book, *Nicaragua: A History of U.S. Intervention and Resistance,* sheds light on how the history of U.S. interventions has shaped the destiny of the Nicaraguan people, a destiny of unyielding commitment to freedom and independence. Kovalick's analysis shows how the current dirty war against President Daniel Ortega uses the same covert techniques and unethical practices deployed numerous times by the U.S. government during the last 150 years, from the bloodshed imposed by the Monroe Doctrine to the Contra scandal under Reagan.

"The recent imposition by the U.S. of economic sanctions and the funding of violent insurrection against the Sandinista government has done serious damage to programs aimed at decreasing poverty, maintaining food independence, and providing social services for millions of Nicaraguans. In that sense, Kovalick provides an accurate portrayal of the abuses of a super power against one of the poorest nations in the Americas, still fighting until this day to defend the dignity and wellbeing of its people.

"Kovalik's book, written from the perspective of someone who has been visiting the country for decades and immersing himself in the Nicaraguan reality of daily life, is a refreshing reminder that it is still possible to write truthfully about history."

—PATRICIO ZAMORANO, Director of the Council on Hemispheric Affairs, COHA.org

NICARAGUA
A HISTORY OF U.S. INTERVENTION & RESISTANCE

Daniel Kovalik

Clarity Press, Inc.

© 2023 Daniel Kovalik

ISBN: 978-1-949762-60-0
EBOOK ISBN: 978-1-949762-64-8

In-house editor: Diana G. Collier

COVER PHOTO: John Paul II Plaza, Managua (Daniel Kovalik, July 19, 2018).

ALL RIGHTS RESERVED: Except for purposes of review, this book may not be copied, or stored in any information retrieval system, in whole or in part, without permission in writing from the publishers.

Library of Congress Control Number: 2022948149

Clarity Press, Inc.
2625 Piedmont Rd. NE, Ste. 56
Atlanta, GA 30324, USA
www.claritypress.com

This book is dedicated to the memory of Socrates Espinoza Muñoz, a brave Sandinista fighter killed in battle on June 28, 1979, just days before the Sandinista Triumph on July 19, 1979. He is survived by many family members who remember and love him, including my good friend Abigail Espinoza Muñoz, the younger sister of Socrates. As she told me with tears in her eyes, it felt as if her life ended when she learned of his death as a child.

CONTENTS

ACKOWLEDGMENTS viii

INTRODUCTION. 1

CHAPTER 1: Lawyers, Guns & Money. 16

CHAPTER 2: Insurrection & Repression 49

CHAPTER 3: The Triumph 87

CHAPTER 4: Reagan's Brutal War Against Nicaragua 105

CHAPTER 5: Dark Days Return 140

CHAPTER 6: The Sandinistas Return 167

CHAPTER 7: The April 2018 Crisis. 194

CONCLUSION. 245

AFTERWORD by Orlando Zelaya Olivas 253

ENDNOTES 273

INDEX 293

ACKNOWLEDGEMENTS

I wish to thank the following individuals whose knowledge, wisdom and encouragement helped me along the way in researching and writing this book: S. Brian Willson, Stephen Sefton, Orlando Zelaya, Jill Clark, Sofia Clark, William Camacaro, Jaime Hermida, Francisco Campbell, Michael Campbell, Becca Mohally Renk, Coleen Littlejohn, John Perry, Abigail Epinoza Muñoz, Nils McClune, Nan McCurdy, Nora McCurdy, Idañia Castillo, Scarleth Escorcia and Erika Takeo.

INTRODUCTION

How did I become interested in Nicaragua and why does it matter so much to me that I have now written a book about it?

In the 1980s, very few would ask such a question, because in 1979, Nicaragua, and the Sandinista Revolution were big topics in conversation and even a subject of popular culture. The Clash's last album was entitled "Sandinista." The Rolling Stones had a song about the Sandinista Revolution on their album *Emotional Rescue,* entitled "Indian Girl," which mentions the pitched battles in the town of Masaya between the guerillas and Somoza's National Guard. There was also a popular film starring Nick Nolte and Gene Hackman about the Sandinista Revolution, entitled *Under Fire.* Now those days are long gone, and for many are a distant memory—if they ever knew about that at all.

My first encounter with Nicaragua and the Sandinista Revolution was in the Fall of 1979. I was eleven years old and attending a small Catholic junior high school, St. Andrew's, in Milford, Ohio, a small town outside Cincinnati. At the start of the school year, two new students enrolled: Juan and Carlos García. They were from Nicaragua but, as I would come to understand later, did not fit the usual profile of a Nicaraguan, at least in the 1970s. They were very big—both in height and weight. Juan, who was in my class, eventually played center on our basketball team. And they both spoke English very well.

At one point, I asked Juan what brought him to Milford to attend school. He told me that he had left his home country of Nicaragua because there was a revolution over the summer which had toppled his father who was president at the time of the revolt. Apparently, Juan and Carlos were the sons of the dictator, Anastasio Somoza, though that name meant nothing to me. I didn't understand then what had taken place in Nicaragua with the revolution or what was taking place even at that time, but the story of the toppling of a government which caused these two boys to flee their country created a lasting impression on me, igniting an ongoing curiosity about Nicaragua and Central America—a region which would be in the news almost daily for the next decade.

Meanwhile, Somoza would soon be gunned down in Asunción, Paraguay by Argentine revolutionaries, and just as suddenly as they appeared in my school, Juan and Carlos left at the end of the year. I never heard from them again.

The other world event that impacted me greatly around this time was the murder of Archbishop Oscar Romero in El Salvador on March 24, 1980.[1] Romero would later be canonized as a saint by the Vatican in October 2018. As a Roman Catholic myself, the gunning down of Romero while he was saying Mass in a hospital chapel was shocking. This was especially disturbing as it became apparent that he was most certainly murdered by forces being funded by the United States. I cannot say enough about how this assassination impacted me. For the first time, I began to question the nature of my country and my government. Was the U.S. really the force for good that we were told it was? This was a question which began to quietly nag at me, though I wasn't prepared as yet to answer this question in the negative, or to embrace all of the implications of this query. But the seeds were now being planted for a radical way of looking at my country and the world.

While at a Catholic high school in Cincinnati in the mid-1980s, I had a very rightwing teacher named Father John Putka, who invited a leader of the Nicaraguan Contras—the terrorist group President Reagan was supporting in an effort to restore the *ancien regime* to power in Nicaragua—to speak to us. The Contra leader (I don't remember his name now) claimed that the Contras were freedom fighters who were battling the allegedly totalitarian Sandinistas in an attempt to restore democracy to Nicaragua. This was indeed the prevailing line at the time, and I largely accepted it, though I also had my doubts. Given that everyone conceded that Somoza had been a corrupt and repressive dictator, what democracy was there to be restored by the Contras? This question became even more relevant when I learned that many of the Contras were in fact former leaders and members of Somoza's brutal National Guard.

By 1986, I was in college, very politically engaged, and still wondering about Nicaragua and what was really going on there. Indeed, the questions gnawed at me, and I felt that I couldn't really know the truth unless I went there to see first-hand for myself.

Then, in the spring of 1987, those of us focusing on Nicaragua and the Contra War were shocked to learn of the death of American Ben Linder in northern Nicaragua. Ben was an amazing human being. He was an engineer working on a hydro-electric project in Nicaragua while also working on the Sandinistas' vaccine campaign and entertaining children as a clown and juggler.[2] On April 28, 1987, Ben, along with two Nicaraguans accompanying him, was shot at close-range by the Contras and killed. He was only 27 years old. It was clear that he had been assassinated. Daniel Ortega, president at the time, served as a pallbearer at his funeral.

Ben's mother stated at his funeral: "My son was brutally murdered for bringing electricity to a few poor people in northern Nicaragua. He was murdered because he had a dream and because he had the courage to make that dream come true. ... Ben told me the first year that he was here, and this is a quote, 'It's a wonderful feeling to work in a country where the government's first concern is for its people, for all of its people.'"[3]

In 1983, Ben Linder wrote a letter to his friends, the words of which still ring true today. As Ben wrote:

> Somoza left the country in shambles. Flat broke. He took everything but the debt. Granted, there are still problems now, but there is a feeling of hope, there is a feeling of building a new country. At times this exuberance leads to false hopes. Many more times it leads to a say in life that has never before been experienced for the majority of Nicaraguans.
>
> It is hard for us to imagine the meaning of a paved street. In Nicaragua there are two seasons—wet and dry. When it is wet the mud is two feet deep. When it is

dry the dust permeates everything. Eating becomes like a picnic at the beach, all the food crunches with dust. Slowly more and more streets are being paved.

But that is only the physical benefits. The more important changes are the feelings of being in control. This is in control of walking out at night and not being afraid of being shot by the police, as was the case before 1979. It is establishing control of the neighborhood and the workplace. It is in education, healthcare and word. This is control. Granted there is still a long way to go, but people are still fighting. Not fighting against the government, but rather fighting old habits, old customs and the results of centuries of oppression.[4]

The death of Ben Linder, far from discouraging American activists from going down to Nicaragua to show solidarity for the people and their fledging revolution, only strengthened our resolve to do so.

In the summer of 1987, I saw an ad in *The Nation* magazine by the Nicaragua Network, offering the opportunity to participate in a reforestation brigade in Ocotal, Nicaragua near the Honduran border. With the money I had saved up working that summer, I was able to just pay for the trip. I took the month of September off from school in order to go.

The experience I had was life-transforming, as it was for so many who visited Nicaragua at that time.

When I landed in Managua, Nicaragua on September 1, 1987, I learned of the tragedy that befell another American trying to stand with the people of Nicaragua and Central America against U.S. intervention and war. On that day, Vietnam veteran turned peace activist, S. Brian Willson, was run over by a train carrying armaments for Reagan's war bound for Central America.[5] Brian, along with other members of Veterans for Peace, was sitting on the tracks to try to prevent the arms from being delivered. The train, instead of slowing or stopping for the protesters, sped up. Brian was unable to get off the tracks in time and was struck. He lost both of his legs above the knee, part of his brain and a

Brian Willson and his partner, Ulda, with Daniel Ortega
DANIEL KOVALIK, JANUARY 10, 2022

shoulder as a result but somehow managed to survive. Despite all of this, Brian became a prolific writer, authoring a number of books, including *Don't Thank Me for My Service*.

As I learned later from Brian himself, who has become a good friend of mine, this was no accident. As Brian explained, he did not have a death wish. He had gone to the site of the protest—a U.S. Naval yard in California—every day for a few weeks before the action and had witnessed the train, which only travelled at about 5 miles an hour at that point, slow and even stop for people who were trying to cross the track. On the fateful day in 1987, the engineer of the train did not slow for the protesters, but in fact sped up. As Brian learned through the process of discovery in the lawsuit he later brought against the government, the engineer had orders from above to run down the protesters if necessary in order to keep going, and that is exactly what he did. The U.S. government ended up settling the case for a handsome sum in light of the evidence of its murderous intentions produced by the lawsuit, and Brian used the proceeds to buy a home in Grenada, Nicaragua where he lives to this day.

I also learned recently from Brian an incredible fact. After he was run down by the train, Rosario Murillo—a Sandinista guerilla in the fight against Somoza, the long-time wife of Daniel Ortega, and the current Vice-President of Nicaragua—came to California with all of her children to visit Brian in the hospital as he recovered.

Brian Willson is considered a hero of the Nicaraguan Revolution and was recently named the 38th Comandante of the Sandinistas. At Daniel Ortega's recent inauguration in January of 2022, which I attended sitting next to Brian and his partner Ulda on the main stage, Daniel spoke of Brian and his sacrifice for Nicaragua and Central America. As I have often noted, the Nicaraguan people are quick to forgive and forget the terrible things done to them by others, but they never forget others' acts of kindness and sacrifice on their behalf. Ben Linder, as an instance, is still well-remembered in Nicaragua where a number of buildings and projects still bear his name. The same can be said of Roberto Clemente, the legendary Pittsburgh Pirates baseball player who died trying to take humanitarian aid to Nicaragua after the 1972 earthquake. Clemente decided to personally deliver such help after reading that Somoza was stealing all of the aid being sent for relief. His plane tragically crashed before making it to Nicaragua. To this day, schools, stadiums, and parks are named after him in Nicaragua. And, when I publicly gave Daniel a Roberto Clemente jersey at his January 2022 inauguration, the crowd cheered, knowing full well who Clemente was, even these many decades later. This reaction of the crowd is even more incredible given the fact that the jersey did not even contain his name, only his number: 21.

The conditions in Managua in September of 1987 were simply shocking. Because of the war, there were frequent blackouts in the city and the poverty was stunning. I vividly remember being at a restaurant with my delegation when at least a dozen children, literally dressed in rags, came to the window, knocking on it and begging for food. I had never witnessed such a sight. It was reminiscent of the final scene of the movie *Suddenly Last Summer* when Montgomery Clift's character is surrounded and accosted by poor children in a foreign land. To see Nicaragua now, with children well-fed, educated and properly clothed, shows how far that country has come since that time.

After a couple of days of orientation, we made the 4-hour or so journey to Ocotal. Many of the roads we traversed on our journey were simply dirt. And the infrastructure of Ocotal was abysmal. Electric power was intermittent at best, clean water was

Children, Ocotal
DANIEL KOVALIK, SEPTEMBER, 1987

non-existent and fresh food was in small supply. As a result, all the members of the delegation were violently ill for the entire month we were there. I lost 20 pounds in that short time. And the poverty in Ocotal was even worse than it was in Managua. When I look at my photos of the children back then it makes me want to cry. Many of the children had no shoes and their clothes were worn to the point of becoming threadbare. Those were difficult times in Nicaragua and especially in war zones such as Ocotal. The Contra war had been going on by that point for about 7 years, the economy had been wrecked and the people were weary. Machine-gun fire could be heard nearly every night. While this provided only a small taste of the war, it was enough to make me understand how terrible and cruel it was.

Ocotal is a historic Nicaraguan city located in the Department of Nueva Segovia. It is famous for being the site of battles between the U.S. Marines and the peasant guerilla forces of Augusto C.Sandino (Sandino's full name is Augusto Nicolás Calderón Sandino, but he is nicknamed Augusto César Sandino) from 1927 to 1933. In 1927, after the U.S. Marines were unable to defeat Sandino's fighters on the ground, the U.S. Navy took to the skies to indiscriminately bomb the town. In short, they hoped to terrorize the population into submission. Some have described this as the first aerial bombing of a civilian population, though it seems that Tripoli, Libya had been on the receiving end of such a bombing by Italy back in 1911. Still, it was one of the first.

Summing up the testimony of those who lived through the U.S. assault, one historian describes the U.S. aerial bombings as "a remorseless faceless enemy inflicting indiscriminate violence against homes, villages, livestock, and people who, regardless of age, gender, physical strength, social status, [and who] lacked any defense except to salvage their belongings."[6] According to a fellow combatant of Sandino who lived through the aerial bombing and the sacking of Ocotal that followed,

> The aviation did much damage to the population between loss of life and loss of property, causing thirty-six deaths in our forces.... Sandino's troops stood up

INTRODUCTION

to the planes as best they could, downing one enemy plane (a Fokker), and after this the Sandinista troops withdrew, and that's when the Yankee troops enter[ed] the already destroyed town, causing the greatest destruction, sacking the images and bells from the ruins of the church and throwing them in the river. . . . There were hundreds of deaths here, among them children, women.[7]

The church mentioned here is the Parish Church of Our Lady of the Assumption, a Roman Catholic Church constructed between 1803 and 1879. That church is still there—right across from what was memorialized as "July 16" Central Park, a park

Our Lady of the Assumption Church, Ocotal
DANIEL KOVALIK, MARCH, 2022

later constructed to commemorate the Battle of Ocotal between Sandino's forces and the U.S. Marines—a battle which took place in part around the Church itself, with Sandino's forces trying to fend off the Marines from the roof and tower of the Church. The Church, moreover, still holds regular services. Indeed, I attended Sunday services at this Church during my stay in Ocotal in 1987.

I returned to this Church in March of 2022. It looks exactly as I remember it, including with the life-sized statue of the bloodied, crucified Jesus laying prone—an almost obligatory accessory to any Catholic Church in Latin America. It is worth noting that Nicolás Antonio Madigral y Garcia—the long-time Bishop of Nueva Segovia who lived from 1898 to 1977—served for 50 years in the Church in Ocotal, including during the Battle of Ocotal. His statue stands just across the street from the Church. Nicolás was a friend to the poor and the indigenous in the area, and he is buried in the poor, indigenous community of Mozonte, which is about a 20-minute drive from Ocotal. The plaque over his tomb explains that he is buried in Mozonte, home of "the indigenous community that loved him." The Sandinista leaders in Ocotal consider Nicolás one of their own, and are very proud of him. I know this because in 2022 they made a point of driving me to the place where he is buried to see his tomb.

The Vatican has begun the process of considering Nicolás for sainthood and has already attributed at least one miracle to him: when he died, his body gave off a holy scent—that of flowers. In that era, while it is possible that the Marines may have seen themselves as righteous Christians attacking the "savages" in Ocotal—despite the fact that they unceremoniously ransacked a church—the very opposite was in fact true.

While the Church looks exactly as I remember it, the city of Ocotal does not. There is no comparison now between its present appearance and the poor town I lived in back then. Most of the roads of Ocotal are now paved, all the residents have electricity, the city has internet and cellphone service, and there are new restaurants and cafes that never existed, including a brand-new Asian fusion restaurant. The people look well-fed, well-dressed and prosperous, and the Sandinista government just inaugurated a brand-new, state-of-the-art hospital there. Nearly all of this progress has come in the past 15 years since the Sandinistas were voted into power after the years of neoliberal misrule from 1990 to 2006 which had done little to nothing to meet the people's needs or to build or attend to infrastructure.

Back when I was going to services at the Church in 1987, the Contras were the ones terrorizing Ocotal and other parts of Nicaragua with the backing of the U.S. I remember sitting there in one of the pews along with hundreds of Nicaraguans who had come to pray for an end to the war. I wondered why God was not answering the prayers of these very poor people, and the absence of any reply to this query would soon lead me to leave the Church. Moreover, the U.S.-backed war against these people made it impossible for me to ever see my country in the same light again. I knew for sure then that the U.S. was not the beacon of freedom and democracy it claimed to be, but a predator that preyed upon peoples and nations much weaker than itself. At the time of the Contra War, Nicaragua was a country of not even 3 million people—most of them under the age of 18—and it was the second poorest country in the Hemisphere. To say that the U.S. picked an unfair fight is a profound understatement, and it made me ashamed to be an American.

Funeral Service of Victim of Contras
DANIEL KOVALIK, SEPTEMBER, 1987

To understand the U.S.'s incessant meddling in Nicaragua, one must go back to the Monroe Doctrine of 1823. Pursuant to this Doctrine, the U.S. government claimed sole dominion and control over the Western Hemisphere and over Latin America, which it saw as its "backyard." Lest one believe this to be a relic of the past, President Joe Biden recently referred to Latin America as the U.S.'s "front yard,"[8] possibly believing that this at least sounds like a more polite reference for the earlier terminology expressing the U.S.'s condescending views towards its southern neighbors. The (Teddy) Roosevelt Corollary to the Monroe Doctrine, moreover, states that the U.S. reserves the right to intervene militarily in the region to protect its claimed interests there. This Corollary, too, is still fully operational as far as the U.S. is concerned.

Besides possibly Haiti, there is no country in the Western Hemisphere in which the U.S. has intervened more often in pursuit of its interests *du jour* than Nicaragua. And Nicaragua has paid a huge price for this intervention. And yet, with each new intervention, the U.S. government and compliant media try to persuade us that all of the instances of intervention, as brutal as they have been, never really took place, and that the U.S. is not really intervening now. Indeed, we are urged to believe that all of this is nothing but the paranoid delusions of Daniel Ortega and his party, the Sandinista National Liberation Front (FSLN).

In his 2005 Nobel Prize acceptance speech, the great British writer Harold Pinter captured this phenomenon precisely:

> The United States supported and in many cases engendered every right wing military dictatorship in the world after the end of the Second World War. I refer to Indonesia, Greece, Uruguay, Brazil, Paraguay, Haiti, Turkey, the Philippines, Guatemala, El Salvador, and, of course, Chile. The horror the United States inflicted upon Chile in 1973 can never be purged and can never be forgiven.
>
> Hundreds of thousands of deaths took place throughout these countries. Did they take place? And are they in all cases attributable to U.S. foreign policy?

The answer is yes they did take place and they are attributable to American foreign policy. But you wouldn't know it.

It never happened. Nothing ever happened. Even while it was happening it wasn't happening. It didn't matter. It was of no interest. The crimes of the United States have been systematic, constant, vicious, remorseless, but very few people have actually talked about them. You have to hand it to America. It has exercised a quite clinical manipulation of power worldwide while masquerading as a force for universal good. It's a brilliant, even witty, highly successful act of hypnosis.[9]

Pinter singles out Nicaragua as a special instance of the U.S.'s brutal interventionist history combined with the simultaneous denial of said brutality:

The tragedy of Nicaragua was a highly significant case. I choose to offer it here as a potent example of America's view of its role in the world, both then and now.

I was present at a meeting at the U.S. embassy in London in the late 1980s.

The United States Congress was about to decide whether to give more money to the Contras in their campaign against the state of Nicaragua. I was a member of a delegation speaking on behalf of Nicaragua but the most important member of this delegation was a Father John Metcalf. The leader of the U.S. body was Raymond Seitz (then number two to the ambassador, later ambassador himself). Father Metcalf said: "Sir, I am in charge of a parish in the north of Nicaragua. My parishioners built a school, a health centre, a cultural centre. We have lived in peace. A few months ago a Contra force attacked the parish. They destroyed everything: the school, the health centre, the cultural centre. They raped nurses and teachers, slaughtered doctors, in the most brutal manner. They behaved like savages. Please demand that the U.S. government withdraw its support from this shocking terrorist activity."

Raymond Seitz had a very good reputation as a rational, responsible and highly sophisticated man. He was greatly respected in diplomatic circles. He listened, paused and then spoke with some gravity. "Father," he said, "let me tell you something. In war, innocent people always suffer." There was a frozen silence. We stared at him. He did not flinch.

Innocent people, indeed, always suffer.

Finally somebody said: "But in this case 'innocent people' were the victims of a gruesome atrocity subsidized by your government, one among many. If Congress allows the Contras more money further atrocities of this kind will take place. Is this not the case? Is your government not therefore guilty of supporting acts of murder and destruction upon the citizens of a sovereign state?"

Seitz was imperturbable. "I don't agree that the facts as presented support your assertions," he said.

Of course, the "highly successful act of hypnosis" Harold Pinter talks about—or "gaslighting" if you will—is intended to lull people, particularly those living in the U.S. who might object to and possibly stop such cruelty, into complacency and passivity, or even worse, to inspire people to cheer such interventions as humanitarian acts.

We see such hypnosis operational today in the case of Nicaragua, with many people who had once defended Nicaragua against U.S. attacks, and who had even visited Nicaragua during the U.S.-backed Contra War of the 1980s, applauding current U.S. sanctions against that country as a means to somehow punish Daniel Ortega—a leader they once admired, but whom they are now convinced is nothing more or less than a petty dictator. Again, it is as if such people had forgotten their own experiences and what their eyes had seen and their ears had heard, so powerful is the assault upon their senses and memory by the U.S. propaganda machine.

The purpose of this book is to remind people of the realities of U.S. intervention in Nicaragua, past and present; of how the Nicaraguans have triumphed over such assaults time and again; and how they are deserving of our continued solidarity in their struggle to pursue their right to sovereignty and self-determination

While many ask why the Sandinistas have not done more and better for the Nicaraguan people, I hope that the reader, after reading this book, will instead ask the more pertinent question: How is it that, in spite of the obstacles presented by the U.S.'s incessant and brutal intervention in Nicaragua, the Sandinistas have managed to do so much for the Nicaraguan people in so short a time?

CHAPTER 1
LAWYERS, GUNS & MONEY
U.S. MARINES AS DEFENDERS OF U.S. CAPITAL

U.S. intervention in Nicaragua must be viewed in the context of the Monroe Doctrine of 1823 which motivates U.S. foreign policy in the Americas to this very day. The Monroe Doctrine was announced in light of Spain's declining hold over the Americas and the response of the U.S. to the intentions of other European nations, and especially Great Britain, to leap into the breach left by Spain. As the U.S. State Department's Office of the Historian explains, the Monroe Doctrine was a reaction to and explicit rejection of Britain's offer to issue a declaration stating that the U.S. and Britain would maintain exclusive *joint* control over the Western Hemisphere. The U.S., however, was not interested in sharing control with any European country.[10] Therefore, President Monroe issued his own proclamation in 1823 stating that

> "The American continents ... are henceforth not to be considered as subjects for future colonization by any European powers." Monroe outlined two separate spheres of influence: the Americas and Europe. The independent lands of the Western Hemisphere would be solely the United States' domain. In exchange, the United States pledged to avoid involvement in the political affairs of Europe ... and not to interfere in the existing European colonies already in the Americas.[11]

As the Office of the Historian freely admits, the Monroe Doctrine quickly became one of U.S. imperial expansion. Thus, the Office explains that

> By the mid-1800s, Monroe's declaration, combined with ideas of Manifest Destiny, provided precedent and support for U.S. expansion on the American continent. In the late 1800s, U.S. economic and military power enabled it to enforce the Monroe Doctrine. The doctrine's greatest extension came with Theodore Roosevelt's Corollary, which inverted the original meaning of the doctrine and came to justify unilateral U.S. intervention in Latin America.[12]

The dream of a U.S.-constructed and controlled canal connecting the Atlantic and Pacific oceans through Central America—thus permitting ships to forgo the long journey all the way around the southern cone of South America—dates back to the earliest days of the nation and Thomas Jefferson, and "bore an affinity to the Monroe Doctrine."[13] In 1850, the U.S. made its first moves towards realizing this objective, initially focusing on the possibilities presented by Nicaragua. However, at this time, Britain controlled the Atlantic coast of Nicaragua. In order to prevent Britain from unilaterally building its own canal, the U.S. entered into an agreement with Britain –without the consultation or consent of Nicaragua, of course—stipulating that it was "desirable that no time should be unnecessarily lost in commencing and constructing the said canal," and that the U.S. and Britain would jointly guarantee the safe construction of the canal and jointly administer and provide security for the canal, once built.[14] This was known as the Clayton-Bulwer Treaty.

As time went on and the U.S. became more powerful than Britain, the U.S. insisted on exercising the sole prerogative to build and control an Atlantic-Pacific canal. As author and historian Stephen Kinzer writes,

Every American president since Ulysses S. Grant had pushed for the canal project. In 1876 a government commission studied possible routes and concluded that the one across Nicaragua "possesses, both for the construction and maintenance of a canal, greater advantage, and offers fewer difficulties from engineering, commercial and economic points of view, than any one of the other routes." Slowly the project gained momentum. In 1889 a private company chartered by Congress began dredging near Nicaragua's Atlantic coast.[15]

Then, in 1901, the Clayton-Bulwer Treaty was officially nullified by President Teddy Roosevelt through the Hay-Pauncefote Treaty of 1901, which then gave the U.S. the sole right to construct and administer a canal across Central America. While this paved the way for the U.S. to build and control the Panama Canal in 1903, the Hay-Pauncefote Treaty did not specify a particular canal route, but rather simply asserts the U.S. right of construction and control over "whatever route may be considered expedient."[16]

The U.S. went ahead with the plans for the Panama Canal in 1903, securing the exclusive rights for itself to such a canal by military means when the Congress of Colombia, of which Panama was then a part, rejected a treaty with the U.S. for such a canal. As the U.S. Department of State's Office of the Historian itself explains,

> President Roosevelt responded [to Colombia's rejection of the treaty] by dispatching U.S. warships to Panama City (on the Pacific) and Colón (on the Atlantic) in support of [rebel forces pushing for] Panamanian independence. Colombian troops were unable to negotiate the jungles of the Darien Strait and Panama declared independence on November 3, 1903. The newly declared Republic of Panama immediately named Philippe Bunau-Varilla (a French engineer who had been involved in the earlier de Lesseps canal attempt) as Envoy Extraordinary and Minister Plenipotentiary. In his new

role, Bunau-Varilla negotiated the Hay-Bunau-Varilla Treaty of 1903, which provided the United States with a 10-mile-wide strip of land for the canal, a one-time $10 million payment to Panama, and an annual annuity of $250,000. The United States also agreed to guarantee the independence of Panama.[17]

President Teddy Roosevelt was unabashed about his brazen act of theft of valuable territory from Colombia, stating "I took the Canal Zone and let Congress debate."[18]

This episode is instructive. First, it demonstrated the willingness of the U.S. to use military force to take whatever it wanted in the Americas, even to the extent of backing rebel forces to carve a separate country from a once-unified nation. The U.S. support for the Contras in the 1980s would greatly resemble this modus operandi. The event is also illustrative of how violence inflicted by the U.S. on other nations, while long forgotten in the U.S., continues to impact these other nations. In the case of Colombia, Gustavo Petro, a former Colombian senator and mayor of Bogota, who has just, in 2022, been elected as the first leftist Colombian president, once explained at a meeting with Senate staffers to which I accompanied him, the initial U.S. assault unleashed against Colombia in 1903 continues to haunt it—a violence prolonged by over a century of U.S. domination and repression that has left it, to this day, torn apart by internal conflict.

Despite the existence of the Panama Canal, the U.S. has never given up on the possibility of another canal passing through Nicaragua to accommodate ever-bigger vessels. A canal through Nicaragua has the potential to be much bigger than the one through Panama because of Nicaragua's giant lake which extends close to the Atlantic on one end and to the Pacific on the other. The U.S. has continued to intervene in Nicaragua to protect what it sees as its sole right to construct and control any such canal in the face of other countries, such as China, showing interest in helping build one[19]

There has been a long history of U.S. interventions in Nicaragua. As historian Howard Zinn noted, "In 1854, [U.S.]

warships were sent to the Nicaraguan town of Greytown on the Atlantic Coast of Nicaragua because a U.S. diplomat suffered a bloody nose" in an assault by Nicaraguans upset about U.S. control over tariffs and transit routes.[20] Greytown, also known as San Juan del Norte, was completely leveled to the ground by a U.S. Naval ship known as the *Cyane*. This initial episode is illustrative not only of the U.S.'s propensity for extreme violence against Nicaragua, even for the smallest slight, but also for the Nicaraguan people's unwillingness to suffer U.S. domination gladly. Time and again, Nicaragua would pay disproportionately for its defiance but defy, it would continue to do.

The first sustained intervention of the U.S. in Nicaragua began in 1855 with the foray of William Walker—a private citizen backed by U.S. bankers and the Democratic Party—into the country.[21] Walker launched his invasion twice (at first without success, then the second time effectively) from the town that the U.S. had just destroyed—San Juan del Norte. He then quickly found his way to Grenada—a beautiful colonial town which remains one of Nicaragua's greatest attractions for foreigners—where he would launch his military attack in earnest. Walker has become the subject of many articles, books and at least one Hollywood movie, *Walker*, starring Ed Harris. Some portray him as attempting to bring democracy to Central America, even while conceding that his first act as self-appointed President of Nicaragua was to reinstate slavery, which had been abolished in Nicaragua decades prior to it being abolished in the U.S.—indicative of the relative orientation of the two countries towards what would later be referred to as "human rights."

Walker was supported in his adventure by the Democratic Party of the U.S., which hoped that he could convert all of Central America into a New Confederacy which could aid the southern U.S. in winning its struggle to maintain slavery in the face of growing opposition in the North and the government in Washington. Despite such contemptible goals, Walker, known as the "grey-eyed man of destiny,"[22] continues to be lionized by many in the U.S. as a freedom-fighter and folk hero. This says much about the U.S.'s self-delusions about the nature of its interventions around the world, and in Nicaragua in particular. Over and over again, what in reality have been attempts to impose slavery on Nicaragua will be passed off by the U.S., George Orwell style, as struggles for Nicaraguan freedom.

For his part, the great Latin American writer, Eduardo Galeano, in his *magnum opus* entitled *The Open Veins of Latin America*, describes Walker and his invasion of Central America, and how this reflected the U.S.'s insatiable quest for Empire, in less sanguine terms:

> In the geopolitical concept of imperialism, Central America is no more than a natural appendage of the United States. Not even Abraham Lincoln, who also contemplated annexation, could resist the "manifest destiny" of the great power to dictate to its contiguous areas.
>
> In the middle of the nineteenth century the filibusterer William Walker, operating on behalf of bankers Morgan and Garrison, invaded Central America at the head of a band of assassins. With the obliging support of the U.S. government, Walker robbed, killed, burned and in successive expeditions proclaimed himself president of Nicaragua, El Salvador, and Honduras. He restored slavery in the areas that suffered his devastating occupation, thus continuing his country's philanthropic work in the states that had just been seized from Mexico. He was welcomed back to the United States as a national hero. From then on invasions, interventions, bombardments, forced loans, and gun-point treaties followed one after the other.[23]

Walker was overthrown and his mercenaries defeated in the battle of San Jacinto, Nicaragua in 1856. The Nicaraguan peasant, Andrés Castro—who, in a scene reminiscent of David and Goliath, threw the rock which incapacitated Walker—is memorialized in a painting entitled, *La Pedrada* ("The Stone") by Luis Vergara Ahumada.[24] This is one of the most ubiquitous paintings in Nicaragua, adorning the walls of nearly every government building and many private buildings as well. I must have seen this painting a hundred times in my travels throughout Nicaragua. This painting, and its enduring popularity, demonstrates how proud the Nicaraguans are of their long and successful history of resistance against foreign invaders—particularly, against invaders from the United States (in addition to the invaders from Spain and the UK which preceded it).

The next and most sustained intervention of the U.S. came in 1910 when Nicaragua's Liberal Party president, José Santos Zelaya, was seen to have defied the Monroe Doctrine by attempting, it was claimed, to partner with Japan to build the coveted canal through Nicaragua. As Stephen Kinzer notes, the claims about Zelaya partnering with Japan on the canal project may very well have been just a rumor spread by U.S. businessmen, and their friend in Washington, U.S. Secretary of State Philander C. Knox, who were wanting to overthrow Zelaya.[25] These businessmen understood quite correctly that just the mere rumor of such a project by Japan would be enough to get the attention of the U.S. government, for, as author Jonathan M. Katz explains, "By that point Teddy Roosevelt had codified his interventionist instinct into a formal policy for the Western Hemisphere," converting the shield of the Monroe Doctrine against foreign interference in the Hemisphere into a sword the U.S. could freely wield to "commit imperial interference of its own in Latin America and the Caribbean—regions Americans would soon start referring to as 'our own backyard.'"[26]

Zelaya was a revolutionary leader who was trying to develop Nicaragua for the Nicaraguans—a verboten project in the view of the U.S., as Nicaraguans would learn time and again. As Pulitzer-prize winning author, Stephen Kinzer, explains in *Overthrow*, his book about the history of U.S. intervention,

> Nicaragua was in the midst of a modernizing revolution.... During the last decades of the nineteenth century, the ideals of social and political reform swept across Central America. Visionary leaders, inspired

by European philosophers and nation builders, sought to wipe away the feudal systems that had frozen their countries into immobility. One of them, President José Santos Zelaya of Nicaragua, took his nationalist principles so seriously that the United States felt compelled to overthrow him.[27]

As Kinzer further relates, Zelaya

> proclaimed a revolutionary program and set out to shake his country from its long slumber. He built roads, ports, railways, government buildings, and more than 140 schools; paved the streets of Managua, lined them with street lamps, and imported the country's first automobile; legalized civil marriage and divorce; and even founded the nation's first baseball league, which included a team called "Youth" and another called "The Insurgency."[28]

As discussed below, these revolutionary projects of Zelaya look a lot like the kind of projects the Sandinistas would carry out in the 1980s, and they too would be punished by the U.S. for such crimes.

As Kinzer relates, the ousting of Zelaya represented "the first time the United States government had explicitly orchestrated the overthrow of a foreign leader." But it certainly would not be its last.

William Howard Taft, Roosevelt's Secretary of War who immediately succeeded Roosevelt as President and who ordered the Marine invasion, himself made it clear that the U.S. would not settle for anything less than control over the whole hemisphere, stating, "The day is not far distant when three Stars and Stripes at three equidistant points will mark our territory: one at the North Pole, another at the Panama Canal, and the third at the South Pole. The whole hemisphere will be ours in fact as, by virtue of our superiority of race, it already is ours morally."[29] Taft further contended that "U.S. foreign policy 'may well be made to include active intervention to secure for our merchandise and our capitalists opportunity for profitable investment.'" [30] True to his word, Taft would use violent and immoral means to achieve such imperial aims.

In addition to the issue, real or made-up, of his reaching out to Japan for help in building a canal, Zelaya made the mistake of stepping on the toes of mining magnates out of Pittsburgh, Pennsylvania whose interests were well represented by Taft's newly appointed Secretary of State—Pittsburgh corporate lawyer Philander C. Knox, who helped form the U.S. Steel Corporation. Knox had also served as Teddy Roosevelt's Attorney General, comically telling Roosevelt, when he asked Knox for a legal justification for the Panama invasion in 1903, "I think it would be better to keep your action free from any taint of legality."[31] Knox would also be helpful in paving a way for the intervention in Nicaragua. As Jonathan M. Katz explains,

> Knox's friends from Pittsburgh were heavily invested in Nicaragua. When Zelaya threatened to revoke the concession at the Pittsburghers' La Luz y Los Angeles gold mine, in Nicaragua's Mosquitia Province on the Atlantic Coast, the investors wrote the new secretary of state to ask for 'protection in the premises.' Unsubtly, they reminded him that La Luz and other nearby mines were owned by "Pittsburgh capitalists, some no doubt known by you."[32]

Dutifully, Knox sprang into action to try to remove Zelaya from office. As Stephen Kinzer explains,

> In the summer of 1909, he began orchestrating a campaign designed to turn American public opinion against Zelaya. He seized on several minor incidents in Nicaragua, including one in which an American tobacco merchant was briefly jailed, to paint the Nicaraguan regime as brutal and oppressive. He sent diplomats to Nicaragua whom he knew to be strongly anti-Zelaya,

and passed their lurid reports to friends in the press. Soon American newspapers were screaming that Zelaya had imposed a "reign of terror" in Nicaragua and become "the menace of Central America." As their sensationalist campaign reached a peak, President Taft gravely announced that the United States would no longer "tolerate and deal with such a medieval despot."

With this declaration, the United States pronounced Zelaya's political death sentence. American businessmen in Bluefields, the main town on the Caribbean coast, rushed to carry out the execution. With tacit approval from the American consul, William Moffett, with whom they shared their plans at every stage, they formed a conspiracy with the ambitious provincial governor, General Juan José Estrada. On October 10, 1909, Estrada declared himself president of Nicaragua and appealed to the United States for diplomatic recognition.

As Kinzer relates, "This revolution was extraordinarily well financed. The chief accountant for the La Luz mining company, Adolfo Díaz, ... served as its treasurer. American companies operating in and around Bluefields sent him large sums of money. The cost of the revolution has been variously estimated at between $63,000 and $2 million." Kinzer relates that most of this money was spent on Nicaraguan militias financed and organized to oust Zelaya, and that these militias, in turn, were supported by U.S. mercenaries, including some working directly for U.S. corporations.

The details of these coup plans are important, for they look a lot like the more recent, and ongoing coup plans against the Sandinista government of President Daniel Ortega. He too is labeled a "despot" and a regional "menace" by the U.S. government and media, and by their quislings in Nicaragua, even as he seeks to defend the interests of his people as Zelaya did. Indeed, Ortega, just as Zelaya, is slandered precisely *because* he acts on behalf of his own people rather than on behalf of Washington. And now, billions of dollars are spent by U.S. government agencies and shady NGOs, working in support of U.S. economic interests, to overthrow him. These monies too have been used to support armed groups and militias (most famously, the Contras, but also the later insurgents of 2018) to violently overthrow the government. It is important to see that these tactics have changed so little in the last century, insofar as this recognition may help people see through the pervasive U.S. government and media lies and deceptions.

Meanwhile, when the internal insurgency was not enough to remove Zelaya, Taft ordered the U.S. Marines, then stationed in Panama, to invade Nicaragua under the command of the colorful and brutally honest Major General Smedley.

Upon hearing of the planned U.S. invasion, Zelaya resigned and fled Nicaragua. Butler, who would become one of the most oft-quoted critics of U.S. imperialist actions in which he himself was involved, was privately critical of the operation he was ordered to carry out, writing to his parents,

> What makes me mad is that the whole revolution is inspired and financed by Americans who have wild cat investments down here and want to make them good by putting in a Government which will declare a monopoly in their favor.... The whole business is rotten to the core, and I am ashamed to think a Republican Administration is, if anything, assisting the revolution.[33]

Of course, this really wasn't a revolution, but in fact a counter-revolution against a progressive Nicaraguan leader who was trying to do something for his own people—an unforgivable crime which would be punished over and over by the U.S., including through support of the counterrevolutionaries in the 1980s called the Contras (literally, "counter-revolutionaries"). While the U.S. would justify intervention in Nicaragua for the next century over alleged concerns about Communism and Soviet encroachment, the Russian Revolution of 1917 had yet to take place when the initial Marines foray into Nicaragua took place.

Meanwhile, as Katz explains, "In May, 1910, Butler's Panama Battalion was rushed to Bluefields [on Nicaragua's Atlantic Coast] to protect" the rebels "who had not yet unseated Zelaya's appointed Liberal successor, José Madriz."[34] Ultimately, Butler's forces were successful in helping the coup leaders overthrow Madriz, and the compliant Adolfo Díaz—the accountant of the U.S. mining company, La Luz—was installed as the new president of Nicaragua. The U.S. planned to use the new government of Nicaragua to seize Nicaragua's assets for the benefit of such banks as Brown Brothers and J.& W. Seligman—these two banks uniting to carry out "an economic coup from Washington" by forming the new National Bank of Nicaragua, which would be a vehicle for bleeding Nicaragua dry.[35] As Katz explains, while under the ousted President José Zelaya, Nicaragua "had enjoyed a good credit rating, a treasury surplus, and a stable economy," the U.S. economic coup against Nicaragua quickly led to the deterioration of the economy which, as Smedley Butler would lament, led to the suffering of average Nicaraguans.

The new president, Díaz, increased the economic woes by draining the Nicaraguan treasury which his predecessor, Zelaya, had built up, and giving the stolen monies to his corrupt cronies. However, Díaz did wonders for U.S. business and banking interests. As Noam Chomsky explains, under the new regime, the National Bank of Nicaragua was run out of New York City by a Board, which "'consisted entirely of Brown Brothers' U.S. representatives, except for a token Nicaraguan' while U.S. banks received the revenues of the national rail and steamship lines and a U.S.-run commission required Nicaragua to pay fraudulent 'damage claims' that exceeded total U.S. investment in the country for alleged 'damages from civil disorder.'"[36]

It must be emphasized that this type of policy toward Nicaragua—a policy in which the U.S. gained control over the government in the interest of U.S. corporate and banking interests to the detriment of Nicaragua's own economy—was not an anomaly. Indeed, this was done pursuant to the explicit policy of President Taft known as "dollar diplomacy." However, as the U.S. State Department explains in its own history, when "diplomacy" failed to achieve such ends, as it often did, the U.S. would turn to military invasion. Indeed, it is fair to say that the word "diplomacy" here is nothing more than a euphemism for much more heavy-handed and forceful pressure against other nations. As the State Department's Office of the Historian explains:

> Taft shared the view held by Knox, a corporate lawyer who had founded the giant conglomerate U.S. Steel, that the goal of diplomacy was to create stability and order abroad that would best promote American commercial interests. Knox felt that not only was the goal of diplomacy to improve financial opportunities, but also to use private capital to further U.S. interests overseas. "Dollar diplomacy" was evident in extensive U.S. interventions in the Caribbean and Central America, especially in measures undertaken to safeguard American financial interests in the region.[37]

For his part, Katz describes "dollar diplomacy" as follows: "In order to accept lucrative loans, targeted countries would have to also accept U.S. financial advisers. Those advisers would then 'reform' the countries' customs collection agencies, putting the country in receivership."[38] Where the "diplomacy" is, here, is difficult to discern. And, as Katz relates, while Taft argued that the use of such economic forces was superior to military means—"substituting dollars for bullets," in Taft's words—"as [Smedley] Butler would learn firsthand, bullets were still very much needed to ultimately guarantee control."[39]

Indeed, in light of his experiences in Nicaragua and other poor countries in the Global South as an officer for the U.S. Marines, Smedley Butler would later utter some of the most famous, and oft-quoted words exposing the truth about U.S. imperial policies abroad. In his book, *War is a Racket*, Butler laid it out in quite blunt terms:

> I spent 33 years and four months in active military service and during that period I spent most of my

time as a high class muscle man for Big Business, for Wall Street and the bankers. In short, I was a racketeer, a gangster for capitalism. I helped make Mexico and especially Tampico safe for American oil interests in 1914. I helped make Haiti and Cuba a decent place for the National City Bank boys to collect revenues in. I helped in the raping of half a dozen Central American republics for the benefit of Wall Street. I helped purify Nicaragua for the International Banking House of Brown Brothers in 1902–1912. I brought light to the Dominican Republic for the American sugar interests in 1916. I helped make Honduras right for the American fruit companies in 1903. In China in 1927 I helped see to it that Standard Oil went on its way unmolested. Looking back on it, I might have given Al Capone a few hints. The best he could do was to operate his racket in three districts. I operated on three continents.[40]

One of the countries where Smedley Butler and the U.S. Marines had also been operating around this time was the Philippines. As a grade-school student, I was told that this operation was to liberate that country from Spain and to bring it democracy and freedom. That is what many at the time believed as well, including one of the U.S.'s greatest authors, Mark Twain. But Mark Twain would eventually learn that this was not in fact the case, and when he did learn this, he helped to found the Anti-Imperialism League. As Twain would write, "...I have seen that we do not intend to free, but to subjugate the people of the Philippines. We have gone there to conquer, not to redeem. And so I am an anti-imperialist. I am opposed to having the eagle put its talons on any other land."[41] In an account dripping with sarcasm, Twain would detail one particular U.S. atrocity in the Philippines which changed his mind about U.S. intentions:

> A tribe of Moros, dark-skinned savages, had fortified themselves in the bowl of an extinct crater not many miles from Jolo; and as they were hostiles, and bitter

against us because we have been trying for eight years to take their liberties away from them, their presence in that position was a menace. Our commander, Gen. Leonard Wood, ordered a reconnaissance. It was found that the Moros numbered six hundred, counting women and children; that their crater bowl was in the summit of a peak or mountain twenty-two hundred feet above sea level, and very difficult of access for Christian troops and artillery. Then General Wood ordered a surprise, and went along himself to see the order carried out. Our troops climbed the heights by devious and difficult trails, and even took some artillery with them. ... Arrived at the rim of the crater, the battle began. Our soldiers numbered five hundred and forty. They were assisted by auxiliaries consisting of a detachment of native constabulary in our pay—their numbers not given—and by a naval detachment, whose numbers are not stated. But apparently the contending parties were about equal as to number—six hundred men on our side, on the edge of the bowl; six hundred men, women and children in the bottom of the bowl. Depth of the bowl, 50 feet....

The battle began—it is officially called by that name—our forces firing down into the crater with their artillery and their deadly small arms of precision; the savages furiously returning the fire, probably with brickbats—though this is merely a surmise of mine, as the weapons used by the savages are not nominated in the cablegram. Heretofore the Moros have used knives and clubs mainly; also ineffectual trade-muskets when they had any.

The official report stated that the battle was fought with prodigious energy on both sides during a day and a half, and that it ended with a complete victory for the American arms. The completeness of the victory is established by this fact: that of the six hundred Moros not one was left alive. The brilliancy of the victory is established by this other fact, to wit: that of our six hundred heroes only fifteen lost their lives.[42]

This episode, and the bloodbath in the Philippines which would cost the lives of perhaps 3 million Filipinos in what some believe was a genocide,[43] is instructive of what type of "racket" the U.S. Marines were running at this time.

It is important to keep in mind that this international "racket," as Butler termed it, and the atrocities that go with it, continue to this day, though it is much more sophisticated and relies less on overt invasions by U.S. troops (though that is still utilized in the last instance) and more on covert operations. A good explication of the modern manifestation of this policy is set forth by John Perkins in his book, *The New Confessions of an Economic Hitman*, which details the current and long-standing U.S. policy of attempting to control, overthrow and/or even assassinate foreign leaders in order to advance the interests of U.S. corporations.[44] As Perkins explains, the U.S. government and corporations utilize people like him who are effectively used as "economic hit men" to try to manipulate and control foreign leaders through bribes, dirty tricks and extortion. If this does not work, the "jackals" are then brought in to try to overthrow and even assassinate the targeted foreign leaders. The modern day "jackals" include the CIA, U.S. Special Forces, such as Navy SEALS and Delta Force, and literally hundreds of thousands of private mercenaries stationed throughout the world. It is only after the efforts of such "jackals" has failed, Perkins explains, that the U.S. will order a full-scale invasion like that of the Marines into Nicaragua addressed here.

Another difference between the current foreign policy of present-day U.S. administrations and that of prior administrations like Taft's is that stability in the targeted nation is not the goal, but rather instability and chaos, which is now viewed as much more optimal for the ability to plunder and exploit foreign lands and peoples. We shall see that goal actively pursued by the U.S. in Nicaragua in later years.

What Taft and Butler's Marines did not foresee was the incredible resistance the Nicaraguans would put up against them and their quislings in Nicaragua. On his visit to Nicaragua in March of 1912, Secretary of State Philander Knox got his first taste of this resistance when "he was greeted with violent demonstrations against Díaz and his American bankers."[45] And, lest he didn't understand the import of these demonstrations, the head of the national legislature, Dr. Ignacio Suarez, invoking the words of General George Washington against the British, made it clear that "Nicaraguans would defend their sovereignty and independence from imperial control as fiercely as the American revolutionaries had, over a century before."[46]

The defense of Nicaraguan sovereignty came quickly in the uprising led by liberal General Luis Mena who, on July 29, 1912, stormed Managua with troops in an effort to overthrow the U.S.-installed president, Adolfo Díaz.[47] Díaz called upon the U.S. to defend his government, and the U.S. was happy to comply. President Taft ordered Smedley Butler's troops, which had returned to Panama after Díaz was installed, to return to Nicaragua to ensure his rule on behalf of U.S. banks. In the face of greater resistance than expected, Taft was forced to order reinforcements, and by mid-September, the U.S. had a full contingent of 2350 troops on the ground in Nicaragua to defend the Díaz regime.[48]

Though in fairly short order Mena, a man in poor health, surrendered to Butler's forces in the town of Grenada, the rebellion continued, nonetheless. As one account explains,

> Mena's surrender stunned his followers, and the revolution began to unravel. Despite this setback, significant resolve remained within the rebel ranks. With Mena's exit, the center of antigovernment resistance shifted to Masaya, where troops under General Benjamin Zeledón blocked the railroad connecting Managua to Grenada. Rebuffing U.S. demands to surrender, Zeledón and 800 rebel troops occupied twin fortified hilltops (known locally as Barranca and Coyotepe) that commanded the train tracks approaching Masaya from the capital. By early October, a force numbering some 1,000 U.S. sailors and marines and 4,000 government soldiers encircled Zeledón's position.[49]

What followed was the Battle of Barranca-Coyotepe in which Zeledón was killed and his troops roundly defeated. The rebellion then quickly collapsed, and U.S. forces went on to take over every major city in Nicaragua.

One leader of the U.S. military effort, William D. Leahy, could not hide his disgust at what he witnessed in Nicaragua and what his forces had done. As an article detailing his diary ruminations relates,

> "Leahy expressed little respect for the Díaz government, which he described as 'weak and tyrannical'—an 'undisguised military despotism.'...Leahy believed they deserved better. Indeed, the extreme hardship and privation observed wherever he traveled in Nicaragua demanded action. Invoking natural law concepts of self-defense and just governance, Leahy argued "that a right to revolt against such conditions is inherent."[50]

As the article continues,

> Leahy aimed his strongest criticisms at the intervention's underlying policy decisions. Writing in a cynical tone, he juxtaposed the U.S. casualty count in Nicaragua with an outcome he deemed unworthy of such sacrifice. His words again called into question the legitimacy of a government that relied upon foreign military muscle, not popular support, to remain in power. "Now that this specific revolution has been put down, with a loss of seven Americans killed and many incapacitated by wounds and sickness," Leahy lamented, "it seems to one that the United States has sustained a weak tyrannical government that can be kept in existence only by the force of our arms." He predicted that the popular will would assert itself once U.S. troops departed Nicaragua, spelling doom for the Díaz regime: "when our withdrawal makes it possible the Liberal [rebel] population will probably start a revolution in self-defense."

These words would prove prophetic. Indeed, the death of Zeledón, and the gloating over his death that followed would sow the seeds of revolutionary self-defense, which would eventually drive the Marines out of Nicaragua. As Jonathan M. Katz explains, the Nicaraguan government troops aligned with the Marines paraded Zeledón's body through the streets of a number of towns as a sign of victory "and a warning to any who dared stand against them and their American allies."[51]

Childhood Home of Augusto C. Sandino in Niquinohomo
DANIEL KOVALIK, JULY, 2021

In the small village of Niquinohomo, the grisly procession passed a white one-story house with blue shutters. Hearing the noise, the [illegitimate] seventeen-year-old son of a wealthy local coffee farmer and a poor native coffee picker went outside to watch. The teenager's eyes grew wide with horror as he recognized the mutilated corpse of his hero—"killed," as he would later remember, "by bullets of Yankee soldiers serving the interests of Wall Street."

It was at this moment, Augusto Sandino would later say, that he swore to carry on Zeledón's fight against the United States and its proxies for the rest of his life.[52]

The U.S. Marines would remain in Nicaragua and occupy it to ensure Conservative Party rule and thus protection for U.S. corporate and financial interests, continuously from the time of Zeledón's death in 1912 until 1933. As the U.S. Library of Congress's Country Study of Nicaragua itself explains, the U.S. sought near total domination over Nicaragua during this time and came close to achieving it. Thus, as the Library of Congress explains,

Nicaragua and the United States signed but never ratified the Castillo-Knox Treaty in 1914, giving the United States the right to intervene in Nicaragua to protect United States interest. A modified version, the Chamorro-Bryan Treaty omitting the intervention clause, was finally ratified by the United States Senate in 1916. This treaty gave the United States exclusive rights to build an interoceanic canal across Nicaragua. Because the United States had already built the Panama Canal, however, the terms of the Chamorro-Bryan Treaty served the primary purpose of securing United States interests against potential foreign countries—mainly Germany or Japan—building another canal in Central America. *The treaty also transformed Nicaragua into a near United States protectorate."* (Emphasis added).[53]

In addition, the U.S. used its control over Nicaragua during this time to make amends to Colombia for the Panama Canal episode at the expense of Nicaragua. It prevailed upon the Nicaraguan government to sign a 1928 Treaty, pursuant to which Nicaragua ceded sovereignty over three islands which it previously had claimed as its own and which reside much closer to Nicaragua than to Colombia.[54] While the Sandinista government would later lose its case before the International Court of Justice (ICJ) trying to win these islands back (largely because the Somoza governments and then the neoliberal governments of the 1990s asserted no interest in the islands), it has now regained legal control over miles of territorial waters also in dispute with Colombia pursuant to a 2022 ICJ decision.[55] However, Colombia, a NATO partner, still does not recognize this latter ICJ decision and continues to engage in provocative incursions into these waters—waters which will be necessary for Nicaragua to control if it wants to go ahead with building a canal of its own.

Not surprisingly, none of this sat well with a great majority of the Nicaraguan people, and the period of U.S. Marine occupation was marked by great instability and resistance.

It was Augusto C. Sandino, with his rag-tag group of mostly peasant fighters, who led the greatest resistance to the U.S. Marines, ultimately forcing them out in 1933. Indeed, while there is a plaque which stands today at Playa Giron in Cuba, in the infamous Bay of Pigs, claiming to be the site of U.S. imperialism's first defeat in the Americas in 1961 at the hands of Fidel Castro's loyal forces, Sandino and Nicaragua could justly lay claim to this honor many years before.

However, Sandino's campaign, which began in 1927, was an arduous one, and faced ever-mounting attacks by the U.S. Marines, including ever-growing indiscriminate attacks against the Nicaraguan civilian population to try to destroy their support for Sandino. Mao Zedong, who began his own anti-imperialist and popular campaign in China around this time, would famously say that "The guerrilla must move amongst the people as a fish swims in the sea." The U.S. military understood this as well, and so set upon what has since become an explicit counterinsurgency goal

Statue of Augusto C. Sandino in his hometown of Niquinohomo
DANIEL KOVALIK, JULY, 2021

of "draining the sea" of the people who supported and sustained Sandino's guerillas in order to destroy those guerillas whom they could not even locate, much less defeat in battle. The reference to Mao here is an apt one, as Chinese guerilla forces themselves became quickly acquainted with the resistance of Augusto Cesar Sandino and even carried banners with his image on it.[56]

The Sandino rebellion began in 1927 in response to the increase of U.S. military involvement in the country the year before. According to the U.S. Library of Congress, the U.S. military contingent had been reduced to 100 in 1913 after a Conservative

Party victory in elections in which the Liberal Party did not even participate. As the Library of Congress itself explains, the U.S. Marine "contingent served as a reminder of the willingness of the United States to use force and its desire to keep conservative governments in power."[57]

However, after tensions rose again after the 1925 fraudulent election of Conservative General Emiliano Chamorro—of the famous Chamorro family which, as described below, continues to figure prominently in Nicaraguan political life to this day and which continues to dutifully serve the interests of the U.S.—the U.S. again upped its military presence in Nicaragua. Thus, "[f]earing a new round of conservative-liberal violence and worried that a revolution in Nicaragua might result in a leftist victory as happened a few years earlier in Mexico, the United States sent marines, who landed on the Caribbean coast in May 1926, ostensibly to protect United States citizens and property."[58] The U.S. would station 5,000 U.S. Marines in Nicaragua to occupy the country and quash the rebellion.[59] In addition, the U.S. Marines at this time began to assist the compliant Nicaraguan government in creating and training the repressive security forces which would rule Nicaragua with an iron hand for the next half a century—the infamous National Guard.[60]

The U.S. Library of Congress describes well the beginnings of the Sandino rebellion which was precipitated by Sandino's refusal to go along with other Liberal Party leaders—including General Moncada who was then leading the Liberal rebellion against Chamorro—who were willing to sign a peace agreement with the Conservative Party, brokered by the United States. Sandino and others objected to the agreement, known as the Pact of Espino Negro, as (1) it would have allowed the Conservative Party President, then Adolfo Díaz, to remain in power through a vote of Congress upon the forced resignation of Chamorro; (2) required the disarming of the Liberal Party forces then fighting the government; (3) consented to the U.S.'s creation of the National Guard; and (4) allowed continued occupation by U.S. forces at least until the next election, which U.S. forces would then "monitor."[61] This was not a peace agreement, in Sandino's view, but a complete surrender. As the Library of Congress put it:

> A rebel liberal group under the leadership of Augusto César Sandino ... refused to sign the Pact of Espino Negro. An illegitimate son of a wealthy landowner and a mestizo servant, Sandino had left his father's home early in his youth and traveled to Honduras, Guatemala, and Mexico. During his three-year stay in Tampico, Mexico, Sandino had acquired a strong sense of Nicaraguan nationalism and pride in his mestizo heritage. At the urging of his father, Sandino had returned to Nicaragua in 1926 and settled in the department of Nueva Segovia, where he worked at a gold mine owned by a United States company. Sandino, who lectured the mine workers about social inequalities and the need to change the political system, soon organized his own army, consisting mostly of peasants and workers, and joined the liberals fighting against the conservative regime of Chamorro. Highly distrusted by Moncada, Sandino set up hit-and-run operations against conservative forces independently of Moncada's liberal army. After the United States mediated the agreement between liberal forces and the conservative regime, Sandino, calling Moncada a traitor and denouncing United States intervention, reorganized his forces as the Army for the Defense of Nicaraguan Sovereignty (Ejército Defensor de la Soberanía de Nicaragua-EDSN). Sandino then staged an independent guerrilla campaign against the government and United States forces. Although Sandino's original intentions were to restore constitutional government ... , after the Pact of Espino Negro agreement his objective became the defense of Nicaraguan sovereignty against the United States. Receiving his main support from the rural population, Sandino resumed his battle against United States troops. ... Sandino's guerrilla war caused significant

damage in the Caribbean coast and mining regions. After debating whether to continue direct fighting against Sandino's forces, the United States opted to develop the nonpartisan Nicaraguan National Guard to contain internal violence. The National Guard would soon become the most important power in Nicaraguan politics.[62]

The first attack launched against the U.S. occupation was symbolically focused on the raison d'être of this occupation—U.S. financial interests. Thus, Sandino, who "had become a Liberal general in the civil war, launched his rebellion, sacking the U.S.-owned San Albino gold mine and issuing proclamations against 'Yankee cowards and criminals' and the 'worm-eaten and decadent' Nicaraguan aristocracy" that served U.S. interests.[63] This gold mine, which is now closed, is located in Nueva Segovia in the region of Nicaragua known as Las Segovias.

The Las Segovias region of Nicaragua, and especially Nueva Segovia on the Honduran border, was the nucleus of the Sandino rebellion.[64] As described by the website entitled, "Sandino Rebellion"—a site containing thousands of source documents about the Sandino resistance (sandinorebellion.com):

> In the late 1920s this rugged region bordering Honduras was home to about 120,000 people spread over some 6,000 square miles of mountains, valleys, forests, and jungles, in several dozen towns and hundreds of villages, hamlets, and homesteads. Even before the Marines arrived, extreme inequality, oppression, exploitation, poverty, and violence dominated the social landscape. After May 1927 Segovianos flocked to Sandino's banner. The Marine invasion intensified; the U.S.-created National Guard grew in power; and by 1932 the Sandinista rebels, based in Las Segovias and organized into a government of their own, threatened to topple the national government."[65]

Nueva Segovia happens to be the region I first visited in 1987, and in which I have spent the most time. To me, and to many Nicaraguans, this is holy ground because of its significance in the fight against the U.S. occupation. The nature and history of the Segovias illuminates what the Sandinista Revolution has always been about—the liberation of the most oppressed peoples in Nicaragua. The Segovias, a major coffee-growing region in Nicaragua, has traditionally been a region of mostly very poor peasants working for a very few rich landowners. At the time of the Sandino rebellion, the life expectancy of the people in the Segovias was around 42 years old, the functional literacy rate was around 2 percent.[66] In addition "[p]overty was ubiquitous, and

Proud Comrade of Augusto C. Sandino, Ocotal
DANIEL KOVALIK, SEPTEMBER, 1987

diseases like hookworm, smallpox, and malaria endemic."[67] It is the peasants of the Segovias, facing such depravations, who have formed the backbone of the Revolution.

It should also be emphasized that, during the insurrection against the Sandinista government in 2018 described in detail below, there was nearly no coup activity or violence in Nueva Segovia which remains one of the most militantly loyal regions to Sandinismo and the FSLN. The residents there, mostly peasant and working class, are not so easily fooled by the propaganda of the U.S. and its Nicaraguan quislings. The other region which saw little disruption in 2018 was the Atlantic Coast which is largely populated by Afro-descendants and indigenous peoples, including the Miskitus who I discuss in detail below.

I have often said that the least educated peasant in Nicaragua is more politically astute than the most educated person in the United States, and this as not a mere hyperbole. As just one example, I recall a recent discussion with a coffee-growing campesino in El Crucero, Nicaragua. Alfonso Guillen, a historic Sandinista combatant, sought me out when I was visiting his coffee cooperative, now owned and controlled by the peasants themselves, thanks to the Sandinista Revolution for which Guillen has fought his entire life. Sitting shirtless and with machete in hand, he eagerly started up a conversation, not about Nicaragua, but about recent events in Ukraine in which Russia had just begun its special military operation in February of 2022. He asked me my opinion about these events, and then he told me his. One observation he made was particularly incisive. He said, "Do you notice that when [Ukrainian President] Zelensky gives a speech, he is always filmed in exactly the same clothes and always with the same background?" He said that this leads him to think that Zelensky was being stage-managed by outside forces—the U.S. and NATO— and that he was more of a figurehead than a real leader operating on behalf of his own people. These were the observations of someone, in my view, who is really paying attention to what is happening in the world.

Given that Las Segovias was the epicenter of the rebellion, it was this region that was marked for the worst brutality by U.S.

Marines who, unable to grapple in a fair fight with Sandino's forces, ultimately took out their rage on the civilian population. The tactics used by the U.S. Marines were so cruel that they even received criticism from the mainstream U.S. media. Thus, as Michael J. Schroeder wrote in his excellent, "Social Memory and Tactical Doctrine: The Air War in Nicaragua during the Sandino Rebellion, 1927–1932,"

> The air war in Nicaragua ... made the headlines early in 1928 when Sandinistas killed six marines and wounded twenty-eight others near El Chipote. In response, the J. Calvin Coolidge administration announced that it would send one thousand more troops.... Ten days earlier, Charles Lindbergh, who had recently returned from his solo flight across the Atlantic, and was taking the Spirit of St Louis on a widely publicized "peace and goodwill tour" of Latin America, changed his flight path on his approach to Managua to avoid flying over the war zone around Quilali [in Nueva Segovia]. The next day, the *New York Times* reported from Managua that, in the northern mountains, "the American planes in their patrols drop bombs in likely spots or wherever there is the slightest indication of the presence of the guerrillas they are seeking." The confluence in January 1928 of the pan-American conference, the aerial assault on El Chipote, and Lindbergh's goodwill tour highlighted the struggle between Sandino and the marines, the tangled history of U.S. imperialism in the circum-Caribbean, and the role of airplanes in modern warfare. Newspapers in the Americas and Europe hailed Lindbergh's message of peace and the high-minded goals of the Havana conference in one column and, in another, assailed the marines' slaughter of men, women, and children in Nicaragua.[68]

The news of what was happening in Nicaragua in 1928 inspired some U.S. workers to denounce the Marines and send messages of solidarity to Sandino and his men and women. Indeed, I discovered a *Daily Worker* edition from 1928 that details how workers in Chicago who were members of the Anti-Imperialist League passed a resolution to support the struggle of Augusto C. Sandino against the United States.

Meanwhile, testimony of survivors of these air assaults given after the Sandinista Triumph in 1979 made it clear what was really meant by the Marines dropping bombs, in the words of the *Times*, "in likely spots or wherever there is the slightest indication of the presence of the guerrillas." Thus,

> Typical was the testimony of José Antonio Ucles Mann, a seventy-eight-year-old campesino from El Jicaro, interviewed in 1983: "the airplanes, when they saw smoke rising, when they saw someone making food for their children, the mothers of the families, they'd bomb them, they'd kill them all. When they saw someone, it was a question of dropping bomb."
> ... Similarly, seventy-year-old Aurelio Osaba Izaguirre of Cinco Pinos recalled: "the airplanes often bombed where there were no combatants, where there were only civilians, they didn't bomb where the muchacho [rebels] were ..."[69]

For his part, Juan Sanchez stated that he joined Sandino's rebel forces after the Marines "'had already destroyed all of these villages...; they had burned, they had killed, they had killed all the animals. In Quilali the airplanes destroyed us. They had killed many people and burned many houses, all this in the invasion.'"[70]

In the end, unable to defeat the guerillas militarily, the U.S. turned to terrorizing the population. Nicaraguans would not forget this horror even though the U.S. had forgotten this long ago. As historian Michael J. Schroeder explains,

> Terror was built into the architecture of the aerial war in Nicaragua. The willingness of the United States to use terror was partly attributable to the airmen's

cultural arrogance, racism, and desire for vengeance, as well as their isolation and lack of supervision. Many Segovianos remembered the marines long after the event; the enduring collective memory was expressed in stories, songs, legends, poems, novels, memoirs, and political mobilization.... Among many Segovianos, an air war seemingly intended to humiliate and dishonour, as well as kill and maim, generated profound individual and collective hatred of the United States and its marines. The hatred, in turn, proved a powerful recruiting tool for Sandino....[71]

The U.S. would turn to terror over and again, especially during the Contra War of the 1980s and the violent insurrection of 2018, to try to achieve its ends in Nicaragua. Not surprisingly, then, Nicaraguans still sing the Sandinista Hymn which includes the line, "We fight against the Yankees, enemy of humanity."

Despite the cruel tactics of bombing defenseless civilians from the air—tactics which the U.S. would continue to use to this day in theaters from Korea, Vietnam, Serbia, and Iraq to Afghanistan, Libya and Somalia—the U.S. was unable to break the resolve of the Nicaraguan people and their leader Augusto César Sandino. Indeed, the resolve of the Nicaraguan people and their resistance to U.S. occupation only grew while that of the U.S. forces, and the public back home, declined. As the U.S. Library of Congress itself explains, "In the United States, popular opposition to the Nicaraguan intervention rose as United States casualty lists grew. Anxious to withdraw from Nicaraguan politics, the United States turned over command of the National Guard to the Nicaraguan government, and United States marines left the country soon thereafter," in 1933.[72] And thus, the U.S. suffered its first defeat in the Global South.

Eduardo Galeano describes it so well in *The Open Veins of Latin America*,

> The epic of Augusto César Sandino stirred the world. The long struggle of Nicaragua's guerrilla leader

was rooted in the angry peasants' demand for land. His small, ragged army fought for some years against twelve thousand U.S. invaders and the National Guard. Sardine tins filled with stones served as grenades, Springfield rifles were stolen from the enemy, and there were plenty of machetes; the flag flew from any handy stick, and the peasants moved through mountain thickets wearing strips of hide called huaraches instead of boots. The guerrillas sang, to the tune of Adelita:

> *In Nicaragua, gentlemen,*
> *the mouse kills the cat.*

Neither the Marines' firepower nor the bombs dropped from planes sufficed to crush the rebels of Las Segovias; nor did the calumnies spread worldwide by Associated Press and United Press International, whose Nicaraguan correspondents were two North Americans who controlled the country's customs houses.[73]

Of course, such "calumnies" and slander against Nicaragua and the children of Sandino continue to this day, regrettably even by those of the "Left," who should know better.

Sadly, the victory of Sandino was short-lived. The new President of Nicaragua, Liberal Party adherent Juan Bautista Sacasa who was elected in 1932, offered a peace agreement with Sandino which included land and amnesty for him and his forces. While Sandino's forces had the upper hand at this point, Sandino was amenable to this deal, especially given that he had effectively taken care of his main concern—the presence of the U.S. occupation forces. Sandino, after all, was as gracious in victory as he was tenacious in battle.

However, this deal was not acceptable to the powerful Director of the National Guard, Anastasio "Tacho" Somoza García. The U.S. Library of Congress itself explains that Somoza "enjoyed support from the United States government.... Having attended school in Philadelphia and been trained by United States marines,

Somoza García, who was fluent in English, had developed friends with military, economic, and political influence in the United States." Unbeknownst to the President of Nicaragua, Somoza plotted to kill Sandino upon his visit to attend a state dinner at the presidential place in Managua where he was to sign the peace agreement. On February 21, 1934, upon leaving the dinner with President Sacasa, "Sandino and two of his generals were arrested by National Guard officers acting under Somoza García's instructions. They were then taken to the airfield, executed, and buried in unmarked graves. . . . After Sandino's execution, the National Guard launched a ruthless campaign against Sandino's supporters. In less than a month, Sandino's army was totally destroyed." The body of Sandino, disposed of effectively by Somoza's henchmen, has never been found and has never been properly grieved over or memorialized.

Somoza would soon oust the President of Nicaragua and assume state power with the full support of the U.S. government. He and his two sons then governed Nicaragua with the iron hand of the National Guard for the next forty-plus years. However, few in the U.S. were concerned about the Somozas and their treatment of the Nicaraguan people. Indeed, President Franklin Delano Roosevelt would famously quip in 1939 that "Somoza may be a son of a bitch, but he's our son of a bitch." I heard President Daniel Ortega reference this quote at the anniversary of the Sandinista Triumph on July 19, 2022.

A very popular song from the era of the early Somoza years underscores the general contempt the U.S. people had for the Nicaraguan people. In 1947, Guy Lombardo recorded the catchy song, "Managua, Nicaragua," the theme of which is that Nicaragua is a place for Americans to go to have fun, buy property for next to nothing and woo young Nicaraguan women, whether they like it or not. The song also portrays the Nicaraguan people (who in reality are some of the hardest working people I have ever known) as lazy people who never work at all. As the song goes, in relevant part:

> *Managua, Nicaragua is a beautiful town*
> *You buy a hacienda for a few pesos down*
> *You give it to the lady you are tryin' to win*
> *But her papa doesn't let you come in*
> *Managua, Nicaragua is a heavenly place*
> *You ask a senorita for a 'leetle' embrace*
> *She answers you, "Caramba! scram-ba bambarito"*
> *In Managua, Nicaragua, that's "No"...*
> *Every day is made for play and fun*
> *'Cause every day is fiesta*
> *And they work from twelve o'clock to one*
> *Minus an hour for siesta*

The Sandinistas would learn time and again, including from Sandino's assassination after trying to make peace with the government, that their willingness to forgive and make peace would always be used against them by the U.S. and its local surrogates. And, when the Sandinistas did fight back in self-defense, the latter were quick to condemn them for doing so. But such condemnation is always the lot of any movement fighting against U.S. imperialism and aggression. Indeed, as my good friend, S. Brian Willson, has explained time and again, the U.S. position—dating as far back as the time of General George Washington and his unforgiving war against the indigenous population—is that those peoples the U.S. attempts to conquer have no right of self-defense, and any attempt to engage in such makes them fair game for the worst of atrocities against their civilian population.

Yet defend themselves the Nicaraguans did. After being wiped out by Somoza in the mid-1930s, rebellion in Nicaragua would rise again. As before, the movement against dictatorship and for national liberation began in Las Segovias with a guerilla struggle against the National Guard, leavened by the success of Fidel Castro's guerillas in Cuba. By 1961, those engaged in the armed struggle against Somoza had organized themselves into the Sandinista Front for National Liberation (FSLN), and would shock the world by completing the job that Augusto César Sandino had begun.

CHAPTER 2

INSURRECTION & REPRESSION

The 1970s brought seismic changes in Nicaragua—both literally and figuratively. In 1972, the country was rocked by a huge earthquake, which devastated Managua. But for the third Somoza to rule over Nicaragua, Anastasio Somoza Debayle ("Tachito" or "Somoza")—the brother of Luis Somoza Debayle who succeeded their father in ruling Nicaragua from 1956 to 1963—that disaster was simply another occasion for gross self-enrichment.

Tachito was the most brutal of the Somozas. Between 1963 and 1967 when Luis Somoza died of a heart attack, politicians loyal to the Somozas ran Nicaragua on an interim basis. Then, according to the U.S. Library of Congress's short history of the Somoza dictatorship:

> In February 1967, Anastasio Somoza Debayle was elected president amidst a repressive campaign against opposition supporters of [Fernando] Agüero.... With his election, Anastasio Somoza Debayle became president as well as the director of the National Guard, giving him absolute political and military control over Nicaragua. Corruption and the use of force intensified, accelerating opposition from populist and business groups.[74]

When the 1972 earthquake came, money poured in from all over the world to help Nicaragua, only to end up in the pockets of Somoza and his cronies. Again, the Library of Congress relates:

On December 23, 1972, a powerful earthquake shook Nicaragua, destroying most of the capital city. The earthquake left approximately 10,000 dead and some 50,000 families homeless and destroyed 80 percent of Managua's commercial buildings. Immediately after the earthquake, the National Guard joined the widespread looting of most of the remaining business establishments in Managua. When reconstruction began, the government's illegal appropriation and mismanagement of international relief aid, directed by the Somoza family and members of the National Guard, shocked the international community and produced further unrest in Nicaragua. The president's ability to take advantage of the people's suffering proved enormous. By some estimates, his personal wealth soared to US$400 million in 1974. As a result of his greed, Anastasio Somoza Debayle's support base within the business sector began to crumble. A revived labor movement increased opposition to the regime and to the deteriorating economic conditions.[75]

For its part, the apolitical British hunger-relief organization, Oxfam, in its important 1985 report entitled "Nicaragua: The Threat of a Good Example"[76]—the "good example" being the Sandinista Revolution, which the U.S. feared would serve as a model for other countries seeking independent development—described the Somoza government's horrifying reaction to the 1972 earthquake as follows:

> The Managua earthquake was to provide new insights into poverty and corruption under Somoza. In the immediate aftermath of the earthquake, Somoza's National Guard went on the rampage looting and stealing. A National Emergency Committee, set up under President Somoza's control and run by the National Guard, institutionalized the misappropriation of emergency relief. Realizing that relief supplies were being

syphoned off and sold by the National Guard, Oxfam's Field Director talked Mrs. Somoza into giving permission to bypass the official distribution system. This meant waiting in the air traffic control tower for the right plane to be spotted, then careening onto the tarmac to get the trucks loaded before the National Guard arrived on the scene.

Huge tents imported in this way were used to set up improvised community centres for food distribution and health care. Special camp committees were formed to run the centres. But these attempts by the earthquake victims to organize themselves were later broken up by the National Guard.

It is important to note that while there is unanimous consensus today about Somoza's extreme corruption after the 1972 earthquake, the media mouthpieces of the U.S. State Department continued to support Somoza and tried mightily to obscure this reality. For example, as Noam Chomsky and Edward S. Herman explain in their book, *The Washington Connection and Third World Fascism*, the U.S.'s paper of record, *The New York Times*, claimed at the time that, after the earthquake, "'immediately, its dynamic young President, Anastasio Somoza Debayle, leaped into the ruins, worked alongside the 2.2 million Nicaraguans, and built a new economy—healthier and stronger than ever before.'"[77] We should always keep these instances of blatant misinformation by our self-designated "trusted" media sources in mind the next time we read/hear claims about what is happening in countries like Nicaragua. A healthy skepticism with regard to such claims is certainly in order, as Chomsky and Herman have told us for years.

Moreover, it is important to note that, as Oxfam explains, the "good example" represented by the Sandinista Revolution was emerging even before their ultimate Triumph in 1979. Even while the Sandinista guerillas were still fighting to topple Somoza, a new world was being created by the poor of Nicaragua themselves. Oxfam gives the following example of people organizing to take and cultivate land in a country in which, at that time, a very few owned and controlled almost all of the land and left 30% of it idle:

> In August 1976, a group of 600 people were successful in taking over idle land on a large estate at Los Arcos, in the department of León. They planted crops and were joined by eight more families who took over some adjoining land. These peasant farmers organized themselves into a cooperative, with help from a small voluntary agency for community development and the Legal Aid Service of León University. Within a year they had built over 50 houses and a communal building that they used as a school, church and weekly clinic. The families faced severe problems including harassment from the absentee landowner. But the whole experience of organizing themselves and taking joint decisions to increase production and set up a clinic, all created confidence in their own abilities and in what might be achieved in Nicaragua without Somoza.[78]

As Oxfam relates, "The experience of the cooperative at Los Arcos was not unique. Throughout the country poor people were coming together and forming peasant associations, trades unions, neighborhoods and women's groups. They began working together on small-scale community efforts to improve health, literacy and food production." However, Somoza had felt threatened by these examples of common people organizing, and his response to such projects was severe repression. Thus, "by 1972 reports were coming in of murder and violence targeted against local community leaders.... As the political and military power of the opposition to Somoza grew, repression became less selective, more brutal and more widespread."

Meanwhile, even his massive graft was not enough for Somoza. He turned to a scheme which earned him the infamous nickname of "Vampire." Somoza, along with his sons, were part owners in a company called Plasmaferesis, which operated on Somoza-owned property and which "bought blood on the cheap from poor and desperate Nicaraguans, separated and froze the plasma, and sent it to Europe and the United States, raking in huge profits."[79] Somoza was even "peddling Nicaraguan blood abroad at a time when the poverty-stricken country needed donations most after a devastating earthquake hit Managua in 1972.... Medical supplies, including blood transfusions, were in short supply."[80]

A report in *Telesur,* written on the anniversary of the Sandinista Revolution in 2016, explains:

> "It was a dark business," former *La Prensa* journalist Roberto Sanchez Ramirez told *El Diario Nuevo* in 2008. "Every morning the homeless, drunks, and poor people went to sell half a liter of blood for 35 (Nicaraguan) cordobas." In 2016, 35 cordobas is less than US$1.25.
>
> Sanchez Ramirez added that the business only existed in Nicaragua and Haiti—the two poorest countries in the Americas.
>
> According to reports published at the time, Plasmaferesis' health standards were dismal, and the clinics would take blood from the same person up to twice a week if they showed up to sell. While health experts suggest that blood plasma is replaced in a matter of days, the body needs more than 30 days to recuperate a normal red blood cell count....
>
> According to Douglas Starr, author of *Blood: An Epic History of Medicine and Commerce,* Nicaragua was "the developing world's largest plasma collector" in the 1970s, taking blood from up to 1,000 people per day at its peak.[81]

As *Telesur* relates, this scandal, originally reported on by Nicaragua's *La Prensa* newspaper in a 1978 series entitled "The Vampire Chronicles," sickened the Nicaraguan people and their rage only increased with Somoza's assassination of *La Prensa*'s editor, Pedro Joaquin Chamorro, just three months after this story ran in the paper. That led to the mass anger, which ultimately toppled the Somoza dynasty.

Somoza's blood profiteering also had earth-shattering international repercussions. Somoza's Plasmaferesis company and others like it around the world were harvesting blood from unhealthy individuals on skid row, many of whom were intravenous drug users. This helped give rise to the tainted blood scandal of the 1980s, in which tens of thousands of people contracted serious diseases, including AIDS, through blood transfusions.[82] This reality was driven home to me in the early 1990s when my two brothers-in-law, Greg and Tim Haas, died as the result of their contracting Hepatitis and AIDS through blood products they took to manage their hemophilia.

Of significance for Puerto Ricans, baseball fans, and particularly for fans of the Pittsburgh Pirates, Somoza's greed led to another tragedy: the untimely death of "The Great One," Roberto Clemente. Clemente was a towering figure in the baseball world. Handsome, and with amazing talent as a fielder, thrower and hitter, Clemente was beloved. He was a World Series MVP, 15-time All Star and twelve-time winner of the Golden Glove Award.[83] He also had a heart of gold. Even as a young player, he fought against segregation and discrimination in Major League Baseball. As the *L.A. Times* explains, Clemente was

> a Black man who spoke out, frequently in his second language, against racism in the United States during a career that paralleled the civil rights movement.
>
> Clemente, a U.S. Marine Corps reservist, admired Martin Luther King Jr. and spent an afternoon with him at his farm in Puerto Rico. He denounced the segregation he confronted during spring training in the Jim Crow era of the South and pushed for the Pirates to make changes to better accommodate Black players.[84]

But what Clemente is most remembered for in Nicaragua is how he died—attempting to bring humanitarian aid to Nicaragua for victims of the 1972 earthquake. Clemente had decided to bring this aid himself after reading that Somoza was pilfering the international aid, including some Clemente, himself, had been sending. As a retrospective on Clemente relates,

> Roberto lost many friends in the quake. He had spent most of November in Nicaragua managing a Puerto Rican all-star team in the Amateur Baseball World Series tournament. He felt the threat to his many colleagues, thousands of fans and friends.
>
> Clemente accepted the honorary chairmanship of an earthquake relief committee and used local media to appeal for help. He worked day and night, even soliciting donations door to door. The relief team raised $150,000, and gathered and shipped nearly 26 tons of food, clothing and medicine by air and sea. Then came reports from Managua—the corrupt regime of General Anastasio Somoza was intercepting the deliveries.
>
> Roberto wanted to make sure the food and medicine got to the people who needed it. On New Year's Eve, he helped load an aging DC-7, then boarded the flight.[85]

However, Clemente never made it to Nicaragua, as one of the plane's engines exploded, and it crashed, killing all those on board, including himself.

In a very real way, Somoza's infamous corruption had led Clemente to his death. The Nicaraguans have never forgotten Clemente's sacrifice. Schools and stadiums in Nicaragua still bear his name and murals of Clemente don many Nicaraguan walls. When I attended Daniel Ortega's inauguration in January of 2022, I gave him a Clemente jersey that I had bought on Clemente Night at PNC Park in Pittsburgh in 2021. Even though the jersey did not bear his name, everyone in the crowd recognized #21 as Clemente's number and cheered when I presented it to Daniel.

In short, while many might think that the U.S.'s propping up of a petty dictator in a tiny Central American country only affects that small nation and doesn't have wide-ranging impacts on the world, this simply is not the case.

The Somoza governments had always aided and abetted U.S. covert operations in Latin America, and even helped initiate some. One of the more notorious instances was Anastasio Somoza García's support for the overthrow of the democratically elected Guatemalan president, Jacobo Arbenz, in 1954. Indeed, according to the CIA's own history of this covert operation, the coup was Somoza's idea. As the history states, the CIA had begun to devise the coup plans, as per President Truman's request, after President Somoza visited Washington in 1952 and stated that "if provided arms, he and Guatemalan exile Carlos Castillo Armas could overthrow Arbenz...."[86] For its part, the U.S. State Department Office of the Historian relates, "Prominent among the [coup] plotters was an exiled army colonel, Carlos Castillo Armas. Castillo Armas, based in Honduras, had the active support of Nicaragua's Anastasio Somoza and the United Fruit Company."[87] The results of this coup were catastrophic for Guatemala, leading to a series of military dictatorships which killed around 200,000 mostly Mayan people in Guatemala in what is now universally recognized as a genocide.[88]

In addition, the Somoza dictatorship provided significant support to the CIA's attempt to overthrow the government of Fidel Castro through the Bay of Pigs invasion of 1961. Luis Somoza Debayle provided the use of Nicaragua's Puerta Cabezas as a staging ground (the CIA referred to it as a "strike base") for an air assault on Cuba by 15 U.S. fighter jets in addition to a sea assault and a base for the training of the expeditionary forces. Somoza also offered the use of a shortwave radio station to broadcast propaganda into Cuba. As the CIA itself, in its history of the Bay of Pigs invasion planning, notes,[89] the same radio station had been used "during the course of operation PBSUCCESS which resulted in the ouster of the leftist Arbenz government in Guatemala..." The U.S. and Somoza also agreed that bodies of the anti-Castro expeditionary team who were killed during the invasion would be shipped back to Nicaragua for burial. On his own initiative, Somoza imprisoned Cuban exiles who mutinied and refused to take part in the invasion, returning them to the U.S. after the operation failed.

In a case of the tail wagging the dog, the CIA explains, "[i]n return for his support, Somoza wanted assurance that once action against Castro started, there would be no backing down by the USG," that is, "until Castro's defeat."[90] Somoza also demanded the approval of $10 million in loans ($2 million directly from the USG as well as $8 million from the World Bank) in return for agreeing to support the covert operations against Cuba. As for these loans, it was General Somoza (Tachito), who insisted on them when in Washington for John F. Kennedy's inauguration. Indeed, he went behind Kennedy's back to meet with Alan Dulles, head of the CIA, to make this demand. The CIA, according to its own history, then put pressure on the U.S. State Department to ensure that these loans were approved.

The CIA's history of the Bay of Pigs operations makes it clear that there were only two countries in the region willing to help in the regime change plans—Nicaragua and (post-coup) Guatemala—demonstrating Somoza's importance for implementing U.S. foreign policy aims. The U.S. government, dominated in its foreign policy at this time by the CIA, had no hesitation in working with Somoza, knowing full well what a pariah he was. Its official History noted that a C. Thomas Barnes, in raising objections to the idea of using Nicaragua as a staging ground for the operations, "introduced what amounted to moral objections to the association—or to the strengthening the association—with the Somoza Government. Barnes emphasized that this would go down hard with the more liberal elements in Latin America." The note goes on to indicate that Barnes' position was in line with the sentiments of the U.S. State Department.[91] But, of course, these concerns were dismissed, and planning with Somoza went ahead.

The Sandinistas and other true patriots in Nicaragua were painfully aware of all this and wanted revolutionary change, not only to improve the lives of the Nicaraguan people, but also to prevent their country from continuing to be used as a pawn in the U.S.'s foreign policy machinations. This goal of the FSLN cannot be overstated. This was both a matter of national pride as well as a matter of solidarity with other peoples in the region struggling for their liberation in the face of U.S. imperialism. So just as Somoza had an outsized role in impacting the wider world, so, too, would the Sandinistas, but in the opposite direction.

It is important to remember that, during the tumultuous 1970s, the U.S. was also supporting right-wing dictators in other countries as well, such as the fascist General Pinochet in Chile and the brutal Shah of Iran, who himself would be overthrown in a popular revolt in 1979, the very same year as the Sandinista Revolution. Pinochet and the Shah were at least as influential as Somoza, with Pinochet spreading his brand of fascism throughout the Southern Cone of South America and ushering in neoliberal economic policies in the Western Hemisphere—all according to Washington's plans, of course—and with the Shah acting as the U.S.'s enforcer in the Middle East.

As for Somoza, there is no doubt that the U.S.'s support for him was critical to his continued reign. One need only read the statements of the U.S. State Department itself on this score. As a 1976 U.S. State Department Cable itemized, concerning a proposed military budget for Nicaragua for 1977:

> 2. NICARAGUA'S MILITARY DEPENDENCY. THE USG IS THE TRADITIONAL SUPPLIER OF MILITARY EQUIPMENT AND TRAINING TO NICARAGUA WHICH LOOKS UPON THE U.S. AS ITS PROTECTOR AND THE GUARANTOR OF CENTRAL AMERICAN-CARIBBEAN STABILITY. SMALL, WEAK COUNTRIES LIKE NICARAGUA NATURALLY SEEK THE PROTECTION OF A STRONGER NEIGHBOR, OR SOME OTHER SYSTEM OF ALIGNMENT, WHICH ENABLES THEM TO FULFILL THEIR PERCEIVED INTERNAL AND EXTERNAL SECURITY REQUIREMENTS.
>
> 3. NICARAGUA DOES NOT HAVE, NOR FOR THE FORESEEABLE FUTURE CAN IT EXPECT TO HAVE, AN INDIGENOUS ARMS PRODUCTION

CAPABILITY OR ADEQUATE TRAINING BASE TO PROVIDE THE MILITARY EQUIPMENT AND TRAINING SKILLS NEEDED TO MAINTAIN A SMALL, EFFECTIVE DEFENSE FORCE. THEREFORE, NICARAGUA REMAINS HIGHLY DEPENDENT ON OUTSIDE SOURCES OF SUPPLY OF ARMS AND TRAINING.

4. THE UNITED STATES IS THE DOMINANT FOREIGN SUPPLIER OF MILITARY . . . EQUIPMENT FOR NICARAGUA, ALTHOUGH SMALL AMOUNTS OF ARMS AND EQUIPMENT HAVE BEEN PURCHASED FROM BELGIUM, THE UNITED KINGDOM AND ISRAEL IN RECENT YEARS. DEPENDENCE ON U.S. MILITARY TRAINING IS NEARLY TOTAL, THE ONLY EXCEPTIONS BEING THIRD COUNTRY TRAINING (SUCH AS IN MEXICO AND VENEZUELA) IN ISOLATED SKILLS NOT AVAILABLE IN THE UNITED STATES BECAUSE OF OUR MORE MODERN OR COMPLEX EQUIPMENT AND TECHNIQUES.

Of course, in recognition of the fact that most Latin American countries rarely war with each other, the U.S. State Department acknowledges in the same cable that Nicaragua's "security threat" was purely internal:

5. NICARAGUA'S SECURITY THREAT. AT PRESENT, THE NATIONAL GUARD FACES A LOW LEVEL THREAT FROM THE PRO-CASTRO FSLN (SANDINISTA NATIONAL LIBERATION FRONT) WHICH IT HAS THE CAPABILITY TO MEET. FOR THE IMMEDIATE FUTURE, A SERIOUS SUBVERSIVE THREAT IS NOT LIKELY TO DEVELOP ALTHOUGH FSLN RETAINS A DIMINISHED CAPABILITY FOR CONDUCTING ISOLATED ATTACKS AND INCIDENTS THROUGHOUT MOST OF THE COUNTRY.[92]

And so, to put a finer point on it, the State Department made it clear that it wanted the U.S. to continue being the main support and trainer of Somoza's military in order to help Somoza retain power in the face of opposition from his own people.

There are two additional notable claims in this statement. First, the State Department uses the usual trope of referring to the Sandinistas as "pro-Castro." Of course, it does so to denigrate the FSLN as sharing the same Marxist-Leninist values as Fidel Castro, and more generally, as some malign force, which is illegitimate and to be opposed. The truth is that, while there was certainly a Marxist-Leninist tendency within the FSLN, this was not the dominant one, and while the Sandinista leaders admired Fidel Castro and his triumph over U.S. domination, the FSLN is not and never has been some cookie cut-out of the Cuban Revolution of 1959.

Moreover, the system of government that the FSLN sought to create, and ultimately did create, bears no resemblance to that of Cuba. Thus, while Cuba is a one-party state which borrowed heavily from the structure of the Soviet Union, the FSLN intended and in fact did create a multi-party democratic system based upon their own, home-grown tenets of *Sandinismo,* which actually pre-dated the Cuban Revolution of 1959 and even Fidel's 26th of July Movement itself, which began in 1953.

Indeed, had the State Department bothered to read it, they would have seen that the Sandinistas had put forth a complete program for the Revolution in 1969, which was quite pluralistic and democratic, and did not resemble the cartoonish caricature of "Communism," which the U.S. has claimed that the Sandinistas espouse. Thus, amongst other policies, the 1969 program, which the current Sandinista government continues to follow, prescribes the following:

> The Sandinista Popular Revolution will establish a revolutionary government that will liquidate the reactionary structure originated by electoral farces and military coups. The popular power will forge a Nicaragua without exploitation, without oppression, without

backwardness, a free, progressive and independent homeland.

The revolutionary government will dictate the following political measures:
- It will give revolutionary power a structure that allows the full participation of all the people, both at the national level and at the local level (departmental, municipal, local).
- It will guarantee to all citizens the full exercise of all individual liberties, respect for human rights.
- It shall guarantee freedom of thought, leading primarily to the vigorous dissemination of popular rights and patriotic rights.
- It shall guarantee the freedom to organize the labor-union movement in the city and in the countryside, freedom to organize peasant, youth, student, women's, cultural, sports, etc. groups....[93]

Moreover, the pluralistic nature of the Sandinista Revolution has been underscored by the historic alliance which the FSLN has made with other groups and parties since before the Triumph. That is, the FSLN has always understood that it could not win and carry forward the Revolution alone. It has needed to make alliances with certain sectors of business, the Catholic Church and other civil society groups in order to succeed.

While many Western leftists have criticized Daniel Ortega for his more recent alliances with such groups, the FSLN has always recognized their importance. For example, the FSLN's 1978 document entitled "Character of the Sandinista Popular Revolution"—a document I was kindly given by the Agricultural Workers' Confederation (ATC)—talks in detail about the need for the FSLN to form an alliance (*Alianza*) with all those forces in society opposed to the Somoza dictatorship and to foreign intervention. Indeed, the FSLN in this document acknowledges that there could be no triumph without such an alliance.

The other pillars of the Sandinista Program, as set forth in 1969, were:

- revolution in culture and education;
- progressive labor and social security legislation;
- honest government administration;
- reincorporation of the Atlantic Coast into the greater Nicaraguan society;
- emancipation of women;
- respect for all religions;
- independent foreign policy;
- Central American unity;
- solidarity between all peoples;
- the creation of a popular, patriotic army; and
- the veneration of the martyrs of the Revolution.[94]

This 1969 Program continues to be a work-in-progress, setting the agenda for the current Sandinista government.

The other notable claim in paragraph 5 of the above-mentioned 1976 State Department cable is that "a serious subversive threat is not likely to develop" in Nicaragua. Obviously, the State Department was dead wrong in this analysis. Within three short years, the Sandinistas would triumph over the U.S.-backed petty dictator. That the State Department did not see this coming shows how tone deaf it has been to the realities of Nicaragua and the true sentiments and capacities of the Nicaraguan people. In short, the State Department believed its own propaganda—always a dangerous thing to do.

But the State Department was not alone in this erroneous assessment of the situation. Much of the world Left, including the Communist Left led by the Soviet Union, also put little stock in the (primarily) peasant guerilla movement of the FSLN, believing guerilla struggle in Latin America to be a thing of the past, and doctrinally captive to their belief that it was the industrial working class, rather than the peasantry, that was the engine driving social change and revolution. Bluntly speaking, the events that would soon unfold in Nicaragua would shock the world—both Left and Right.

Yet another 1976 U.S. Department of State cable demonstrates that the State Department was quite aware the U.S. economic and military support of Somoza was leading to the kind of repressive measures that he in fact put in place.[95] There, the State Department expressed concern that future aid and loans could be jeopardized by the "Harkin Amendment," which forbade aid to countries with a "consistent pattern of gross violations of human rights," and that Somoza's government certainly could be viewed as one such country. In this regard, the State Department specifically noted "issues of detention incommunicado, treatment of detainees, [lack of] provision of fair trials, etc." It also listed "the practice of holding suspected FSLN detainees incommunicado, without access to their families and legal counsel," "numerous cases of disappearances brought to Somoza's attention by the Nicaraguan Bishop," the "state of siege" imposed by Somoza, and "the suspension of constitutional rights and press censorship."

These were not minor human rights abuses, but profound and systematic ones, which should have made aid to Somoza illegal under the Harkin Amendment but for which the State Department invariably found workarounds in order to maintain the Somoza dictatorship. The State Department continues to find such workarounds to evade the similar and more recent (Senator Patrick) Leahy Amendment, which forbids aid to miliary units guilty of serious human rights abuses—now all but a dead letter due to its utter disregard.

Another human rights abuse singled out by the State Department was "the elimination of Carlos Fonseca and other leaders" by the Somoza government. The murder of the legendary FSLN founder and leader Carlos Fonseca is worth discussing here as it continues to be a source of trauma for the Nicaraguan people. Other than Sandino himself, Carlos Fonseca is certainly the most famous and revered of the Sandinista leaders. His image, with his iconic glasses and goatee, is ubiquitous in Nicaragua. He is largely credited with keeping the memory and philosophy of Sandino alive during some of the darkest days in Nicaraguan history.[96] Fonseca had a thirst for justice for his people, and particularly for the poor majority of Nicaraguans, and had lived a revolutionary life from an early age. As my dear friend Stephen Sefton, an

Irishman who has lived in Estelí with his Nicaraguan wife, Luisa, for many years, explains:

> The revolutionary life of Fonseca consisted of clandestine conspiracy and organizing, constant studying, spells of harsh imprisonment, torture, exile and, finally, combat. On Jan. 6, 1965, after being deported to Guatemala—the third time he received such punishment because of his struggle against the Somoza dictatorship—Fonseca wrote, "One thing the oppressors of my motherland must be sure of. They may expel my body from Nicaraguan soil, but they will never expel from my soul the decision to fight for the freedom and sovereignty of the nation, and for the people's happiness."[97]

Fonseca did not live to see the success of the revolution he had fought for so long and hard, having been killed in battle with the National Guard on November 8, 1976, after losing his glasses and struggling to see as a result. Legend has it that his severed head was brought to Somoza as a prize. The rest of his remains were brought to Managua after the Triumph and his tomb, with an eternal flame illuminating it, resides in the Plaza of the Revolution. I remember the tomb as one of the first things I was taken to see when I first visited Nicaragua in 1987, and it moved me greatly.

Canadian singer-song writer, Bruce Cockburn, memorializes this tomb in his song, "Nicaragua," written in 1983 in Managua:

> *Breakfast woodsmoke on the breeze —*
> *On the cliff the U.S. Embassy*
> *Frowns out over Managua like Dracula's tower.*
> *The kid who guards Fonseca's tomb*
> *Cradles a beat-up submachine gun —*
> *At age fifteen he's a veteran of four years of war*
> *Proud to pay his dues*
> *He knows who turns the screws*
> *Baby face and old man's eyes*

These lines capture my memories of Nicaragua and visiting the tomb back in 1987 perfectly.

The State Department, in the same 1976 Cable, expresses concern that Somoza's human rights violations might impair future aid and that a meeting should be scheduled with Somoza to address these issues. The State Department specifically references Henry Kissinger's meeting with fascist dictator General Augusto Pinochet earlier that year as an example of how that discussion should go. It is therefore worth looking at that meeting to see what such a discussion looks like in practice.

Far from demonstrating a bona fide concern about human rights, U.S. Secretary of State Kissinger had made it clear to Pinochet that the Gerald Ford administration was fighting hard against measures in Congress, at that time being sponsored by Senator Edward Kennedy, to more closely link military aid to other countries based upon their human rights compliance and that he was meeting with Pinochet as a means to show Congress that such legislation—legislation which was being pushed forward due to Chile's human rights abuses—was not necessary. However, the gist of the meeting indicated that Kissinger and the administration really didn't care about human rights compliance, just the bare appearance of such.

As the transcript of the meeting demonstrates, Kissinger praised Pinochet for overthrowing the democratically elected president of Chile, Dr. Salvador Allende, on June 8, 1976.[98] Kissinger told Pinochet, "We want to help, not undermine you. You did a great service to the West in overthrowing Allende." Kissinger further stated, "We welcomed the overthrow of the Communist-inclined government here." Of course, Allende was not "Communist-inclined," but rather a democratic socialist—an irrelevant distinction as far as the Americans were concerned. Further, Kissinger made it clear that the U.S. was happy with the demise of Allende, who was killed in the coup. Kissinger never expressed concern about the fact that Pinochet's forces also killed around 3,000 Chileans and tortured nearly 30,000 more in the aftermath of the overthrow.[99] As we will see, Somoza would dwarf these figures even in a far smaller country.

Kissinger went on to assure Pinochet that, while he was compelled to have this meeting with him about human rights to try to fend off Congress's overzealousness on this issue, he and the Administration really were not concerned about such matters. As Kissinger explained:

> In the United States, as you know, we are very sympathetic with what you are trying to do here. I think that the previous government was headed towards Communism. We wish your government well. At the same time, we face massive domestic problems, in all branches of the government, especially Congress, but also in the Executive over the issue of human rights. As you know, Congress is now debating further restraints on aid to Chile. We are opposed. But basically we don't want to intervene in your domestic affairs. We can't be precise in our proposals about what you should do. But this is a problem which complicates our relationships and the efforts of those who are friends of Chile. I am going to speak about human rights in the General Assembly. I delayed my statement until I could talk to you. I wanted you to understand my position. We want to deal in moral persuasion, not by legal sanctions. It is for this reason that we oppose the Kennedy Amendment.

In other words, Kissinger is telling Pinochet that he has to make a show about human rights to placate the pesky members of Congress who care about such niceties and hoped, by so doing, that the U.S. would thereby not be hindered in delivering Pinochet the weapons (specifically, F-5E combat jet aircraft) he was asking for.

In a chilling passage, both Kissinger and Pinochet mention their joint concern about General Orlando Letelier, an ally of the late President Allende, who was engaged in lobbying Congress in favor of the Kennedy human rights amendment. Handwritten arrows and underlines highlight both Letelier's name and Pinochet's statement: "Letelier has access to the Congress." Three months later, Letelier's car would be blown up in an upscale section of Washington, D.C., killing Letelier, his driver and Ronnie Moffitt, a young intern from the Washington-based think-tank, the Institute for Policy Studies.[100] General Pinochet personally ordered this car-bombing, and uncontroverted evidence exists that the assassin who carried out the hit "was paid by the CIA before the bombing and was in regular contact with top officials at the spy agency."[101] So much for Kissinger's little pep talk with Pinochet about human rights.

Finally, it is worth noting that, in this same year of 1976, Kissinger also met with Admiral Cesar Augusto Guzzetti, the foreign minister of the new fascist junta of Argentina, telling him that the junta should destroy the left opposition in Argentina, and with all due haste. As *The Guardian* explained in 2004:

> Henry Kissinger gave Argentina's military junta the green light to suppress political opposition at the start of the "dirty war" in 1976, telling the country's foreign minister: "If there are things that have to be done, you should do them quickly," according to newly declassified documents published yesterday.
>
> State department documents show the former secretary of state urged Argentina to crush the opposition just months after it seized power and before the U.S. Congress convened to consider sanctions.
>
> "We won't cause you unnecessary difficulties. If you can finish before Congress gets back, the better," Mr. Kissinger told Admiral Cesar Augusto Guzzetti, the foreign minister, according to the State Department's transcript.[102]

Kissinger, demonstrating his cynical disregard for human rights, further told Admiral Guzzetti, "Look, our basic attitude is that we would like you to succeed. I have an old-fashioned view that friends ought to be supported. What is not understood in the United States is that you have a civil war. We read about human rights problems but not the context. The quicker you succeed the better." And the junta completed its assignment accordingly, forcibly disappearing 30,000 individuals in Argentina's "dirty war" that followed in coordination with other Southern Cone countries, such as Pinochet's Chile, in what was known as Operation Condor.[103] That Kissinger is still regarded in the U.S. as a respected, elder statesman tells one everything they need to know about the true nature of U.S. foreign policy and the U.S. government's views of human rights. However, it must be noted that outside the U.S., Kissinger's reputation is much different. Thus, he is almost universally considered a war criminal, with the Spanish Judge Baltasar Garzon, who famously ordered the arrest of Pinochet himself, issuing a warrant for Kissinger to appear before his bench to answer questions about his role in "'Operation Condor'—a concerted effort by the ruling regimes of Brazil, Argentina, Chile, Uruguay, and Paraguay to suppress political dissent in the 1970s."[104]

In Nicaragua, the human rights situation became more dire as the Sandinistas became more successful in their struggle to topple Somoza. Indeed, in his desperate attempt to cling to power, Somoza would claim more victims in one year—1978–1979—than Chile and Argentina combined. Fifty thousand Nicaraguans would be killed in this year.[105]

The 1978 human rights report of the Inter-American Commission on Human Rights (IACHR)[106]—a body of the usually pro-U.S. Organization of American States (OAS)—reveals just how deadly this year was. Per the IACHR, Somoza suspended the exercise of constitutional rights in Nicaragua beginning in September of 1978, and this is when the worst human rights abuses began.

Taking a page out of the U.S. Marine playbook from the 1920s and 1930s, Somoza engaged in the aerial bombing of Nicaragua's towns and cities, leading to most of the huge death tolls. Indeed, around eighty percent of the 50,000 Nicaraguans who lost their lives at this time were killed in these aerial bombings.[107] As the IACHR concluded in its report: "The Commission is totally convinced that the Nicaraguan National Guard not only used its firepower indiscriminately causing a great number of casualties and tremendous suffering to the civilian population, but that it also ordered the people to remain inside their homes before the bombing, without even allowing them to evacuate, thus violating a basic humanitarian norm."[108] In other words, Somoza waged a total war against his own people, and it was specifically aimed at terrorizing the civilian population.

The IACHR gives significant details of the carnage which these bombing wrought, based on eyewitness accounts. Here is testimony about the bombing, for example, from the city of Chinandega:

> It was Thursday, September 14, when the airplanes began to strafe our houses in Barrio La Libertad. My husband, my 5-year-old daughter and I were crouched in a corner of our house, crying and thinking that we would die right then and there because the bullets and shrapnel were destroying our small wooden house. We decided to go out and seek shelter in a safe place; we left by the kitchen, my husband with our daughter in his arms. A plane flew very low, it seemed as if it was coming straight at us and fired some rockets which hit my daughter's shoulder and my husband who was carrying her. Everywhere I looked I could see the heart and intestines of my child; she was in pieces, destroyed. My husband, who had already lost his arms, took about thirty steps, with blood spouting everywhere until he fell dead. He had a wound in the chest; he had a part of a still-smoking rocket stuck in his leg. The left leg was bare to the bone.
>
> I wanted to lift my child but she was in pieces; I didn't know what to do. I ran and I got her little arm and I tried to put it on her, I tried to put everything that was coming out of her back in but she was already dead. She was my only daughter, and I had a difficult time having her; and I used to dress her up for parties and spoil her. I don't know what I'm going to do, I'm going to go crazy.[109]

Here is further testimony from a professional association in the historic city of León, Nicaragua:

> On Thursday the 14th, early in the morning, we heard on the radio about the suspension, decreed by the government, of all constitutional rights and the implantation of the State of Siege. The army announced through loudspeakers in an airplane and a helicopter that people should remain in their houses with the doors locked and not allow strangers in because the National Guard was going to fight. There had been rumors that the President was going to order the bombing of the city but no one had believed such rumors since we didn't consider that a person could do such a thing, that an army would bomb its own people; nevertheless, at around 9 in the morning, several helicopters and planes, it's impossible to say how many, flew over the city and to the surprise and terror of the people of León, the impossible happened. The airplanes and helicopters suddenly dived and started to drop shrapnel, bombs and rockets which spread panic among the civilian population. While the civilians remained inside their houses, innocent victims of the massacre, the insurgents moved to more secure places. For many more hours, the National Guard continued the destruction and genocide of this unprotected city. After a brief period of respite, at noon, the stunned population was victimized by another bombing which started around 4:30 in the afternoon and ended around 7:30 in the evening. The moon illuminated the city and facilitated the continuation of the bombing during the first hours of the night.[110]

According to the IACHR,

> Estelí was the city which suffered the greatest material damage. But, above all, it was at the human level where there was the most devastation. The Special

Commission was able to confirm that a large number of people from Estelí, especially members of the Bar Association, Medical Society, Chamber of Commerce, Red Cross, Dental Association and firemen, priests, journalists and workers, were dead, wounded, imprisoned, in asylum or in exile, harassed or threatened with death.[111]

What the National Guard did not bomb in Estelí, it torched. According to one resident of Estelí, "My house was burned in the presence of my husband and children. We begged the [National] Guard not to burn it down but he answered that he had orders from his superiors to burn 'this fucking town.'" Another resident corroborated this account, explaining that "The Guard also went around with gasoline cans and started fires. It was horrible. All of us were sick with nervousness. We lived horrible days. Twenty-one days of anguish and terror, without water, electricity, or food. The Guard arrived at the house where we were sheltered and

Memorial to Victims of Somoza's bombing campaign, Masaya
DANIEL KOVALIK, MARCH, 2022

started to search. It's incredible that the Guard took the jewelry right off of me."

I recently visited the city of Masaya where bombings also took place. There is a park there, built where a bomb was dropped, leaving untold numbers of dead and leveled buildings. In that park is a modest monument which reads, "In memory of the fallen heroes and martyrs of the 500-pound bomb launched by the genocidal air force on July 3, 1979."

And then, after the bombings and burnings, the National Guard moved into the targeted cities to engage in further atrocities. As the IACHR explains:

> When the bombings were over, the National Guard carried out a military operation, which has come to be known as "Operation Mop-up," designed to annihilate the last pockets of resistance. According to complaints received by the Special Commission even before they went to Nicaragua, the National Guard during this phase carried out a cruel attack summarily executing numerous non-combatants, for the mere fact that they lived in neighborhoods or small hamlets where members of the Sandinista Front had fought. Among some of the places mentioned are Monimbó in Masaya, Subtiava and Fajas William in León, El Calvario in Estelí, and Colonia Venerio in Chinandega.[112]

The IACHR visited a number of these sites and interviewed numerous people about these operations, leading to the following conclusion: "All the proof gathered by the Commission has led to the conclusion that the Nicaraguan National Guard's actions during the phase called 'Operation Mop-up' were marked by complete disregard for human life, that they shot numerous people, in some cases children, in their own homes or in front of the same and in the presence of parents and siblings."

The IACHR report contains numerous accounts of the atrocities committed during "Operation Mop-up" in various cities and towns. The following account is from León:

In the days after the bombings and coinciding with the desperate exodus of a large part of the population, the National Guard, in its efforts to destroy the resistance, broke and destroyed closed doors of houses, warehouses and stores, and also furniture, looking for rebels or documents and compromising objects. We know several cases of those abuses. But even more painful and enraging is the fact that a true manhunt has been organized, where there are no prisoners but only death for young men over 14 for simple suspicion, or rather fear, that they might be rebels. Horrible massacres have been committed by the military who show up in different places, indiscriminately shooting the male population, leaving widows and unprotected orphans. There are places in which whole blocks have been left without men. Other times, unarmed youths fleeing from the ferocious persecution head for the countryside where they are victims of the deadly action of an informer, respectable citizens are captured with their sons and cruelly tortured. Sometimes when they don't find the right person, they capture women as hostages to force the men to present themselves. This persecution must immediately cease because it constitutes a crime against humanity and is depriving our city of its youth, the necessary manpower for the reconstruction and progress of the country.[113]

The National Guard also had no problem with assassinating children whom they saw as helping the cause of the Sandinistas. Thus, in the town of Diriamba, witnesses gave the following testimony to the Commission:

> Manuel Jesús Ribera was a child of 12, very popular and well-loved in the neighborhood, called "the mascot." During the fighting he helped the Sandinistas, bringing them messages and food but without fighting with them. This fact later caused the Guard to search for

him implacably, even killing another child whom they mistook for "the mascot." As vengeance, the father of the other murdered child looked for him until he found him in the Diriamba market and denounced him to the National Guard. Soldiers of the National Guard found him there on Thursday, October 5, hiding inside a box, and then took him out and machine-gunned him, killing him.[114]

The murder of this child was freely admitted to the IACHR by National Guard Commander Lola, "who, as an explanation, answered that he 'helped the guerrillas.'"

Even after this brutal operation, the National Guard was not finished. According to the IACHR, "At the end of military operations in the cities most affected, a new phase began around September 21, in which the National Guard is charged with carrying out a systematic campaign of persecution and killing young men who are suspected of having some link with the Sandinista Front, or for the simple fact that they sympathize with it."

When one reads of the brutality of the National Guard, it is important to remember that all of its ranks were trained at the U.S. Army School of the Americas (SOA), then located in the Panama Canal Zone.[115] Indeed, as journalist Stephen Kinzer noted at the time, "'Nicaragua is the only country which sends the entire annual graduating class of its miliary academy for a full year of training'" at the SOA.[116] So notorious did the SOA—now located in Columbus, Georgia—become (particularly after its infamous torture manual was discovered[117]) that it was later renamed the Western Hemisphere Institute for Security Cooperation (WHINSEC) in an attempt to give it a make-over.

Then, there are the forcible disappearances. Argentina is the most famous for such disappearances, having "disappeared" about 30,000 people during the "dirty war" of the 1970s and early 1980s. More recently, close U.S. ally Colombia dwarfed those figures, with the Red Cross reporting over 92,000 disappeared by 2014.[118] And Mexico has recorded around 100,000 disappeared in the course of its recent U.S.-backed "war on drugs."[119] In the late 1970s, the Somoza regime had carried out its own share of disappearing people, particularly peasants—the backbone of the Revolution. There, according to the IACHR, at least 321 peasants were disappeared by the National Guard.[120]

Even the Catholic Church was not immune from the assaults by Somoza's National Guard, with Catholic priests from the U.S. reporting that the Guard had taken over 28 rural churches which they converted "into barracks and places of torture."[121]

Another serious human rights concern addressed by the IACHR was the conditions to which prisoners were being subjected throughout Nicaragua. This is an issue of particular note given that nearly all of the Sandinista leadership, including Carlos Fonseca, Daniel Ortega and Tomás Borge (the only FSLN founder to survive to the Triumph), spent significant time as political prisoners in Somoza's dungeons. It is impossible to understand the struggle of the Sandinistas without understanding the abuses their leadership suffered while in detention, the incredible strength they showed in enduring, persisting, and rising above it, and the magnanimous ways in which they responded to their abusers later.

The IACHR visited 12 prisons within Managua and spoke to numerous prisoners. As it reported:

> During the conversations with the prisoners, the Special Commission repeatedly received charges of physical and psychological torture. The great majority of the prisoners alleged that while under detention they had been severely beaten by rifle butts, pistol-whipped, beaten with fists and kicked. On several occasions, the prisoners, very frightened that they might be seen by the guards, showed scars on their heads and other parts of their bodies, black and blue marks, and broken ribs and bones. The Commission also took note of the easily visible scars on the wrists of many prisoners in different locales of the country who stated that they had been hung by their arms. The Special Commission's attention was drawn to the similarity of the scars.

The Commission also received claims related to the application of electrical shocks through the use of electric prongs or cables connected to generators, batteries or "jumper cables." The places where the claimants alleged that electric shock was most used as a means of torture were the National Guard Command Posts in Masaya and Jinotepe and the National Security Office of Managua.[122]

The use of electric shock administered on political prisoners, particularly on their genitals, was of course standard operational procedure in Latin America, as the CIA trained security forces throughout the region in such techniques.[123] However, it appears that the CIA first honed its skills in such techniques in the U.S. war on Vietnam, then later in Latin America in the 1970s and 1980s, and later still in the "war on terror" in places like Iraq, Afghanistan and Guantanamo Bay, Cuba.[124]

The specifics of the torture visited upon the top Sandinista leadership seem to be much worse than reported by the IACHR. For example, Daniel Ortega was a prisoner of the Somoza regime for 7 long years, from January of 1967 to December of 1974 at La Modela prison in Tipitapa—a prison I myself visited in 2018, though conditions were much better by then under the Sandinistas. Daniel's prison experience would leave him psychologically and physically damaged, though certainly not broken. As one biographer notes, he suffered "the usual kicks and beatings, sometimes while hooded, ... [and] electric shocks directly to the testicles."[125] In addition, while Daniel does not talk openly about his prison experiences, the poetry he wrote during his confinement insinuates that being kicked in the testicles, face and ribs; threats of and possibly actual forced sodomy (including by a police baton); and being made to eat his own feces were other forms of torture visited upon him and other prisoners. Being left handcuffed alone in a "tiny" space merits special mention: [126] it is rumored that Daniel was kept in a coffin for nine months straight.

And yet, Daniel endured. Indeed, in addition to keeping up on the news of the world with the help of some sympathetic guards who provided him and his comrades with access to a radio, he read voraciously, including Proust's *Remembrance of Things Past*, one of the most famously difficult books to read. (I tried to read it once and got no further than five pages in).[127] He also learned something about Nicaraguans in prison which would become important in the future:

> Ortega and the other prisoners quickly learned that some of the prison guards privately sympathized with the FSLN. They were simply doing their job to support their families. In prison, Ortega learned that it was difficult, almost impossible, to draw a sharp line between the Nicaraguans who supported the revolution and those who did not. Later in life, he would show that he had learned this lesson well by extending merciful amnesty to those who became caught up in the counterrevolution.[128]

Daniel would ultimately be freed due to a daring feat by his Sandinista comrades who stormed a fancy party on December 27, 1974, which included the head of the Nicaraguan Central Bank, the U.S. Ambassador and two relatives of Somoza.[129] The comrades took 14 big wigs hostage and were able to thereby force the release of a number of political prisoners, including Daniel; the publication of hitherto-censored Sandinista messages; and one million dollars in ransom. Daniel, once released, would quickly return to helping lead the struggle.

In light of this history, I can only shake my head when I see cartoonish references to Daniel Ortega in books like Jonathan M. Katz's very recent *Gangsters of Capitalism*—an acclaimed and well-reviewed book focusing on the crimes of the big bankers and U.S. Marines in the earlier part of the 20th Century.[130] Given the subject of Katz's book, he doesn't discuss Ortega or his contemporaries much at all, but what he does say would lead you to believe that Ortega was a non-entity in the struggle who somehow emerged out of nowhere ("maneuvered" Katz puts it) to lead Nicaragua after the Triumph. Based upon the statements of a single disgruntled former Sandinista leader, Katz portrays Ortega as "very lazy" and not a significant Sandinista leader in the struggle leading up to the overthrow of Somoza. Lazy? A man who endured 7 years of torture only to turn around and start fighting again is lazy? If he was so insignificant, why was Ortega elevated to the National Directorate of the FSLN during his incarceration,[131] and why did the Sandinistas bother engaging in a high-stakes operation to free him?

Authors like Katz don't even try to answer such questions because a narrative disclosing this important history in Ortega's life would itself give the lie to his dismissal of Ortega. To the contrary, Katz extolls how courageous his one witness, Monica Baltodano, was because she was "imprisoned for nine months" under Somoza "before resuming her guerilla activity and helping to bring down the dictatorship." Daniel's seven years of captivity is apparently of no moment in comparison and is never mentioned. Katz doesn't try at all to explain how Daniel became the leader and public face of the FSLN. Indeed, when he asks Baltodano how the Sandinistas came to be led by Daniel, she sidesteps with, "I do believe that it will be necessary to do much deeper research to answer that." As far as we can tell, Katz did no such research and simply leaves the apparent mystery of the re-emergence to prominence of Daniel Ortega unexplained. This is what passes for great historical writing these days.

As for Tomás Borge, his treatment was even worse than Ortega's, and indeed indescribable. Tomás was forced to endure the rape and murder of his wife, Yelba Moyorga, by the National Guard as well as the rape of his 16-year-old daughter, Bolivia, also by Somoza's guardsmen. Bolivia, who was the light of Borge's life, would later commit suicide at Christmas time as a consequence of the emotional suffering brought about by the rape. According to his daughters Valeria and Ana with whom I spent some time in Managua, Tomás would never celebrate Christmas again.[132] Tomás was also held in prison for two years, from 1976 to 1978, during which time he was subject to grave torture. While it is rumored that he was castrated, his daughters assured me he was not. Indeed, Valeria, born two years after the Triumph in

Ana Borge, Valeria Borge and José Antonio Guevara Miranda at the tomb of Tomás Borge
DANIEL KOVALIK, JULY, 2022

1981, is living proof that he was not. However, Valeria did tell me that many of Tomás's fellow prisoners were castrated and indeed forced to eat their own testicles. While this may seem overly graphic to relate, it is important to emphasize that this type of ritual and grisly torture by the security forces of U.S. client states in Latin America and beyond was quite common. Indeed, as Noam Chomsky has often pointed out, this type of torture, bordering on the Satanic, was not happening in the USSR or its client states at this time.[133] In the name of fighting what was portrayed as "the evils" of Communism, the U.S. and its allies were engaged in much greater evils. This point cannot be emphasized enough.

Meanwhile, Tomás, whom Ronald Reagan would single out as a particularly evil Marxist-Leninist, would vow to find his torturers after the Triumph of the revolution and exact his revenge. And here is how Tomás himself describes his revenge:

> After having been brutal tortured as a prisoner, after having a hood placed over my head for nine months,

after having been handcuffed for seven months, I remember that when we captured these torturers I told them: "The hour of my revenge has come: we will not do you even the slightest harm. You did not believe us beforehand; now you will believe us." That is our philosophy, our way of being.[134]

And Tomás made good on his word. As Amnesty International would report after the Triumph:

> When the government of Anastasio Somoza Debayle was overthrown thousands of National Guard soldiers laid down their arms and surrendered at a number of camps and establishments under the supervision of the International Committee of the Red Cross and the Red Cross of Nicaragua. Shortly afterwards they were handed over to the Government of National Reconstruction as prisoners. At that time the Minister of the Interior, Commander Tomás Borge, declared that no prisoner would be ill-treated, that neither the death sentence nor torture would be used in Nicaragua and that all the accused would be tried in accordance with the existing criminal laws. He also asserted on various occasions that previous members of the National Guard would be considered prisoners of war.[135]

Tomás Borge went on to write a poem, "My Personal Revenge," with Luis Enrique Mejía Godoy (the legendary songwriter of the Sandinista Revolution) about his act of personal forgiveness against his torturers

This poem would later become the basis of a song performed by Jackson Browne in 1989, entitled, "My Personal Revenge."

The reader may be curious about guerilla leaders like Daniel and Tomás writing poetry, but anyone who knows anything about Nicaragua is aware of the Nicaraguan people's unique appreciation for poetry and the fact that nearly all Nicaraguans are poets. Indeed, Salman Rushdie quotes Daniel Ortega as saying,

"'In Nicaragua, everybody is considered a poet until he proves to the contrary.'"[136] And, alongside the guerilla, Augusto Cesar Sandino, who himself was a poet, the other most celebrated figure in Nicaraguan history is poet Rubén Darío, whose image often appears alongside Sandino on murals and paintings throughout the country.

> **My Personal Revenge**
>
> My personal revenge will be the right
> of your children to school and to flowers;
> My personal revenge will be to offer you
> this florid song without fears;
> My personal revenge will be to show you
> the good there is in the eyes of my people,
> always unyielding in combat
> and most steadfast and generous in victory.
> My personal revenge will be to say to you
> good morning, without beggars in the streets,
> when instead of jailing you I intend
> you shake the sorrow from your eyes;
> when you, practitioner of torture,
> can no longer so much as lift your gaze,
> my personal revenge will be to offer you
> these hands you once maltreated
> without being able to make them forsake tenderness.
> And it was the people who hated you most
> when the song was language of violence;
> But the people today beneath its skin
> of red and black* has its heart uplifted.
>
> [*THE COLORS OF THE SANDINISTA FLAG]

But before leaders like Daniel and Tomás could show such magnanimity to the torturers of themselves and their people, they had to defeat Somoza and his National Guard.

By late 1977, it was becoming clear to all in Nicaragua, including the business community, that Somoza no longer had legitimacy to rule and was going down, one way or another. However, there was great disagreement over what would take Somoza's place. The ruling economic elite wanted to make sure that Somoza would be removed before the Sandinistas, with their revolutionary program, forced him out.[137] However, the U.S. was reluctant to give up on its man in Managua on whom it had been able to count for so long, and it was the U.S. that was, of course, calling the shots.[138]

It was obvious why the U.S. continued to back Somoza for as long as it did. Somoza protected its business interests across the boards. As Chomsky and Herman note, as late as May of 1977, the *Wall Street Journal* was still touting Nicaragua as "'[a]n investor's dream come true,'" and predicting that "'Nicaragua will continue to enjoy political stability and a bright economic future.'"[139] Among other benefits Nicaragua offered, the *WSJ* pointed out, were "'no capital gains or dividend tax,'" and "'low-abundant labor' which 'takes pride in its task,' with no compulsory union affiliation."[140]

These benefits reflected the fact that the Nicaraguan people's per capita income was $130 a year in the countryside, and disregarded that they suffered high levels of malnutrition, infant mortality and illiteracy.[141] Chomsky and Herman, quoting John Huey in another *WSJ* article, explain that, for example, "'the colonial city of León—before it erupted into full-scale guerilla warfare—reveals a degree of poverty and desperation that is startling, even by Latin American standards.'"[142] León would be the first city liberated by the Sandinistas, and they are proud of this, as I witnessed when there during the celebration of the 40th Anniversary of the liberation of León.

Clearly, something had to give, and even most of Nicaragua's ruling elite had come to realize this. The bourgeoisie eventually settled on a strategy of "Somocismo without Somoza."[143] "Somocismo without Somoza" entailed convincing Somoza to step down while maintaining his brutal National Guard in place. The Carter Administration, which was never able to bring itself to publicly call for Somoza's ouster and which even sent a letter to Somoza praising him, eventually settled on this strategy in the face of the reality that Somoza could no longer provide the stability needed for U.S. investments.[144] This strategy required "'replacing the Somoza dictatorship with an equally conservative, though less brutal successor.'"[145] Even Carter, the self-dubbed "human rights President," abided by his administration's policy of "searching for stability rather than social and economic change or even human rights—repeating, as they see it, American policy during its occupation of Nicaragua between 1912 and 1933, and its subsequent support of the Somoza family.'"[146]

U.S. aid to Nicaragua, though reduced, continued to flow to the Somoza government until the bitter end, and Somoza's Guard continued to be trained at the U.S. Army School of the Americas.[147] Moreover, as per usual, any deficit Somoza suffered in U.S. military aid was made up by the U.S.'s loyal client state, Israel, and also by the right-wing military dictatorship of Brazil, which, installed by Washington in 1964, was also closely aligned with the U.S.[148]

The revolutionary FSLN wanted the entire system overturned. It wanted to thoroughly democratize the country and insisted that the National Guard be replaced in its entirety by an army of the people, with ranks drawn from the masses who actually participated in the fight against Somoza.[149] And the Frente further wanted real economic and social change, which would include "the confiscation of natural resources and of enterprises that exploited them; the nationalization of maritime, air, and urban public transport; an agrarian reform program that would promote and diversify production, limit landowning property and national idle latifundios; freedom of trade union organization; reforms in legislation; and so on...."[150] Finally, the FSLN insisted on non-interference in Nicaragua's affairs from other countries, most notably the U.S. In other words, they insisted on an anti-imperialist agenda.[151]

It was these demands that impelled the people of Nicaragua in droves to the side of the Sandinistas and away from the agenda led by the economic elite. As Carlos M. Vilas, who served in the Sandinista government after the Triumph from 1980–1984, explains:

> The alliance that the non-Somocista bourgeoisie tried to establish with the U.S. Embassy had to compete with the revolutionary struggle of the FSLN and its frontal opposition to the Somicista regime. The open participation of the popular classes in the Sandinista struggle was on the rise.... Failing in its mass actions, the bourgeoisie opted for palace strategies: a military coup, pressure from the U.S. Embassy. But this could not win over the FSLN's strategy that combined mass insurrectional action, popular organization, rural guerilla warfare, conventional military combat, international diplomacy, and the opening toward all forces opposed to Somocismo on the basis of an uncompromising program. The Nicaraguan bourgeoisie ... could not present itself to the peasants, workers, students, unemployed, the poor of the countryside and the city, in other words the majority of the country, as a real alternative to the FSLN.[152]

By this time, the FSLN was being led by nine Comandantes—three for each of the three different, and sometimes competing, tendencies in the party—the Prolonged People's War group (led by Tomás Borge and most favored by Fidel Castro), the Proletariat Tendency (an Orthodox Marxist faction led by Jaime Wheelock, who studied in Europe and Chile), and the Terceristas (or Insurrectionist) tendency.[153] The Tercerista tendency of Daniel Ortega and his brother Humberto (their youngest brother Camillo was killed fighting the National Guard when he joined a spontaneous uprising in Monimbó), while considered the most moderate of the tendencies in terms of program, was also considered most militant in terms of tactics, and led some of the boldest assaults such as an attack on three National Guard quarters in October of 1977.[154]

And, it was Daniel and Humberto who were the most decisive in wanting to move forward and quickly towards victory over Somoza before the bourgeoisie was able to succeed in convincing Somoza to step down while then carrying forward with their non-revolutionary "Somocismo without Somoza" plan.[155] Quite possibly the most dramatic action the Ortega brothers led, along with Eden Pastora (Comandante Zero) and Dora Marie Téllez, was the storming of the National Palace in August of 1978—an event which sparked the major insurrectionary period, catalyzed national support for the FSLN and helped lead to ultimate victory in less than a year.[156]

This event, which inspired a mass uprising in September of 1978, also sparked a great repression by Somoza, who massacred 3,000 Nicaraguans to put this uprising down.[157] This massacre was met with silence by the Carter Administration.[158] Indeed, as Chomsky and Herman note, it was Carter's refusal to "openly call for his [Somoza's] resignation or entirely withdraw support from him" which

> set the stage for Somoza's suppression of a virtually unified Nicaraguan population and the death of thousands in September, 1978, again compliments of the U.S.-trained and -armed national guard. With U.S.-supplied helicopters and gunships and other sophisticated weaponry, Somoza demonstrated that U.S. counterinsurgency techniques may now permit pacification of a unified hostile population.[159]

But even this repression could not hold back the tide of the revolution, led by a Sandinista leadership with remarkable resolve. When Carter tried at the 11th hour to "piece together a joint U.S.-Latin American intervention that would prevent a total Sandinista victory.... Not a single nation in the hemisphere would join him."[160]

Clearly this history simply belies any claims that somehow Daniel "came late to the party" in leading the struggle and emerged only after the Triumph to take top leadership. While it is beyond the scope of this book to analyze deeply the different divisions within the FSLN, suffice it to acknowledge that they were there, as in any revolutionary struggle, and they were there from the beginning. In Nicaragua, "[t]he tendencies did not turn on each other with the kind of violence and constant public attacks that ripped apart other leftist movements around Latin America, but they did not collaborate either."[161]

Moreover, Daniel played a key role in uniting the three factions in 1978 to push for a unified effort to unseat Somoza. As one historian notes, most of Ortega's efforts

> at personal persuasion [to unite the factions] were successful, seemingly because they were fair. One of his main goals in late 1978 and early 1979 was to negotiate a reunification of the FSLN. In part it was a personal goal. Since his teenage years, Ortega's whole life had been devoted to and enveloped by the FSLN, and he could not imagine winning a revolution without it. While he was obviously willing to act independently, he wanted the victory to be for the Sandinistas, not for the Terceristas alone.[162]

All of this is important to keep in mind when, later, different FSLN leaders would fall out, fall back in, and then fall out again with the party and the top leaders thereof, most notably with Daniel. As in other revolutionary situations, some of the former disgruntled FSLN leaders would even turn to counter-revolutionary activity—some very violently so.

CHAPTER 3

THE TRIUMPH

On July 17, 1979, as the Sandinista fighters approached Managua, the last Somoza fled the country. July 17 is now known as the "Día de la Alegría" (Day of Joy) and is celebrated every year. Two days later, on July 19, the Sandinistas entered Managua and the Plaza containing the National Palace and the original Catholic Cathedral—still in ruins from the 1972 earthquake. The Plaza, now the "Plaza of the Revolution," filled with thousands of fighters and ordinary Nicaraguans waving the red and black flags of the FSLN in what became a celebration of epic proportions, marveled around the world.

A ragtag bunch of poorly armed guerillas had defeated a brutal dictatorship and its National Guard which had been trained and armed to the teeth by the United States—the Colossus to the North. This truly was a people's Revolution, and a people's victory. While the Revolution certainly had its leaders, the fighters were mostly regular people who battled the National Guard, sometimes with the most rudimentary of weapons, in order to achieve their freedom. As one historian wrote, "So the revolution came. When it did, it was most visibly led by *los muchachos* (the kids)—men, women, and children who fought with rocks, .22 rifles, anything they had, in order to overthrow their hated dictator.... Combining the numbers, approximately one in every twenty Nicaraguans was killed or injured in the revolution, yet most fought on."[163] And they fought on to victory in one of the most storybook revolutions in history.

David had slain Goliath. The world was mesmerized as guerillas literally dangled from the remains of the Catholic Cathedral in jubilation. Only the hardest of hearts would have been unmoved by the sight. To this day, I cannot see photos or footage of this scene without tears welling in my eyes. July 19 is now the national day of celebration of the Revolution, and I have been there in the Plaza several times to enjoy this day.

As Andrew Reding wrote in the Forward to *Christianity and Revolution*, a compilation of writings by Tomás Borge, "It is a revolution without parallel in recent history. In the political realm, a vanguard party organized along the Leninist model but inspired by the moral example of Augusto Sandino" began to democratize the political life of Nicaragua.[164] "In the economic realm, the Sandinistas ... set up a system that combines capitalist and socialist characteristics in such a way as to give priority to production for satisfying human needs. And in the religious realm, the FSLN has integrated Christians and Marxists in one revolutionary movement, entrusting top government ministries to Catholic priests and lay persons."[165] Most notably, the new government famously included three Catholic priests—Father Miguel D'Escoto Brockmann, a U.S.-born Maryknoll priest who served as the revolutionary government's first Foreign Minister, who was elected the 63rd President of the UN General Assembly and who would remain loyal to Daniel and the FSLN unto his death in 2017; and the two Cardenal brothers, Father Ernesto and Father Fernando, both Jesuit priests.

All three of these priests were adherents to the tenets of Liberation Theology, a philosophy that attempted to synthesize Christianity with Marxism, focused on building the Kingdom of God on Earth, right here and now and advocated "the preferential treatment of the poor." This was a philosophy that the U.S. had violently opposed from its inception after the Second Vatican Council in 1962, and which the Vatican itself would come to oppose after the death of Pope John XXIII who had initiated the sweeping, humanistic changes of the Council.[166] It must be said: the institutional Church in Nicaragua was definitely not in favor of Liberation Theology and has been and continues to be quite conservative and reactionary. The official Church of both Rome and Nicaragua would pose many challenges to the new Sandinista government, the presence of priests in the government notwithstanding, and would play a quite treacherous role during the tragic events of 2018.

The most prominent victim of the U.S.'s crusade against Liberation Theology would be slain shortly after the Sandinista Revolution. El Salvador's Archbishop Oscar Romero, a conservative priest turned radical after becoming bishop and seeing fellow priests, including his good friend Father Rutilio Grande, murdered by U.S.-backed forces, was gunned down while saying Mass in a field hospital on March 24, 1980. He was killed by death squads armed and trained by the U.S. only one month after he had written a letter to President Jimmy Carter asking him to stop arming the soldiers who were killing his people.[167] Romero was recently canonized a Saint by the Roman Catholic Church under the leadership of Pope Francis, an Argentine cleric who has openly stated that his chief mentor in life was a Communist and who is more amenable to Liberation Theology than his predecessors. Shortly after the death of Archbishop Romero, 4 American churchwomen—Maryknoll Sisters Maura Clarke and Ita Ford, Ursuline Sister Dorothy Kazel, and lay missionary Jean Donovan—were raped and murdered in El Salvador by U.S.-backed death squad forces upon returning to El Salvador from a conference in Nicaragua.[168]

As one of my friends who lived in El Salvador for years, explained, the murder of Saint Romero would "begin the Salvadoran Civil War in earnest," and that war in El Salvador would become linked with the Sandinista Revolution, with the Reagan Administration hell-bent on destroying the progressive movements in both countries. The rebels leading the charge in El Salvador—the Farabundo Martí National Liberation Front (FMLN), named after El Salvador's own liberation leader of the 1920s and early 1930s—also carried a red and black flag as did the Sandinistas. Traditionally, the red and black flag has been associated with anarcho-Communism, and the Sandinistas and Sandino himself certainly have some roots in anarchism as well as socialism, but also in Christianity.

The Salvadoran civil war would end similarly to how it began—with the murder of six Jesuit priests and their housekeeper and daughter in 1989. As the Center for Justice and Accountability puts it succinctly, "the Salvadoran Civil War was "punctuated by three well-known atrocities: the 1980 assassination of Archbishop Oscar Romero that sparked the conflict, the rape and murder of four American churchwomen that caused international outrage, and the 1989 Jesuits Massacre that finally compelled the international community to intervene."[169] All told, 75,000 Salvadorans would be killed by the U.S.-backed government forces during this conflict.[170]

As discussed above, in the spirit of Christian forgiveness, one of the first acts of the new government was to suspend the death penalty, and many National Guardsmen—men who had killed, tortured and raped so many in Nicaragua—were set free and allowed to flee across the border. Tomás Borge himself personally stayed the hands of Nicaraguan citizens who gathered to kill National Guardsmen after the Triumph. Again, Andrew Reding explains,

> Borge carried his personal forgiveness to public office. When, in the tumultuous days following the collapse of the dictatorship, a lynch mob gathered outside the Red Cross building where National Guardsmen had found refuge, Borge hurried to the scene before the building could be overrun. "To what end did we carry out the revolution," he asked the crowd, "if we are going to repeat what they did?" The mob was stilled."[171]

José Adán Rivera Castillo told me how he helped facilitate the National Guards' exodus into Honduras. José was in his late teens when he quit school and joined the guerillas. I had the honor of interviewing him in Managua in March of 2022. His family was from the northern coffee region of San Rafael del Norte, which formed one of the main bases of Sandino in his fight against the U.S. Marines. José pointed out that Sandino's wife was from this region as well.

José was now 63 years old—around the same age as the Cuban Revolution, he was proud to tell me. He had grown up as an agricultural worker on his family's medium-sized farm, which grew coffee and raised cattle. José's grandparents helped Sandino's troops in the 1920s and 30s by providing them with horses and mules. José's grandmother had even met the elusive Sandino back in the day. He explains that his grandparents supported Sandino because they were (nationalist) Liberal Party members of the stripe represented by former President José Zelaya, as was Sandino, and because he was fighting for the benefit of the peasants. His family knew they were risking their lives to support Sandino because this also meant fighting the North American troops.

José Adán Rivera Castillo
DANIEL KOVALIK, MARCH, 2022

José explained that he came to the Revolution via his interest in the Cuban Revolution. He began listening to Radio Havana when he was six years old, and he began to read revolutionary literature. He has never ceased in such studies. Indeed, he was reading a book on the Sandinista Revolution at the time I interviewed him. He proudly took it out to show me and explained that he reads a book a week.

José left his studies in Managua and joined the FSLN and the armed struggle up in the Carlos Fonseca Northern Front because he wanted to fight for a more just and equitable society. It was both his own political studies as well as his lived experience as someone who had worked in the fields as a young person and saw the horrible inequalities in Nicaraguan society that led him to the struggle. José was part of the final offensive of the Sandinistas from 1978 to 1979, and he was 20 years old when the day of the Triumph came.

José's squadron did not make it all the way to Managua in time for the Triumph. And so, they stayed behind and oversaw the exodus of the National Guardsmen. His squadron's job was to make sure that the Guardsmen were not armed and the Sandinistas escorted them safely to Honduras. "They went with the white flag, and their escort respected this," José explained to me after I expressed my surprise at the fact that they just let these monsters go free. José simply explained that "in battle, [the revolutionaries] were implacable; in victory, they were gentle."

This, of course, was true, and explains why the Sandinistas won the love and adulation of people around the world. That said, this kindness and forgiveness would be used against them in a big way by the United States, bringing to mind the maxim I learned early on as a union lawyer—"no good deed goes unpunished."

President Jimmy Carter, having failed in his attempt to pressure the Sandinistas to form a new government with National Guard officers,[172] was beginning to assemble the Guard in Honduras as the nucleus of what would become, with the support and organization of the CIA and the fascist junta of Argentina, the Contras. In fact, Carter organized an air lift of National Guard leaders to Honduras for this purpose. He did so in airplanes marked (falsely) with Red Cross insignia—a war crime, as Noam Chomsky often reminds us.[173] Thus,

> In March 1980, Carter, alarmed at this loss of a U.S. investor haven, ordered Major General Robert Schweitzer to Honduras to confer with its armed forces about becoming a "bulwark" against communism in the Central American region. Carter authorized $1 million for the CIA to support anti-Sandinista labor groups, media, and political organizations. In mid-November 1980, newly elected, but not yet inaugurated, President Reagan's transition team met with a small group of exiled Nicaraguans in Honduras in preparations to fight the Sandinistas.[174]

Meanwhile, one of the major tasks the new revolutionary government set out to do was to teach the largely uneducated population how to read and write. To do so, they set up a popular literacy campaign headed by Father Fernando Cardenal, in which thousands of mostly young volunteers were sent out throughout Nicaragua, and in particular to the countryside, to teach the illiterate. The number of volunteers numbered around 95,000[175]—an extraordinary figure given that Nicaragua had a total population of only around 2.2 million at that time. This demonstrates the popular support the Revolution had and the enthusiasm with which the people met the Sandinistas' agenda.

Berta Sanabria, who was involved in the literacy campaign—which they actually termed, a "Crusade"—shared her experience with me when I visited the education center in Estelí where she currently works—still a teacher, after all these years. In 1980, Berta had joined other volunteers going out to the very poor peasant areas of Estelí. She was only 18 years old at the time. As she explained, her brigade, the Irline Cacares Brigade, spent 9 months living with the peasant community. At that time, the community had no lights and no running water. The experience taught the *brigadista*s themselves about the daily lives and experiences of the people in their country, who toiled to grow their food. Her brigade taught 300 people. As Berta explained,

> We lived with them in all respects. We ate with them, met with them. We taught them basic reading and writing. Some couldn't even write their names. Before this, these were forgotten people. We taught them the importance of learning. They then made other decisions for their own children. This opened their eyes. They began then to think of a different future, for example of a profession for their children beyond the campo. This was the principal purpose of the Revolution as articulated by Carlos Fonseca.

Berta then told me how, when the U.S.-backed Contra War started, the Contras, quite tellingly, killed the *brigadistas* who were trying to teach those that the Somoza regime had neglected and even persecuted. But the campaign continued in spite of the dangers. Everyone, regardless of political affiliation, was involved in this movement, Berta explained. She, for example, was not a Sandinista at the time, but she is now.

The other big initiative of the new Revolutionary government was the Agrarian Reform—a major goal of the Sandinistas, going back to Sandino himself. Under the Sandinistas' Agrarian Reform program, between 1981 and 1984 nearly 50,000 poor families were given new titles to their own land.[176] By 1990, a full 60 percent of Nicaraguans benefited from the land reform program.[177]

In March of 2022, Lola del Carmen Esquivel González described to me at the women's coffee collective she lives and works at—the Gloria Quintania Cooperative—how she had been supporting the Revolution since she was only 14 years old. This was back in 1976, three years before the Triumph. At that young age, she was already organizing unions and youth. After the Triumph, she too joined the Literacy Crusade and went out and taught fellow peasants how to read and write. The other task she took on was defending the 2100 manzanas (approximately 3500 acres) of land which the Revolutionary government had distributed to peasants in her region. When the Contra War came, she and other women kept the land productive while the men went out to defend the country.

I asked Lola what the Revolution meant to her. She explained it to me quite proudly:

> One of the biggest benefits of the Revolution is that we can live well. We have between 80 and 90 social programs—education, land, health care. We have food sovereignty [meaning they grow all the food they eat]

Lola del Carmen Esquivel González
DANIEL KOVALIK, MARCH, 2022

...We are the Revolution, and we have been able to improve our lives. I was a sad worker, a nomad before the Revolution. I was paid 3 Cordobas a day. Now, I have land, I grow coffee, I am an entrepreneur. It is not we who are poor, but you. We have water, we have land, we have love, we have life, we have peace. We feel quite happy.... We are not in war even though they want us to be. I'm 60 years old. I have 11 children. I feel young and ready to defend the Revolution. Soon, we will have a Revolution which is totally red and black. My mother gave birth to me, the ATC [the Peasant Workers Union] collected me, and the Revolution allowed me to develop into what I am today.

Lola was one of many poor Nicaraguans who benefited very swiftly from the overthrow of Somoza and the rise of the FSLN. As Oxfam pointed out in its report, "Nicaragua: The Danger of a Good Example," when the Sandinistas took over in 1979, they inherited a country where the vast majority of the people were impoverished and completely neglected. As Oxfam then explains in detail: one baby in eight under one year's of age died; two out of three children under five were undernourished; 93% of rural homes had no safe drinking water; six out of ten deaths were caused by preventable and curable diseases; over half the population was illiterate; two out of three peasant farmers were either completely landless or had plots too small to meet their basic needs; 90% of medical services in the country served only 10% of the population, with more than half the country's doctors clustered in the capital city; less than 20% of pregnant women and children under five years of age received health care; and 94% of rural children were unable to finish primary school.[178]

Not only that, Somoza looted the Nicaraguan treasury before fleeing the country, leaving the Revolutionary government a balance of exactly zero to work with. As the writer Salman Rushdie put it so eloquently in his short book on the Nicaraguan Revolution, *The Jaguar Smile*,

When Don Anastasio Somoza fled the country, he took with him everything he could carry, including all the cash in the national treasury. He even had the bodies of Tacho I and Luis Somoza dug up and they, too, went into exile. No doubt he would have taken the land as well, if he'd known how. But he couldn't, and nor could his cronies who fled with him, and so the government of the new Nicaragua found itself in the possession of the abandoned estates, amounting to half the arable land of the country."[179]

Rushdie makes a point of saying that all of the land distributed to the peasants as part of the agrarian reform program came exclusively from this abandoned land.

The Sandinistas moved quickly to turn the situation of the country around with the scant resources they had, and they were quite successful. Oxfam, citing a World Council of Churches report from 1983, sums up the gains of the Revolution, which had triumphed only 4 years before:

What we see is a government faced with tremendous problems, some seemingly insuperable, bent on a great experiment which, though precarious and incomplete at many points, provides hope to the poor sectors of society, improves the conditions of education, literacy and health, and for the first time offers the Nicaraguan people a modicum of justice for all rather than a society offering privilege exclusively to the wealthy ... and to the powerful.[180]

Oxfam explained that the Sandinistas swiftly began to develop the country from the bottom up, and in a democratic fashion:

After what Nicaraguans call the "triumph" on 19 July 1979 when the old Government fell, rapid changes were set in motion....

The cornerstone of the new development strategy, spelled out by the Sandinista Front some years before taking power, was to give priority to meeting the basic needs of the poor majority. This was to be achieved by involving people in implementing change at a local level, through their neighborhood groups, peasant associations and other organizations; at a central level, representatives of these organizations were to cooperate closely with the Government Ministries.

The new Government of National Reconstruction stressed its desire to develop a mixed economy and political pluralism in a country that had no tradition of democracy or free elections. Great importance was also attached to achieving a high degree of national self-sufficiency and an independent, nonaligned foreign policy.[181]

Oxfam concluded that the Revolutionary government's dedication to real development for its people was indeed exemplary. Thus, "[f]rom Oxfam's experience of working in seventy-six developing countries, Nicaragua was to prove exceptional in the strength of that Government commitment."[182]

As Oxfam details,[183] the achievements of the Revolutionary government were extraordinary, with illiteracy slashed from 53 to 13 percent. In 1980, just a year after the Triumph, Nicaragua would receive the UNESCO Literacy Award for its achievements. By 1984, Nicaragua had built over 1400 new schools, mostly in rural areas. Oxfam cites the prestigious *New England Journal of Medicine* for the proposition that "'[i]n just three years, more has been done in most areas of social welfare than in fifty years of dictatorship under the Somoza family.'" In addition to the Literacy Crusade, the Sandinistas embarked upon an inoculation campaign, which eradicated polio and nearly eradicated malaria.

Furthermore,

A significant expansion of workers' rights, especially the right to form unions and engage in collective bargaining, was a definitive achievement of Sandinista power. Prior to 1979 only about 30,000 Nicaraguans (less than 10% of the workers) were trade union members and strikes or even collective bargaining were made virtually impossible by the Somoza regime. By the end of the 1980s there were more than 2000 workplace unions with some 55% of the working population unionized....[184]

There were also huge advances for women's rights achieved from the early days of the Revolution. This should not be surprising, given the critical role that women played in leading the struggle from the very beginning. As Erica Takeo and Rohan Rice write in their recent article, "Women's Struggle in Nicaragua: From liberation fighters to building an alternative society":

> Firstly, it must be said that it is impossible to separate the women's movement in Nicaragua from the Sandinista revolution. They are mutually interdependent. The reason is quite simple: women's lives are dramatically better under Sandinista governance. During the Somoza dictatorship, supported by the U.S. and its allies, many women lived in slave-like conditions. They were prevented from owning property, accessing health care, directly receiving salaries, or attending formal education. Reproductive rights and information on sexual health were non-existent. Rape was extraordinarily common, particularly on the plantations. Under Somoza's tyranny, women existed for expropriation and nothing more....
> Much of this changed after 1979: women were instrumental in the overthrow of Somoza, both as combatants and in supporting roles. Throughout the 1980s women fought for all the basic human rights, many of which were immediately granted by the socialist FSLN. In Nicaragua's first democratic elections in 1984, 67

percent of the women who voted in that election voted for the FSLN.[185]

As Takeo and Rice note, 30 percent of the Sandinista guerillas at the time of the Triumph were women, with many serving in all-women militias, while a number "then went on to senior military positions in Sandinista society and have worked tirelessly to progress the revolution ever since, like Doris Tijerino, who led the Sandinista Police, or Leticia Herrera, who directed the Sandinista Defense Committees."[186] I myself met and interviewed Doris Tijerino, who is a Comandante of the Revolution—the highest honor anyone could have—as part of a documentary I helped make, entitled "Nicaragua: The April Crisis and Beyond." She made it clear to me that she is still firmly committed to the Revolution, the FSLN and to Daniel, and that she believes that the leadership is still committed to their original principles and to the cause of women's rights. It is curious, as I told her, that she is never interviewed in the U.S., including by the progressive press, even when they are seeking women's voices from Nicaragua. She just smiled and shrugged her shoulders.

Indeed, the concrete gains for women after the Triumph were substantial:

> The first major victory was the Agrarian Reform and Co-operatives laws of 1981 whereby Nicaragua became the first country in Latin America to recognize women's rights to wages, land, and co-operative organizing as equal to that of men. This was soon followed by "the Law Regulating Relations Between Mothers, Fathers and Children [1981] . . . which created equal rights over children for both parents; and the Law of Nurturing [1982] which obliged all men to contribute to their children's upkeep and to do their share of household tasks" . . . In these early revolutionary years, single women also won the right to legally adopt; the trafficking of Nicaraguan children was banned; and

women began to fill various positions in the National Assembly.[187]

And then, after seven years of intense lobbying and pressure by women's organizations, the FSLN published the *Programa* which recognized the double oppression of women for the first time in Nicaraguan history.[188] Specifically, the *Programa* acknowledged that "women suffer additional exploitation specific to their sex and that struggles within the revolutionary process were legitimate; it also roundly condemned *machismo*. Most importantly, it argued that women's issues could not be 'put off' till after the war...."[189]

In addition, there were great advances in women's health—something which had been all but neglected in the past. There was a concerted effort to train midwives, especially in the northern part of Nicaragua, to assist women, particularly in rural areas, with childbirth without the assistance of a doctor.[190] Mothers were encouraged by *brigadistas* to breastfeed as opposed to feeding with bottles, which often contained contaminated water that could lead to life-threatening diseases for babies.[191] And for babies—who did suffer from diarrhea, a condition many could die from—the government set up rehydration centers throughout the country.[192]

The FSLN, clearly the predominant force of the Revolution, also moved quickly to form a national unity government that was inclusive and pluralist, and had representation from all groups, including the bourgeoisie, which had opposed Somoza. That is, the FSLN did not insist on ruling alone, though it certainly could have. Again, this was quite consistent with the Frente's long-time position of working in alliances with all sectors of society in order to succeed. As Carlos Fonseca put it,

> We are conscious that socialism is the only perspective that the people have to achieve a profound change in their living conditions. This does not suggest that we will exclude persons that do not think as we do, and ... we are disposed to march alongside people with the most diverse beliefs who are interested in the

overthrow of the tyranny and in the liberation of our country.[193]

And so, while the FSLN had significant representation in the new transitional government, including Daniel Ortega, Sergio Ramirez and Moises Hassan, only two of the first government Ministers were from the FSLN—Tomás Borge, who became Minister of the Interior, and Jaime Wheelock, who led the Nicaraguan Institute of Agrarian Reform (INRA).[194] As Carlos M. Vilas notes, the FSLN, magnanimous in victory, gave the bourgeoisie greater representation in the new government than their actual role in overthrowing Somoza would have warranted or necessitated.[195]

As this make-up of the new government would suggest, the Sandinistas did not push for a purely socialist economy, but rather for a mixed market/socialist economy which resembled something closer to that of countries in Scandinavia as opposed to those in the Eastern Bloc. And indeed, the FSLN was and is a member of the Second International, which includes the U.S.'s Democratic Socialists of America (DSA)—that is, the party of Bernie Sanders and AOC—and not the Third International, which included the Communist Parties of the world, including the Communist Party of the Soviet Union and the Communist Party of Cuba. Indeed, I remember a representative of the FSLN being warmly received at a national DSA conference I attended at Columbia University in the spring of 1987. This is important to remember when one assesses the claims of people like Ronald Reagan and his henchmen like Elliott Abrams (a man who still lurks around in the halls of Washington D.C.) who have demonized the Sandinistas as evil Marxist-Leninists and have justified their crimes against them and Nicaragua on this basis.

Within five years of the Triumph, the Sandinistas would hold the first truly free and fair elections in Nicaraguan history. The 1984 elections engaged seven parties, including the FSLN led by Daniel Ortega as Presidential candidate; all were given the right to freely campaign throughout the country and on TV and radio.[196] Of the six parties running against the Sandinistas, three were from the left and three were from the right of the political spectrum.[197] The Sandinistas won with 67% of the vote. Numerous independent observers, including a parliamentary delegation from Ireland and the U.S.-based Latin American Studies Association, concluded that these elections were free and fair.[198]

Shamelessly, the U.S. government, which had supported the brutal Somoza dictatorship for 45 years, refused to recognize these elections. And indeed, as demonstrated by a leaked National Security Council document, the U.S. was attempting to undermine the credibility of the elections even before they began, knowing full-well that the Sandinistas were the popular choice of the people and that elections would prove this fact to the world.[199] Furthermore, the U.S. had already launched the Contra War against Nicaragua before the elections even took place—making the very holding of these elections a victory in and of itself. By waging war against Nicaragua at the time of these elections, the U.S. disadvantaged the FSLN in the electoral process, given that the electorate was keenly aware that voting for the Sandinistas would ensure more war.

Nothing the Sandinistas could do or not do, could save them or Nicaragua from more aggression by the United States, which simply could not abide the fact that an independent, sovereign country in Central America had dared to go its own—though albeit moderately leftist—way. Nicaragua was in for more suffering imposed by its neighbor from the North, and the gains of the Revolution described above would be greatly undermined by a brutal and quite illegal military and economic war against this tiny country.

Indeed, by the late 1980s, the Revolution would effectively be stalled, not to return to its forward momentum again until 2007. Instead, the Revolution had to shift its focus from social advance to defending itself—as every other Revolution in the world has had to do—and many compromises had to be made in the process, which few of us from the outside could hardly understand in full—though this has not stopped many arm-chair intellectuals in the West from being quick to criticize these compromises. As one of my favorite historians and social critics, Michael Parenti, has opined on this subject:

> It occurs to me that when people as smart, different, dedicated and heroic as Lenin, Mao, Fidel Castro, Daniel Ortega, Ho Chi Minh and Robert Mugabe—and the millions of heroic people who followed and fought with them—all end up more or less in the same place, then something bigger is at work than who made what decision at what meeting. Or even what size houses they went home to after the meeting....
>
> To be sure, the pure socialists are not entirely without specific agendas for building the revolution. After the Sandinistas overthrew the Somoza dictatorship in Nicaragua, an ultra-left group in that country called for direct worker ownership of the factories. The armed workers would take control of production without benefit of managers, state planners, bureaucrats, or a formal military. While undeniably appealing, this worker syndicalism denies the necessities of state power. Under such an arrangement, the Nicaraguan revolution would not have lasted two months against the U.S.-sponsored counterrevolution that savaged the country. It would have been unable to mobilize enough resources to field an army, take security measures, or build and coordinate economic programs and human services on a national scale.[200]

When one considers the brutality of the counter-revolutionary war the U.S. waged against Nicaragua, it is hard to believe that the Revolution, or even the country of Nicaragua, survived at all.

CHAPTER 4

REAGAN'S BRUTAL WAR AGAINST NICARAGUA

When I think of the Contra War what makes me most angry is the thought of what could have been. Had Nicaragua been able to simply pursue the path it set in 1979 to teach the ignorant, feed the hungry, provide land to poor farmers, guarantee health care for all, treat women with respect—that is, to carry out the mandate of the Gospels—where would Nicaragua be today? What if the U.S. government had heeded the very simple and reasonable demand of the U.S. peace movement to "let Nicaragua live"? Of course, we will never know for sure. But I think when we judge Nicaragua and the Sandinista Revolution today these are very important questions to consider.

The reality was, of course, that the U.S. government could not abide by Nicaragua's post-Triumph progress, and it set out to destroy it. The Reagan White House was so desperate to do so even in the face of Congressional opposition that it resorted to selling cocaine on U.S. city streets, and illegally selling arms to Iran to keep its project of destruction going, as will be discussed below. Rolling back the Nicaraguan Triumph was truly an obsession. When CBS's *Face the Nation* asked Che Guevara what Cuba wanted from the United States, he had answered quite simply that they wanted the U.S. to forget Cuba entirely.[201] Nicaraguans desperately prayed for the very same. But this was not to be. The Eye of Mordor had seen Nicaragua and its gaze was now firmly set upon it.

According to the U.S. State Department's own Office of the Historian, the first major attack of the Contras against Nicaragua took place in March of 1982—just over two and a half years after the Triumph. And, as discussed below, there were actually smaller attacks as early as December of 1981. The Revolution was never given a real chance to breathe. Rather, the goal was to strangle the infant revolution in its crib.

Even more telling, the Office of the Historian admits that

> These "Contras," as in "counterrevolutionaries," were primarily ex-Nicaraguan National Guard members who had gathered in Honduran territory.... In response, the Sandinistas undertook a dramatic build-up of military manpower assisted by Soviet and Cuban advisers and weaponry, mostly from the Soviet bloc.[202]

There is a bit to unpack here in these pregnant two sentences. Note that the U.S. State Department admits that the Contras were primarily former members of Somoza's National Guard—an inconvenient truth that apologists of the Contras would try to deny. As a comprehensive study from Brown University reports,

> The main contra force, the FDN, grew out of the Fifteenth of September Legion, which was established by Somoza's National Guardsmen who had fled into neighboring Honduras, El Salvador, and Guatemala as the Sandinistas took power in July 1979. A July 1982 [U.S.] Defense Intelligence Agency Weekly Summary described the Legion as a "terrorist group." Some 50,000 Nicaraguans had died in the revolution to rout the National Guard and overthrow the 44-year Somoza family dictatorship. National Guardsmen were responsible for the rape, torture, and wounding of thousands of other Nicaraguan women, men, and children.[203]

The Brown study notes that "[i]n a staff report, the Congressional Arms Control and Foreign Policy Caucus found that 46 of the 48 positions in the FDN's military command structure were held by former [National] guardsmen."[204]

Given the composition of the Contra leadership, there is no doubt that the ultimate goal of the Contra War was to bring back the old regime—one that anyone would have to concede was both brutal and undemocratic. In other words, the goal was *not* about restoring a democracy which the U.S. pretended had existed prior to the Sandinistas' victory. Indeed, the Contra leadership's history of horrendous human rights abuses against the Nicaraguan people during the Somoza dictatorship was a fair predictor of their conduct in their new, counter-revolutionary war against Nicaragua.

What the Office of the Historian neglects to point out is that the Contras were entirely the creature of the CIA, working hand-in-glove with the Argentine fascist military junta, which organized, funded and directed them. The CIA had begun organizing the Contras almost immediately after the Sandinistas' Triumph—that is, before it was even possible to know how the fledging government would conduct itself. It therefore should come as no surprise that all of the claimed justifications for arming the Contras were simply made up. The entire Contra program was based on lies.

As the Brown study relates,

> In late 1981, the Reagan Administration settled on a policy of providing arms, money, and equipment to the Argentinean-backed Contras. This followed President Carter's authorization, in early 1980, of CIA financial support to the Nicaraguan opposition (for the purposes of "organization and propaganda," but not "armed actions")...[205]

Then,

> In December 1981, President Ronald Reagan signed a secret directive authorizing an expenditure of $19 million to conduct paramilitary operations in Nicaragua. Administration officials claimed before Congressional intelligence committees that the purpose

of aid to the Contras was interdicting arms allegedly being supplied to the Salvadoran revolutionaries by the Nicaraguan government. Despite this claim, David MacMichael, a CIA intelligence analyst from 1981 to 1983, charged in June 1984 that the CIA had "systematically misrepresented" Nicaraguan aid to the Salvadoran rebels. Since April 1981, he said, there had been no verified reports of arms shipments from Nicaragua to El Salvador.[206]

The other truth buried in the Office of the Historian's statement is that major military support from the Soviets did not come until *after* the Contras began attacking Nicaraguan soil. This too is important, for it belies claims that the Contra War was somehow a response to the Soviet domination of Nicaragua. Indeed, none other than Fidel Castro had counseled the Sandinistas early on not to cozy up too closely with the Soviets lest they invite attack from the U.S., and lest they lose some of their hard-fought national independence to the Soviet Union. Daniel and the FSLN initially heeded this counsel. But, just as it had done with regard to countries like Vietnam and Cuba itself, the U.S. drove Nicaragua closer to the Soviet Union by its violent assaults. Then it used the resulting relationship to justify further attacks. This was the classic Cold War playbook, and it worked like a charm.

Another lie perpetuated to justify the U.S.'s war against Nicaragua was that the Sandinistas were systematic human rights abusers. However, while the Sandinistas were certainly guilty of their own share of mistakes and excesses, the facts demonstrated that they had made great efforts to respect human rights, especially if measured by the standards of other Central American countries and in the face of the pressures put on them by the counter-revolutionary activities which followed so quickly upon the heels of the Triumph. Thus, the Brown study quotes a 1985 report of America's Watch (a division of Human Rights Watch), which concluded:

The misuse of human rights data has become pervasive...When inconvenient, findings of the U.S. Embassy in Managua have been ignored; the same is true of data gathered by independent sources. In Nicaragua, there is no systematic practice of forced disappearances, extrajudicial killings or torture—as has been the case with the "friendly" [counterrevolutionary] armed forces of El Salvador. While prior censorship has been imposed by emergency legislation, debate on major social and political questions is robust, outspoken, even often strident.... Nor has the Government practiced elimination of cultural or ethnic groups, as the [Reagan] administration frequently claims; indeed in this respect, as in most others, Nicaragua's record is by no means so bad as that [of] Guatemala, whose government the administration consistently defends. Moreover, some notable reductions in abuses have occurred in Nicaragua since 1982, despite the pressure caused by escalating external attacks... [The] description of a totalitarian state bears no resemblance to Nicaragua in 1985."[207]

One of the most enduring allegations against the Sandinistas was their treatment of the Miskitu Indians on the Atlantic Coast. The U.S. government claims that the Sandinistas simply set out to assimilate the Miskitus—for example into the dominant Latin, Spanish-speaking culture—a claim belied by the fact that the Sandinistas' literacy crusade in the Atlantic Coast actually focused on maintaining and promoting the spoken and written indigenous languages there. As Michael Shapiro explains in his, "Bilingual-Bicultural Education in Nicaragua's Atlantic Coast Region":

Within the first 18 months of the revolution, the Sandinistas took two decisive steps in shaping their Atlantic Coast educational policy. First the new government brought to the Atlantic Coast its National Literacy Crusade. In March 1980 a national effort was launched to raise the staggeringly low literacy rate inherited from the Somoza years. Seven months later, in October of that year, a parallel *Cruzada de Alfabetización en Lenguas* was initiated in the English, Miskitu, and Sumo languages of the Atlantic Coast. This three-language literacy campaign, the first recognition by any Nicaraguan central government of the need for native language education on the Atlantic Coast, proved a decisive event in terms of both political and educational relations between the Miskitu and Creole communities and the Sandinistas.[208]

The earliest and most severe allegations against the fledgling Sandinista government in regard to their treatment of the Miskitus—allegations which became the centerpiece of the U.S.'s propaganda war against the FSLN and the justification for the backing of the Contras—were either entirely fabricated or grossly misrepresented and were indeed an integral part of the CIA's explicit plan to undermine the credibility of the Sandinistas and inspire armed insurrection against them by the Miskito communities. Quite notably, the allegations center around events which allegedly took place in December of 1981—coinciding with Reagan's December 19, 1981, authorization of monies for the CIA's backing of the Contras as well as the bombing of a Nicaraguan airline at the Mexico City airport.[209]

The most infamous allegation surrounds the events along the Rio Coco River in the Northern Atlantic Coast region, which quickly came to be known as "Red Christmas." The claim was that the Sandinistas had engaged in attacks on Miskitus living in this region around Christmas time, and that this was part of a planned "ethnocide" by the FSLN.[210] But in actuality, it was members of the Miskitu community aligned with the CIA and Contra leader Steadman Fagoth Muller—a Miskitu Indian and former Somoza collaborator—who had carried out attacks with the goal of provoking a wider conflict. As Michael Fredette explains in an insightful paper entitled "Contemporary American Print Media Coverage of Nicaragua's Miskito People during the Contra War":

Around Christmastime 1981 a series of attacks did in fact occur along the Rio Coco, but that is where the similarities end. These attacks, which were dubbed *Navidad Roja* (Red Christmas), actually marked the beginning of the Miskito rebels' violent campaign against Nicaragua. As Reynaldo "Ráfaga" Reyes recalls it, Navidad Roja began on Christmas Day when a band of Miskitos mostly armed with clubs and bows, attacked a Sandinista garrison at San Carlos on the Rio Coco. They killed everyone there besides the radio operator, who they used to lure the area commander to the town and laid in ambush for his arrival. Lucho, the commander, was found "tied to a tree, disemboweled. His heart had been removed." Historian Roxanne Dunbar-Ortiz, who was in Nicaragua at the time but not near the site of these attacks, recounted similar but slightly different details. Rather than Christmas Day, Dunbar-Ortiz says it took place on the December 21, 1981. Dunbar-Ortiz theorizes that there were dual purposes for carrying out these attacks on the border. First, to create a northeastern front that would necessitate a large Sandinista presence to control, drawing forces away from other areas in the country. Secondly, she proposes that "the CIA's objective was to place civilians—Miskitus—in the crossfire, so that the U.S. could accuse the Sandinistas of massacring the Indians." [Historian Jane] Freeland concurs with this assessment of rebels and the Central Intelligence Agency sharing responsibility for Red Christmas, with the intent to create a "U.S.-recognized liberated zone."

This version of events is confirmed by Michael Shapiro in his journal article, "Bilingual-Bicultural Education in Nicaragua's Atlantic Coast Region." And both Fredette and Shapiro explain that the Sandinistas' forced evacuation of thousands of Miskitos—another event used against them for propaganda purposes—was in response to the "Red Christmas" attack and intended to move Miskitus out of harm's way of future attacks.

Note, moreover, that the Contra assaults in the Atlantic Coast assault took place on December 21, 1981—just two days after Reagan had directed monies toward CIA operations with the Contras.

Oxfam, which had people on the ground in the Miskitu Coast, gives the Sandinistas their due for trying to make the best of a terrible situation:

> The Contra military build-up escalated from the beginning of 1981, with 96 separate border incidents reported between January and April. The level of attack led to the evacuation of isolated communities along the border, who were moved inland for their safety. In January 1982 the Nicaraguan Government took the highly controversial decision to move the Miskitus from their settlements along the River Coco. The Miskitus understandably resented the suddenness of their removal and the loss of their homes and crops, which were destroyed to prevent their being used by the Contras. About 10,000 Miskitus fled north across the border, some of them subsequently joining the counter-revolutionary forces.
>
> Whilst criticism must be made of the handling of the situation, Oxfam feels that genuine efforts were made to help the 8,000 or more Miskitus who were resettled inland. In contrast to the totally inadequate resettlement provisions made for the Miskitus 20 years before [by Somoza], the Government took steps to try to provide the five new settlements at Tasba Pri with housing, agricultural and public health services.[211]

Oxfam relates that even their staff were not immune from the attacks by the Contras, as one of their employees who was working on new water pumps in Tasba Pri was fired upon by Contra soldiers in 1983. While he survived, he had to leave the area for his own safety before his work on the pumps was finished.

The second of the two chief allegations, allegedly made by the Honduran government, was that the Sandinistas had entered Honduras in December of 1981 and carried out the brutal killing of 200 or so of the 3,000 Miskitus who had (voluntarily) followed Steadman Fagoth Muller into Honduras to join the Contra forces, who were just being organized. However, within two weeks, the Honduran government issued a correction to the InterPress Service on the initial report wherein it "denied making the statement and denied its accuracy as well."[212] In addition, the 1982 report of the United Nations High Commissioner of Human Rights (UNHCR) regarding its activities in the area of this alleged event contained absolutely no mention of such an attack.[213] Not surprisingly, the mainstream U.S. press, which had reported on the initial allegation, failed to report on either the Honduran government's correction or the UNHCR report, and therefore, this allegation has endured in the memories and beliefs of the American public, including the American Left.[214]

Demonstrating the Sandinistas' good faith in regard to the Miskitu peoples, they were able to even make peace with the Miskitus who had joined the counterinsurgency well before the overall Contra War ended in 1990, and this was because the Miskitus quickly recognized that the Sandinistas had their interests at heart much more than did the Contras and their CIA masters. As Philippe Bourgeois wrote in 1988 in his journal article entitled "The Miskitu Conflict: CIA Incompetence Matched by Sandinista Reforms and Indian Pragmatism,"

> Indeed on the Atlantic Coast of Nicaragua, the U.S. had already lost control of the political and military process by 1985.... In fact, in several regions it is the former anti-Sandinista Miskitu squadrons who are now patrolling to keep the Hispanic contra troops from being able to enter their territory. Indeed, the Sandinistas negotiated different cease-fire arrangements with almost every single individual Miskitu comandante.

Some indigenous fighting units have retained complete autonomy from the Sandinista army. The only difference now from during the war is that today they receive their bullets, guns, uniforms, and medicine from the Nicaraguan government instead of from the CIA. Other Indian squadrons have been organically integrated into the Sandinista army.[215]

Philippe attributes these developments to the Sandinistas' willingness to address the Miskitus' longing for more autonomy, unlike the CIA, which based its decisions regarding its ever-shifting alliances in the Atlantic Coast, not upon what was good for the Miskitus and other indigenous groups, but upon its own single-focused desire to overthrow the Sandinistas. The CIA's counterinsurgency goals inevitably meant continuing the war at all costs, including increasing the suffering and loss of life of the Miskitu peoples. In other words, while the Sandinistas strove for peace and meaningful reconciliation, the CIA pursued a policy of fighting the Sandinistas to the last Miskitu Indian.

As Philippe explains, the Miskitus rejected

> the continued racism and dogmatism of the CIA operatives who are in charge of renewing the blood bath in Indian territory. Up until now they have systematically insisted on promoting the least Indian-oriented leaders who are most willing to accept outside orders and who willingly subsume their struggle to the dictates of the Hispanic contra whose military leadership continues to be dominated by ex-Somoza National Guardsmen.

Indeed, why would anyone think that the CIA and Reagan Administration—which were simultaneously waging a genocidal war against the Mayan Indians in Guatemala—would act in any other way; that they actually cared about the indigenous peoples in Nicaragua or anywhere else?

It should also be noted that former Miskitu Contra leader Steadman Fagoth Muller has since become a staunch supporter of the FSLN and President Daniel Ortega, just as have a number of other former Contra leaders. Indeed, former Contra leader Jaime Morales Corazo ran as Daniel Ortega's vice-presidential candidate during Daniel's successful 2006 Presidential bid, which focused on peace and reconciliation.[216] Jimmy Carter, who observed these elections, lauded them as free and fair and praised the conciliatory tone of Ortega's campaign.[217]

Daniel's willingness to work with former Contras has certainly been criticized by some on the Left, and, truthfully, was not readily accepted by many Sandinista adherents. As Sandinista militant José Antonio Guevara Miranda, the husband of one of Tomás Borge's daughters, Valeria, explained to me over a great Chinese lunch in Managua, "Daniel was the first person to start calling the former Contra leaders 'brothers.' This was hard for many of us to accept at first, but then we came to the understanding that this was important for bringing about national unity and reconciliation." For her part, Valeria herself explained that her father, Tomás Borge, himself considered Jaime Morales Corazo, the former Contra who ran as Daniel's running mate, as a friend. Here again, Daniel and the FSLN demonstrated their incredible capacity to forgive, and to put aside differences in order to bring peace to a country torn asunder by civil conflict brought about by the U.S.'s imperial machinations. Still, as we shall see below, Daniel's actual policies stayed true to the Sandinista values even as he worked with people like Morales.

Indeed, many people focus on the former friends and allies of Daniel Ortega who have turned against him—while of course ignoring the many friends and comrades who remain with him—and few regard this turn of events as demonstrating Daniel's ability to make peace and even friendship with his enemies. Daniel's willingness and skill in being able to do this throughout his life is laudable, and indeed has made enduring peace in and for Nicaragua possible.

A further great example of Daniel's ability to reconcile with those who had betrayed both him and the Revolution was his enduring friendship with Eden Pastora, also known as "Comandante Zero." Pastora, a handsome, charismatic, though albeit womanizing and egotistical FSLN leader who fought alongside Daniel in overthrowing Somoza, would go on to fight with the southern front of the Contras in Costa Rica from 1983–1986. This Contra front, too, was backed by the CIA.[218] Most assume Pastora joined the Contras out of spite because he was rejected for the position of Defense Minister in favor of Daniel's brother, Humberto.[219] However, Pastora would later regret his efforts on behalf of the Contras and return in 1989 to Nicaragua, where he was welcomed back by Daniel and the FSLN. Pastora would eventually become a staunch and vocal Daniel supporter and remain so until his death in 2020. He was ultimately allowed to be remembered as a hero of the Revolution and is generally recalled as a Sandinista Comandante, and not a Contra fighter. I, myself, see all of this as a great strength of Daniel and the FSLN, and not as a weakness. Indeed, I see Daniel as a figure like Abraham Lincoln—a leader grappling with the terrible difficulty of leading a nation facing civil war and internal strife, and struggling mightily to keep it all together and bring about reconciliation.

Meanwhile, whatever deficits the Sandinistas may have had in terms of human rights simply cannot be compared to the systemic and quite intentional violations of human rights and humanitarian law norms of the Contras and their CIA masters. The Contra War, accompanying CIA operations and punishing economic measures against Nicaragua were terrible and inhumane—rivaling the worst assault against the people by Somoza himself. This is an incredible fact, for the Sandinistas had yet to be able to fully rebuild from the rubble Somoza had left them during his counterinsurgency war against them—a war which included Somoza's bombing of his own cities—when they then had to fend off but a second counterinsurgency war. That Nicaragua continues to exist at all as a nation is, therefore, more than a small miracle, and a miracle pulled off by the resolve of the FSLN and its leaders like Daniel Ortega.

It is a truism that a guerilla movement is only able to succeed in its efforts to take over a country to the extent it has popular support among the people on whom it depends to hide them, feed them and fill their ranks. This is why the Sandinistas were so successful, and why the Contras could not succeed, at least as a force that could actually take over and hold territory. Insofar as the Contras were never a true liberation force as we were being told, they were never able to hold so much as one blade of grass within Nicaragua. Instead, they resorted solely to terrorist attacks launched from Honduras, and to a lesser extent from Costa Rica, in order to put fear in the hearts of the Nicaraguan people and destroy the gains of the Revolution, hoping that, by doing so, they could coerce the nation into surrendering to their will.

Former CIA officer John Stockwell dramatically outlines some of the tactics of the Contras in a speech that I heard for the first time on cassette tape with my college buddy Jon Wentz in our college dorms:

> I don't mean to abuse you with verbal violence, but you have to understand what your government and its agents are doing. They [the Contras] go into villages, they haul out families. With the children forced to watch they castrate the father, they peel the skin off his face, they put a grenade in his mouth and pull the pin. With the children forced to watch they gang-rape the mother and slash her breasts off. And sometimes for variety, they make the parents watch while they do these things to the children.[220]

Lest one doubt such grisly claims, a 24-year-old mother named Olivia de la Vides Mesa recounted a typical Contra attack, this time in May of 1984 in the town of Castillo Norte:

> The Contra attacked us at 11 am. I was in the kitchen. They began with mortars. There were about 600 of them. We only had 20 militia. One of the mortars fell and killed an old woman in the shelter. When they got nearer, my little sister begged them: "You already killed an old woman, please don't kill our children". But they tortured and slit the throats of our militia. I know, because there were so few and they had no more

ammunition, they gave themselves up with their hands in the air. And when I got out, they had castrated one of the boys, and cut another's tongue out. And a militia girl who was 4 months pregnant, they raped her and cut off her breasts while she was still alive. They left them all naked. Then they burned them. About 20 campesinos were kidnapped.[221]

Clearly, such tactics were not designed to win over the people, but rather, to inspire maximum terror and fear of resistance. The other purpose was, in the words again of John Stockwell, to rip "apart the economic and social fabric" of the country. Stockwell explains how this was done:

> What we're talking about is going in and deliberately creating conditions where the farmer can't get his produce to market, where children can't go to school, where women are terrified inside their homes as well as outside their homes, where government administration and programs grind to a complete halt, where the hospitals are treating wounded people instead of sick people, where international capital is scared away and the country goes bankrupt....
> To destabilize Nicaragua beginning in 1981, we began funding this force of Somoza's ex-National Guardsmen, calling them the Contras (the counter-revolutionaries). We created this force, it did not exist until we allocated money.... Under our direction they have systematically been blowing up graineries, saw mills, bridges, government offices, schools, health centers. They ambush trucks so the produce can't get to market. They raid farms and villages. The farmer has to carry a gun while he tries to plow, if he can plow at all.[222]

The attempt to strangle the Nicaraguan economy were taken to absurd lengths, as I personally witnessed. In 1988, I had attempted to travel by truck from the United States to Nicaragua with the Veterans Peace Convoy, a project of Veterans For Peace. The goal of the convoy was to bring humanitarian aid, including the trucks themselves, to Nicaragua and to challenge the U.S. embargo against that country. The truck I drove was designated for a prostitution rehabilitation center in Nicaragua. When we tried to cross the U.S. border into Mexico at the initial steps of our journey, U.S. Customs and Immigration officials stopped us, violently breaking the windows of some of the vehicles in the front of the convoy and pepper spraying the vehicle occupants, all of whom were Vietnam veterans. They also seized four of the vehicles and prevented the remainder of us from continuing. The U.S. government claimed that the trucks, most of which were four-person pick-up trucks, could theoretically be used by the Sandinistas for troop movement and were therefore contraband and not humanitarian aid as permitted by statute to be sent to Nicaragua.

Nicaraguan children welcome Veterans Peace Convoy
DANIEL KOVALIK, 1988

We waited for two months to try to cross the border, living most of the time in tents in Laredo, Texas. We ended up being able to go across the border one-at-a-time over a period of several days and to bring the aid to Nicaragua, though most of the drivers, with jobs and families to return to at home, had to leave with their trucks before we finally crossed. For my part, I was on summer break between my sophomore and junior years of college and was therefore able to carry on with the convoy. This became quite possibly the most profound experience of my life.

Throughout our journey through the length of Mexico, Guatemala and Honduras, there were groups of people who organized housing, food and even entertainment for us. By and large, these were poor people who did this because they, too, supported Nicaragua and opposed what the U.S. was doing to that country. And they offered help to us even though their lot in life was not so much better than the Nicaraguans, and not nearly as good as ours. The kindness and hospitality shown to us was humbling, and still moves me when I think about it. This experience recalls the words of John Steinbeck that "If you're in trouble, or hurt or need—go to the poor people. They're the only ones that'll help—the only ones."

One memory from our journey that stands out to me is a homily given by a Catholic Bishop in Mexico City at a special Mass said for the safety and success of the Convoy. In his speech, the cleric, known as the "Red Bishop," urged that if one is to be a true disciple of Jesus Christ, he/she must follow Christ's living disciples on Earth, "Saint Fidel Castro" and "Saint Daniel Ortega." As a practicing Catholic at the time, this made a huge impression on me, and it inspired my political awakening. I had quite the opposite experience, also in Mexico City, when I tried to bond with a Russian journalist from *Pravda*—the chief newspaper of the USSR and the Communist Party of the Soviet Union—at a press conference. I went up to him and shook his hand and told him that I was very interested in Marxism-Leninism. He smiled at me and said dismissively, "That's too bad, because we aren't, anymore." Remember, this was only 1988; the USSR would not fall for another three and a half years, and almost no one, not even the CIA, saw it coming. Still, the writing was on the wall, and this signaled to me that the world was poised to change in a very big way, and probably not for the better as far as I was concerned.

Sandinistas welcome Veterans Peace Convoy to Nicaragua
DANIEL KOVALIK, 1988

When we reached Nicaragua, we were received as heroes. As we entered the country, Sandinista soldiers lined both sides of the highway, greeting us with their AK-47s raised in the air to salute us. When we reached Managua, President Daniel Ortega himself received us at an event to celebrate our successful arrival. The aid that we carried with us was not much in truth, but the gesture of defying our government to bring it was what the Nicaraguans appreciated so much.

I am still close friends with a number of those who made this journey, and we all carry the memory of this experience with us every day, even decades later.

In the meantime, with the help of the Center for Constitutional Rights and other legal organizations, we sued the U.S. Secretary of State, George Schultz, in U.S. federal court, demanding the right to proceed with our humanitarian efforts. On September 29, 1988, after those of us who continued had already made it to Nicaragua, the U.S. District Court for the Southern District of Texas, in the case of *Veterans Peace Convoy, Inc. v. George P. Schultz*, 722 F.Supp. 1425, ruled in our favor and granted us declaratory relief, holding: "The President has no authority to regulate or prohibit, directly or indirectly, donations by persons subject to the jurisdiction of the United States of articles, as distinguished from funds, which the donor intends to be used to relieve human suffering if the articles can reasonably be expected to serve that purpose." While we had already delivered our goods, the decision probably saved us from the criminal prosecution that the U.S. government had been threatening us with. And more importantly, the decision represented a small victory against Reagan's vicious war in Nicaragua.

Meanwhile, in 1986, over half-way through the war, the Washington Office on Latin America (WOLA), a non-governmental human rights organization, sent a team to Nicaragua to investigate the human rights situation in light of Reagan's attempts to obtain continued support for the Contras. What WOLA found was that it was the Contras who were committing the lion's share of the human rights abuses in Nicaragua. As the UPI, reporting on WOLA's findings, explained:

> In its report the Washington Office on Latin America cited 139 cases of attacks against Nicaraguan civilians last year involving assassination, kidnapping, rape, mutilation and torture.
> Of the total, 118 were committed by the Contras, who are trying to overthrow Managua's Sandinista government, and 21 by members of the Nicaraguan armed forces, said the report released Wednesday....
> Reagan . . . continued efforts to win congressional approval of his request for $100 million for the Contras—$70 million of it to be spent on military hardware.[223]

Significantly, WOLA found that the Contras' abuses were systematic and integral to the Contras' strategy of counterinsurgency, while Sandinista abuses appeared to be the actions of individual rogue soldiers. The UPI, summarizing WOLA's findings, put it this way: "The presence of Contras in a given locale 'seemed to give rise to a pattern of indiscriminate attacks against civilian targets,' while violations by government troops 'appear to be relatively isolated cases of abuses of authority and breaches of military discipline. There was no evidence that violations were condoned by superiors,' the report said."[224] And, of course, if there had been no Contra war to begin with, and therefore no fighting, it is most unlikely that the Sandinista soldiers would have been committing the abuses attributed to them in the report; rather, these were occasioned by a war imposed upon them by the United States.

Meanwhile, in 1984, Nicaragua had begun a case against the United States before the International Court of Justice (ICJ), also known as the World Court, for injunctive relief to stop the war against Nicaragua, as well as seeking compensation for economic damages resulting from the war and accompanying economic sanctions and blockade. This case, captioned as *Nicaragua v. United States of America, Case Concerning Military and Paramilitary Activities in and against Nicaragua*, was the brainchild of Father Miguel d'Escoto, Nicaragua's Foreign Minister, who was dedicated to the United Nations system and international law. Father D'Escoto would later become President of the United Nations General Assembly. Conversely, demonstrating its utter contempt for international law—believing it to apply only to the weaker nations of the world—the U.S. refused to even appear to defend itself on the merits of the case and ultimately refused to abide by the decision of the ICJ. Rather, the U.S. made only a limited appearance before the Court to raise objections to the very exercise of jurisdiction by the ICJ over the case.

After initially concluding that it had jurisdiction over Nicaragua's case against the U.S., the ICJ decided the merits of the case in 1986, ruling resoundingly in favor of Nicaragua. This decision has become one of the most important and most cited in the history of international law. In addition, the opinion of the ICJ gives a good and authoritative summary of the U.S. war against

Nicaragua and is worth examining here on this basis. The ICJ framed the case as follows:

> The dispute before the Court between Nicaragua and the United States concerns events in Nicaragua subsequent to the fall of the Government of President Anastasio Somoza Debayle in Nicaragua in July 1979, and activities of the Government of the United States in relation to Nicaragua since that time. Following the departure of President Somoza, a Junta of National Reconstruction and an 18-member government was installed by the body which had led the armed opposition to President Somoza, the Frente Sandinista de Liberación Nacional (FSLN). That body had initially an extensive share in the new government, described as a "democratic coalition", and as a result of later resignations and reshuffles, became almost its sole component. Certain opponents of the new Government, primarily supporters of the former Somoza Government and in particular ex-members of the National Guard, formed themselves into irregular military forces, and commenced a policy of armed opposition, though initially on a limited scale.[225]

As the ICJ explains, the U.S. supported the Contras at first secretly and then publicly with the explicit authorization of the U.S. Congress. The ICJ thus relates that

> after an initial period in which the "covert" operations of United States personnel and persons in their pay were kept from becoming public knowledge, it was made clear, not only in the United States press, but also in Congress and in official statements by the President and high United States officials, that the United States Government had been giving support to the contras, a term employed to describe those fighting against the present Nicaraguan Government. In 1983 budgetary

legislation enacted by the United States Congress made specific provision for funds to be used by United States intelligence agencies for supporting "directly or indirectly, military or paramilitary operations in Nicaragua." According to Nicaragua, the contras have caused it considerable material damage and widespread loss of life and have also committed such acts as killing of prisoners, indiscriminate killing of civilians, torture, rape and kidnapping. It is contended by Nicaragua that the United States Government is effectively in control of the contras, that it devised their strategy and directed their tactics, and that the purpose of that Government was, from the beginning, to overthrow the Government of Nicaragua.

As to the allegation of Nicaragua that the Contras were under the effective control of the United States, and that the United States was therefore liable for the conduct of the Contras, the ICJ would not go quite that far, though it concluded, largely based upon the testimony of Edgar Chamorro—a Contra leader who became disgusted with the conduct of the Contras and the CIA, and who went over to the side of the Sandinistas—that the U.S. exercised a great deal of authority over the Contras and many of their tactics and strategies.

According to Chamorro, the CIA took over training the Contras, whom he himself described as former National Guardsmen, in 1981 from the Argentine trainers of the fascist junta who themselves were being paid by the CIA to perform this task. From that time forward, the Contras, including Chamorro himself, received a salary from the CIA. The CIA also provided all of their weapons, uniforms, radios and small aircraft. The CIA also provided the Contras with intelligence, for example on Sandinista troop movement, and gave the Contras specific orders about tactics and strategy. In addition, "[a]ccording to the affidavit of Mr. Chamorro. who was directly concerned, when the FDN was formed 'the name of the organization, the members of the political junta, and the members of the general staff were all chosen or approved by the CIA'; later the CIA asked that a particular person be made head of the political directorate of the FDN, and this was done." As the ICJ further commented, "Mr. Chamorro attributes virtually a power of command to the CIA operatives: he refers to them as having 'ordered' or 'instructed' the FDN to take various action." From all this, the ICJ stated, "the Court holds it established that the United States authorities largely financed, trained, equipped, armed and organized the FDN."

One of the most infamous ways the CIA directed the Contras was through its notorious "terrorist manual," officially called "Psychological Operations in Guerrilla Warfare." According to Edgar Chamorro, about 2,000 copies of this manual were supplied to the Contra forces by the CIA. Amongst other things, as the ICJ notes, there was a

> section on "Implicit and Explicit Terror" which included "directions to destroy military or police installations, cut lines of communication, kidnap officials of the Sandinista government, etc. Reference is made to the possibility that 'it should be necessary ... to fire on a citizen who was trying to leave the town,' to be justified by the risk of his informing the enemy."

In addition, the ICJ pointed out,

> a section on "Selective Use of Violence for Propagandistic Effects" begins with the words: "It is possible to neutralize carefully selected and planned targets, such as court judges, mesta judges, police and State Security officials, CDS chiefs, etc. For psychological purposes it is necessary to take extreme precautions, and it is absolutely necessary to gather together the population affected, so that they will be present, take part in the act, and formulate accusations against the oppressor."

The ICJ emphasized that another section of the manual advised that,

> "If possible, professional criminals will be hired to carry out specific selective 'jobs.' Specific tasks will be assigned to others, in order to create a 'martyr' for the cause, taking the demonstrators to a confrontation with the authorities, in order to bring about uprisings or shootings, which will cause the death of one or more persons, who would become the martyrs, a situation that should be made use of immediately against the regime, in order to create greater conflicts."

Some of these very tactics, curiously, would be used by the opposition in 2018 in an event which the Sandinista government, I believe quite rightly, characterized as an attempted coup.

In the end, the ICJ concluded that "the support given by the United States, up to the end of September 1984, to the military and paramilitary activities of the contras in Nicaragua, by financial support, training, supply of weapons, intelligence and logistic support, constitutes a clear breach of the [customary international law] principle of non-intervention" for which the United States is liable. On the other hand, the ICJ conclusion referred to public records showing that the U.S. Congress had passed legislation limiting U.S. operations in Nicaragua; that, beginning in October of 1984, U.S. support for the Contras was limited solely to humanitarian aid; and that this in and of itself did not violate international law. However, what neither the ICJ nor the U.S. Congress knew at the time was that the Reagan Administration was secretly continuing to supply lethal aid to the Contras via an arcane configuration which, when revealed, came to be referred to in its totality as the "Iran-Contra Scandal." More on this shortly.

Significantly, the ICJ also found that the United States was directly responsible for various acts of war against Nicaragua separate and apart from the activities of the Contras. For example, the ICJ found that in 1983 or 1984, President Ronald Reagan himself explicitly authorized the CIA to mine Nicaragua's harbors, causing damage to both Nicaraguan and other foreign ships alike. Incredibly, as the ICJ explicitly concluded, so callous was the United States that it failed to warn other nations, including its own allies, that it had mined the harbors, and allied ships were ultimately damaged by these mines. Thus, as the ICJ notes, this concerned, "[a]ccording to Nicaragua, vessels of Dutch, Panamanian, Soviet, Liberian and Japanese registry.... Other sources mention damage to a British or a Cuban vessel." The mining of the harbors became one of the more infamous crimes of the U.S. in its war against Nicaragua as it clearly constituted a war crime—and the ICJ concluded as much—by failing to distinguish between military and civilian vessels, including vessels of nations that had nothing to do with the conflict.

In addition to the mining of the harbors, the ICJ found that the United States was directly responsible for the following acts, which could only be described, in my view, as acts of state terrorism:

(1) the blowing up of an underwater oil pipeline (on two separate occasions) and part of the oil terminal at Puerto Sandino;
(2) an air attack upon the port of Corinto, "involving the destruction of five oil storage tanks, the loss of millions of gallons of fuel, and the evacuation of large numbers of the local population";
(3) the attack by speedboats and helicopters using rockets against the Potosi Naval Base; and
(4) the attack upon oil and storage facility at San Juan del Sur by speedboats and helicopters.

For its part, the ICJ found that these acts violated customary humanitarian law norms established as far back as the Hague Convention of 1907.

Moreover, while the U.S. defended itself before the ICJ largely on the claim that it was protecting El Salvador from arms shipments being sent from Nicaragua, this was a quite dubious claim, especially by the time of the ICJ case. Indeed, there is a quite interesting and at times humorous story about how the U.S. claims in this regard fell apart, which highlights the incredible bravery of the Nicaraguan revolutionaries. It revolves around the case of Orlando José Tardencilla Espinosa, who became quite famous in the early 1980s. It was well-documented in the 1982 *New York Times* story, "Recanter's Tale: Lesson in Humility for State Department."[226] Mr. Tardencilla was a young Sandinista revolutionary who, on his own accord, joined the Salvadoran FMLN guerillas in 1980. He was later captured by Salvadoran security forces and jailed. While in jail, he was subjected to severe torture. The CIA discovered the existence of Mr. Tardencilla in a Salvadoran jail and hoped to use it to prove Nicaragua's involvement in the Salvadoran civil war. The CIA offered to take Tardencilla out of El Salvador and to the U.S. if he could corroborate such claims. Tardencilla swore up and down that he could and would, and he was brought to the U.S. The stage was set for a press conference in which he would spill the beans on Nicaragua and Cuba as well. Tardencilla's handcuffs were undone just before he took to the microphones. Once on air, he stated instead that Nicaragua and Cuba were not in fact aiding the FMLN in El Salvador, and that he had gone there entirely on his own. It was a huge embarrassment for the United States. The twenty-something Tardencilla had outsmarted both the CIA and the U.S. State Department, which had also bought his original story. Ultimately, Tardencilla was released back to Nicaragua where he received a hero's welcome by all nine Comandantes and by hundreds of Sandinista combatants who briefly left their posts fighting the Contras to come to Managua and greet him. Tardencilla, still loyal to the Revolution and Daniel, is currently working as special assistant to President Daniel Ortega in the diplomatic corps of Nicaragua.

While the U.S. claims that Nicaragua was aiding the rebels in El Salvador were debunked, the truth was just the contrary—it was El Salvador which was actually engaged in real armed attacks against Nicaragua. It appears that El Salvador had begun to support the ex-National Guardsmen in Honduras as early as 1979, with Chomsky pointing out that "Salvadoran pilots bomb Nicaragua under CIA control from their sanctuaries in Honduras and El Salvador, and according to U.S. officials in Central America, fly as many as a dozen sorties a week from El Salvador deep into Nicaraguan territory to supply *contra* forces."[227] It should also be noted that the U.S. itself, through the 101st Airborne Division based in Kentucky, directly engaged in bombing operations against Nicaragua.[228] In short, as usual, the claims the U.S. was making against Nicaragua in relation to El Salvador—which, by the way, even if true would not, according to the ICJ, have amounted to "an armed attack" triggering the right to self-defense—was another classic case of the pot calling the kettle black.

Furthermore, Nicaraguan President Daniel Ortega had made offers of major concessions to the U.S. to try to stop the devastating war against Nicaragua. As the ICJ writes, Daniel gave an interview to the *New York Times* in which he stated,

> We've said that we're willing to send home the Cubans, the Russians, the rest of the advisers. We're willing to stop the movement of military aid, or any other kind of aid, through Nicaragua to El Salvador, and we're willing to accept international verification. In return, we're asking for one thing: that they don't attack us, that the United States stop arming and financing ... the gangs that kill our people, burn our crops and force us to divert enormous human and economic resources into war when we desperately need them for development.

The other huge step Ortega and the Sandinistas took was to hold elections in the midst of the armed conflict, despite how challenging this was to do. While the Sandinistas had vowed in 1980 to hold free and fair elections within five years—that is, by 1985—they moved these elections up to 1984, hoping "that a competitive election with heavy turnout would help deter a [direct] U.S. military intervention in Nicaragua."[229] And indeed, they pulled off just such an election. Thus, as explained by the (U.S.-based) Latin American Studies Association (LASA), which was on the ground during the elections, 93.7 percent of the voting-age population were registered to vote within just four days, and a whopping 75% of registered voters cast ballots in the election, this despite the fact that the U.S. and the Contras encouraged voter abstention in order to try to discredit the elections.[230] As LASA also noted, "The electoral process was marked by a high degree of 'open-endedness,'" with the Sandinistas making a number of concessions to the six opposition parties which ran in the election on how that election was to be run.[231] LASA concluded that "The actual voting process was meticulously designed to minimize the potential for abuses. The vote was truly a secret ballot and was generally perceived as such by voters. We observed no evidence of irregularities in the voting or vote-counting process." [232]

In a stinging critique of the Reagan Administration's policies towards the Nicaragua elections, LASA concluded that, to the extent that there was undue pressure on these elections which would make them less than free and fair, it came from the United States itself which, amongst other things, put pressure on opposition candidates to drop out, "and in at least one case ... [bribed] lower-level party officials to abandon the campaign of their presidential candidate, who insisted on staying in the race."[233] The U.S. military and the Contras also engaged in military acts during the week before the election to frighten potential voters, with the Contras carrying out attacks in the Miskitu Coast which effectively shut down some polls while the U.S. conducted aerial flights over Nicaragua which caused sonic booms and instilled "a sense of near panic among the population."[234]

As LASA explained, "the Reagan Administration used a combination of diplomatic, economic, and military instruments in a systematic attempt to undermine the Nicaraguan electoral process and to destroy its credibility in the eyes of the world." LASA ultimately concluded that

> Clearly, the Nicaraguan election was manipulated, as the U.S. Government so often charged. However, the manipulation was not the work of the Sandinistas—who had every interest in making these elections as demonstrably fair, pluralistic, and competitive as possible—but of the Reagan Administration, whose interest was apparently in making the elections seem as unfair, ideologically one-side, and uncompetitive as possible.[235]

The Reagan White House realized that if the elections went forward in any unimpeded way, the Sandinistas, who clearly had the support of the people, would win. And indeed, the Reagan Administration's worst fears were realized, with the Sandinistas winning the elections handily. Luckily, the U.S. press corps was there to either ignore the result of the election entirely or to simply repeat the smears of the electoral process by the Reagan Administration.

If the real reasons behind Reagan's war against Nicaragua were that country's relations with Cuba and Russia, its alleged military support for the FMLN in El Salvador, and/or the desire to see democracy in Nicaragua, the concessions offered by Daniel, combined with the holding of elections in 1984, should have ended the war. But the war did not end. And that is because these were not the real reasons. Rather, the effect that Daniel stated that the war was having—interference with the attempts of the Sandinistas to independently develop Nicaragua—was indeed an intended goal of the war.

As former CIA analyst David MacMichael, who testified on behalf of Nicaragua before the ICJ, explained, two of the chief goals of the Contra War were (1) "to undermine its [Nicaragua's] shattered economy"; and (2) "to pressure the Nicaraguan government to 'clamp down on civil liberties within Nicaragua itself, arresting its opposition, demonstrating its allegedly totalitarian nature and thus increase domestic dissent within the country.'"[236] This latter goal is quite typical of U.S. government regime-change efforts in other countries. Far from trying to democratize the targeted country and attempting to improve its human rights policies, the U.S. intentionally tries to provoke anti-democratic and repressive responses in order to cause mass discontent and disunity among the population as well as to justify its efforts to overthrow that country's government. But these are only the subsidiary goals of the U.S. regime-change efforts.

The U.S.'s overarching aim in countries like Nicaragua is to maintain its neo-colonial control of that country, just as it was the goal of the U.S. in Korea, Vietnam, Cuba and various other countries. As Hugo Chavez explained in a speech I heard him give in Caracas in 2010, the great struggle of the 20th Century was the struggle against Western colonialism, represented by the Mexican, Russian, Chinese, Cuban, Vietnamese and Nicaraguan Revolutions, amongst many others. By the end of WWII, the United States had arisen as the primary defender of colonialism against the mass movements in Latin America, Asia and Africa attempting to loosen their colonial chains. The Soviet Union almost invariably supported the anti-colonial efforts in this world, and, as writers such as Jean Bricmont have noted, the success of these movements that the USSR helped bring about was its greatest achievement (next to its defeat of Nazism)—an achievement which would ultimately exhaust it.

Given the true aims of the U.S., there were simply no concessions the Sandinistas could make, short of complete capitulation, to end the U.S. war against them. As a result, the progress the Sandinistas were making for Nicaragua was greatly stunted and rolled back.

Indeed, so hell-bent was the Reagan Administration on destroying the Sandinista Revolution that neither the loss at the World Court in 1986, which explicitly ordered the U.S. to halt the war against Nicaragua, nor Congressional measures known as the Boland Amendments, which ended military assistance to the Contras by 1984, would deter it.[237]

Lacking funding from Congress, Reagan created a special task force to find monies elsewhere for the Contras. Two sources were found which appeared to be in complete contradiction to U.S. foreign policy elsewhere: (1) the team found a way, with the help and facilitation of Israel,[238] to sell arms to Iran which was officially under an arms embargo from the U.S., and which was then involved in a devastating war with Iraq; and (2) the team facilitated the sale of cocaine in the U.S., the proceeds of which went to the Contras.

In terms of the sale of arms to Iran, Reagan's secret team sold a total of 1500 missiles to Iran in this deal, diverting $12 million of the proceeds to the Contras.[239] It also happened that the U.S. was bankrolling Iraq in its prosecution of the war with Iran at the very same time. Thus, in a profoundly cynical move, the Reagan

Administration was fueling both sides of the Iran/Iraq armed conflict, making the conflict more deadly and extending its length for a total of eight years—from 1980 to 1988, that is, for the entirety of Ronald Reagan's two terms. This was optimum for the Reagan Administration, which actually liked the idea of pitting Iran and Iraq against each other and weakening both countries in the process. As Christopher Davidson explains in his book, *Shadow Wars*, "[i]n many ways, the West's position ... is reminiscent of Harry Truman's views on Nazi Germany before the U.S. entered the Second World War. After all, as his well-documented remarks on Adolf Hitler's invasion of the Soviet Union reveal, he and others did not really want to see either side winning, while any long-drawn-out fight between the two side was seen as ultimately suiting U.S. interests."[240] Davidson cites William Blum for the proposition that the Iran-Iraq War "had the effect of 'enhancing the ability of the two countries to inflict maximum devastation upon each other and stunt their growth as strong Middle East nations.'" The results for the Iranians and Iraqis of this diabolical plan were terrifying, with more than one million people on both sides dying during this war.[241]

Not only were Iraqi and Iranian lives sacrificed to enable the Contra War, but so were the lives of Americans, and especially African Americans, and for many years to come. As William Blum explains,

> In August 1996, the *San Jose Mercury News* initiated an extended series of articles linking the CIA's "contra" army to the crack cocaine epidemic in Los Angeles. Based on a year-long investigation, reporter Gary Webb wrote that during the 1980s the CIA helped finance its covert war against Nicaragua's leftist government through sales of cut-rate cocaine to South Central L.A. drug dealer, Ricky Ross. The series unleashed a storm of protest, spearheaded by black radio stations and the Congressional Black Caucus, with demands for official inquiries. The *Mercury News'*

Web page, with supporting documents and updates, received hundreds of thousands of "hits" a day.

While much of the CIA-contra-drug story had been revealed years ago in the press and in congressional hearings, the *Mercury News* series added a crucial missing link: It followed the cocaine trail to Ross and black L.A. gangs who became street-level distributors of crack, a cheap and powerful form of cocaine. The CIA's drug network, wrote Webb, "opened the first pipeline between Colombia's cocaine cartels and the black neighborhoods of Los Angeles, a city now known as the 'crack' capital of the world." Black gangs used their profits to buy automatic weapons, sometimes from one of the CIA-linked drug dealers.[242]

This was the second source of funding accessed by the Reagan administration to fund its Contra assault on Nicaragua. Bluntly put, the Reagan Administration played a key role in starting the crack cocaine epidemic, which cost the lives of thousands of African Americans and destroyed entire communities. As the National Bureau of Economic Research (NBER) concluded in 2018, the "murder rates of black males aged 15 to 24 doubled soon after the crack epidemic hit their cities and that 17 years later, these rates were still 70 percent higher than they might otherwise have been."[243] The NBER further concluded that "... even today, nearly 25 years after the peak of the systemic violence in the retail crack market, crack-related violence and suicide may explain approximately one-tenth of the gap in life expectancy between white and black males." But again, no cost was too steep in pursuing the war against Nicaragua. Or perhaps, even worse, the Reagan Administration saw helping destroy the Nicaraguan Revolution and the African-American community along with it as killing two birds with one stone.

The cruel hypocrisy of Reagan's authorizing the sale of crack cocaine in U.S. cities cannot be understated, as he also claimed to be a crusader against drug use. Indeed, Reagan oversaw the passage of draconian drug legislation which put hundreds of thousands of Americans in jail for drug-related offenses, including for the possession and sale of the very drugs his CIA was selling to fund the Contra War—crack cocaine. As the addiction rehabilitation group, Landmark Recovery, relates:

> One of the most significant pieces of legislation of the entire drug war was passed by the Reagan administration in 1986....
>
> The Anti-Drug Abuse Act is one of the most important federal laws that passed in United States history regarding drug punishment. The law was signed by President Ronald Reagan in October 1986 and was partially a result of Nancy Reagan's "Just Say No" campaign efforts. The act gave over a billion in funding for the drug war and substantially increased the number of drug offenses with mandatory minimum sentences, including marijuana.
>
> One of the most controversial aspects of this act is the changes in the sentencing for possession of crack cocaine. The 1986 act instituted a five-year minimum penalty without parole for the possession of five grams of crack cocaine. Meanwhile, the same sentence was given for the possession of 500 grams of powder cocaine. This 100:1 disparity was criticized by some as racially biased because crack cocaine was more likely to be used by poor Americans, many of whom were African Americans.[244]

The result of this legislation, combined with the CIA's peddling of drugs, was the mass incarceration of Americans. Landmark Recovery explains that "the number of people behind bars for nonviolent drug law offenses increased from 50,000 in 1980 to over 400,000 by 1997. According to Pew Research and many other sources, the country saw a sharp growth in overall incarceration between 1980 and 2008. In 1980, there were 500,000 incarcerated in the United States, that number rose to 2.3 million in 2008."

Panamanian lives were also expendable in the war against the Sandinistas. For 20 years, the U.S. had a close, though albeit strange, relationship with Panama's Manuel Noriega, who was trained as an army intelligence officer by the CIA.[245] Three U.S. administrations, from Carter to Reagan to Bush (Sr.), openly tolerated Noriega's drug smuggling, money laundering, illegal arms trafficking and other criminal activities, and later his dictatorial rule when he took over leadership of Panama, because of the intelligence he gave the U.S. and because of his support for the U.S.'s Contra War.[246] This changed in 1989 when Noriega announced that he would no longer continue to offer Panama as a training and staging ground for Contra activity.[247] At this point, the U.S. invaded Panama, attacking working-class neighborhoods in Panama City with state-of-the-art weaponry, killing hundreds if not thousands of Panamanians—the true numbers are still not known.[248] The U.S. captured Noriega and successfully charged him in the U.S. for drug-trafficking—a great irony, given the CIA's role in running drugs for the Contras. Once again, innocent civilians, this time Panamanians, were sacrificed on the altar of the Contra War.

And, of course, civilians in Nicaragua paid a huge cost for the war. As an editorial board opinion piece in the *New York Times* summarized in 1990, "[i]n nearly 10 years, 30,000 Nicaraguans were killed, many more wounded, the economy shattered and Washington ensnared in horrors like assassination manuals, the clandestine mining of Nicaraguan harbors and the still-reverberating Iran-contra scandal."[249] To say nothing of the toll that the war took upon on the progress towards development and social justice that the Sandinistas had initiated.

As the war was still raging, diseases which the Sandinistas had made huge gains in eradicating came roaring back with a vengeance. Oxfam stated that "the impact on the control of infectious diseases is particularly serious," quoting the respected medical journal *The Lancet,* which noted:

> Several anti-malarial workers and many volunteers have been killed by Contras. Their disruption of the health system and communications, and attacks on

peasants, have resulted in new malaria problems. It appears that only a termination of hostilities will make it possible for the border areas to achieve the successes in malaria control noted in the rest of the country.[250]

As Oxfam further related,

> Tragically, the effects of the war are now affecting the lives of all Nicaraguans to some degree, through direct attack, military call-up for national defense, higher prices, chronic shortages of food and imported commodities, and breakdown of public and private transport. 90% of the most important basic foods (rice, beans, maize and sorghum) are produced in areas seriously affected by the fighting. The war is fueling a vicious circle: agricultural production is disrupted, so foreign exchange earnings fall. This makes it impossible to import all the spare parts ... and agricultural inputs vital to ensure next year's harvest.
>
> For Nicaragua's poor majority, the Contra war poses a direct and growing threat to hopes for a better future. It is a senseless diversion from the real war against poverty and underdevelopment. Nicaraguans who have invested time and effort in setting up schools and cooperatives have suffered the morale-sapping experience of having to start all over again once these have been destroyed. The imperative of defending the country from attack is now draining a massive 40% of Government funds. Inevitably, the poorest are worst hit by the diversion from development to defense and, as long as the war continues, there will not be time, energy or funds to focus on long-term solutions to the escalating economic crisis that threatens the living standards of the poor.[251]

Noam Chomsky quoted the director of medical affair for the New York State Department of Health, visiting in 1985, who reviews the deleterious impact of U.S. military and economic actions on health care, education and food production, devoted to the poor for the first time in history, observing that we are 'slowly strangling a poor people' who are 'struggling for a better life' and 'who should find it difficult to comprehend that they are alleged to be a threat to the Giant of the North.'"[252]

It was in the face of all of this that Nicaraguans approached new elections in 1990—elections which the Sandinistas held earlier than planned, again in an effort to bring an end to the war that was being waged against them. The truth, however, was that the only way the war would end (if this was not clear enough after the 1984 elections) was if the Nicaraguan electorate voted "the right way," meaning, voting the Sandinistas out of power. And, lest there were any doubts, the U.S. made it abundantly clear to the Nicaraguan people in public statements by the State Department and the U.S. Ambassador to Nicaragua that this was the stark choice confronting them when they went to the polls.

CHAPTER 5

DARK DAYS RETURN
THE 1990 ELECTIONS AND THE NEOLIBERAL PERIOD

While I was not on the ground in Nicaragua for the 1990 elections or their aftermath, I felt pain and shock at hearing that the Sandinistas had lost. It marked the end of an era—an era that had also meant so much to so many non-Nicaraguans, who had been so inspired by the Revolution of 1979. According to all the accounts of my friends in Nicaragua at the time, the Nicaraguans themselves were also shocked and saddened by the results. While the Nicaraguan voters ultimately pulled the poll levers (or the triggers, if you will) that put the Sandinistas out of office, they were, by and large, not happy with this choice. Clearly, it was a choice that had been forced upon them, and, apparently, the streets in Nicaragua were quiet and somber the day after the elections when it became clear what happened.

As William I Robinson writes in his book, *Faustian Bargain*, about the U.S.'s intervention in the 1990 elections, even President George H.W. Bush was shocked, albeit pleased, by the election results.[253] Indeed, these results were 10 years in the making; the Contra War had simply worn down the Nicaraguan people to the point that they capitulated to the pressure. As Robinson notes, "[t]hroughout the 1980s, Nicaragua was under relentless external pressures—military, economic, political, diplomatic—that took a heavy toll on the incumbent party. In the final years of their rule, the Sandinistas presided over a desperate economic crisis marked by hyperinflation and a tumultuous drop in living standards."[254] When combined with the collapse of the Eastern Bloc, which had been so helpful to the Sandinistas, Robinson opines that, in fact, what was surprising was that the Sandinistas did as well as they did in the 1990 elections, garnering 42 percent of the vote to the opposition's 54 percent.

To the factors mentioned by Robinson, I would add the immediately preceding U.S. invasion of neighboring Panama, and the ousting of Manuel Noriega in December of 1989—just a few short months before the February 1990 elections. This event demonstrated to the Nicaraguans the U.S.'s willingness to go so far as to invade a nearby sovereign country contrary to international law, deposing its leader without warning and without authorization from the UN Security Council. This surely signaled that Nicaragua could be the next target of such an operation, and this indeed remained the worst fear of Nicaraguans for years.

Former President Jimmy Carter, whose Carter Center had accepted the FSLN's invitation to observe the 1990 elections, explained the impact of the Panama invasion:

> The December 20 invasion of Panama by the United States, followed by the intrusion into the residence of the Nicaraguan ambassador in Panama, promoted alarm and a state of military alert in Nicaragua as well as the expulsion of U.S. diplomats from Nicaragua. These actions had an indirect effect on the electoral process in Nicaragua as a result of a communique issued by Minister of Defense Humberto Ortega outlining contingency plans in the event of a U.S. invasion of Nicaragua. [Opposition] UNO leaders particularly objected to one clause of the communique calling on the army, in the case of "Yankee intervention," to "apply the plans of neutralization, judgment and execution of all those recalcitrant traitors ... that had advanced the intervention."[255]

Thus, as Carter confirmed, the Sandinistas fully understood the message that the Panama invasion was meant to send to them, and Nicaraguan voters did as well.

In the transition from the 1980s to the 1990s, it appeared as if the United States was entering into an *Empire Strikes Back* period. Bush's invasion of Panama shouted this loudly to the world: that the U.S. could now, with the Eastern Bloc gone and the USSR in severe decline, act wherever and whenever it wanted without fear of reprisal or resistance. Lest there be any doubt about this, Bush announced the "New World Order" in which the U.S. would now reign alone and supreme in the world. "What we say, goes," is how he put it. This had a huge impact on liberation movements throughout the world, which now were in near full retreat. By the way, without making too much of the *Star Wars* analogy here, I feel compelled to tell the reader that George Lucas has made it clear that the Empire in his films was in fact the United States while the rebels were the Vietnamese, the Vietnam War having just ended with the victory of the Vietnamese rebels when Lucas began making the first *Star Wars* installment.[256] And, as for Princess Leia, her character's hair style and dress were inspired by that of Mexican female revolutionaries, known as *"soldaderas,"* in the early part of the 20th Century.[257] I suspect that these truths have been lost on nearly all fans of the *Star Wars* films. *Que lastima!*

As an instance of how liberation forces were influenced by the "New World Order," by the time Nelson Mandela went to the bargaining table with South Africa's leader, F. W. de Klerk, to dismantle Apartheid, the Soviet Union had already collapsed. Mandela was aware that this greatly weakened his hand in negotiating the future of South Africa. This ultimately led him to make concessions on the ANC's longstanding demands for economic redistribution and socialism.[258] In the end, South Africa became a democratic country ruled politically by its majority Black population, but to this day facing as bad or even worse economic circumstances than they did under Apartheid.[259] In a profound way, then, the ANC's victory was a Pyrrhic one.

This is all to say that the Sandinistas and Nicaraguans were up against powerful historical forces in the face of which, even the best liberation fighters in the world had succumbed. And as if all the foregoing were insufficient, the U.S. directly intervened in the Nicaraguan elections of 1990 to make sure that their candidate won.

It is largely undisputed that the Nicaraguan government, led by the FSLN, conducted elections in 1990 that were free and fair by international standards. For example, the Carter Center, while acknowledging some shortcomings and missteps preceding the polling, concluded:

> (1) During the entire electoral process, the political system in Nicaragua gradually opened so that by election day, the major political parties acknowledged that they had an adequate opportunity to explain their positions to the Nicaraguan people. The Council of Freely-Elected Heads of Government shared the conclusion of the parties: the Nicaraguan people were free to vote their preferences in a fair election, and the official results reflected the collective will of the nation.
> (2) For the first time in Nicaraguan history, all of the political parties that began the electoral campaign completed it, and all agreed to accept and respect the vote both before the election and afterwards.
> (3) The people of Nicaragua were eager to vote; 89 percent of those eligible registered, and 86 percent of these voted.[260]

What wasn't fair, however, was how the U.S. and its Contra allies coerced the voters in their decision. As William I. Robinson put it so well in his book, *Faustian Bargain*:

> In terms of the procedure, the elections were free and fair. But these were not normal elections under normal circumstances. They can perhaps best be described as "transnational elections" in which the will and material resources of a foreign power with deep

vested interests in the outcome were superimposed on
the internal political system of a sovereign nation. [261]

S. Brian Willson, former U.S. Air Force Captain and peace activist, explains that between CIA and National Endowment for Democracy expenditures, the U.S. spent around $50 million to influence the outcome of the election.[262] This money, which amounted to over $25 per each registered voter in Nicaragua, went to fund opposition political parties and NGOs, anti-Sandinista trade unions, and newspapers like the infamous *La Prensa* which was openly pro-Contra.[263] *La Prensa* was, and continues to be, owned by the wealthy Chamorro family and in the 1980s was run by Violeta Chamorro, who, in the 1990 elections, was the U.S.'s preferred candidate. Of course, the $50 million in monies directly allocated to influence the outcome of the elections was only the tip of the iceberg. Robinson quoted Democratic Congressman George Miller as bragging, "'[w]e are going into this election [spending] $1 billion dollars. We funded the Contras, we have destroyed [Nicaragua's] economy, we have taken Mrs. Chamorro and we pay for her newspaper to run, we funded the entire operation, and now we are going to provide her the very best election that America can buy.'"[264] To put this into perspective, the entire Gross National Product of Nicaragua in 1990 was $1.29 billion, falling to $.92 billion in 1991,[265] meaning that the U.S. had spent around as much money trying to unseat the Sandinistas through economic, political and military warfare as Nicaragua's entire economy generated in one year. Could one imagine what Nicaragua could have done with $1 billion if the U.S. had just decided to gift it that money for its development? Instead, that money went to destroying Nicaragua.

As Brian S. Willson explains, the U.S.'s "extraordinary" bankrolling of opposition forces during the 1989–1990 election campaign

> was only one of three prongs in the U.S. strategy to overthrow the Sandinista-led government. The second prong was economic strangulation through the economic

embargo and associated U.S.-imposed trade and credit blockades that continued to force most Nicaraguans to suffer significant misery. The U.S. hoped that, in the process, more and more of Nicaragua's citizens would cry "uncle." The third prong, of course, was the continued financial and military support of the Contras as a terrorist military force operating throughout the country. The terrorist campaigns continually caused widespread suffering and damage through ambushes, assassinations of various community leaders, kidnappings and disappearances of other important citizens, and attacks on cooperatives.[266]

As for the economic embargo, President Bush promised at the end of 1989 that this would be lifted immediately if Violeta Chamorro were elected President.[267]

Conversely, the Bush Administration made it clear that the Contras would continue to be funded and to operate against Nicaragua if Chamorro was not elected. To show that it was not bluffing, the Bush Administration continued to fund the Contras and to encourage them to launch attacks within Nicaragua into 1990, despite the fact that this violated the peace agreement which had been brokered by Costa Rican President Óscar Arias, earning a Nobel Peace Prize for his efforts, and signed by the Nicaraguan government and the heads of the Contras.[268] As Willson relates:

> I was personally travelling with a small delegation in Nicaragua during December 1989, beyond the mandated December 5 date for *completion* of Contra demobilization. Visiting nine of Nicaragua's fifteen departments, we documented numerous up-to-the-minute Contra terrorist activities. These included assassinations of FSLN leaders in a number of communities, destruction of a cooperative including the murders of several of its members, and an ambush of a public transport, killing or wounding over 20 civilians. Additionally, a number of the roads we desired to travel

on were considered too dangerous due to roving bands of Contras.... On January 1, 1990, just seven weeks before the elections, the Contras ambushed a vehicle in the Rosita mining region, killing two nuns, one a U.S. citizen, Sister Maureen Connelly from Wisconsin.

As Willson relates, "[t]here was a realization that as long as the Sandinistas remained in power, the U.S. embargo and Contra terrorism would never relent in their campaign to overthrow them. President Bush had virtually told them this." And lest the Nicaraguan voters did not get Bush's message, the Contras were "communicating to virtually all rural campesinos, through word of mouth, distribution of U.S. funded leaflets, and direct threats, that they will 'make the war worse than ever if the FSLN wins the elections.'"[269]

Willson quotes Paul Reichler, a U.S. lawyer representing the Nicaragua government at that time, who concluded that "'[w]hatever revolutionary fervor the people once might have had was beaten out of them by the war and the impossibility of putting food in their children's stomachs.'"

In spite of it all, Daniel Ortega and the FSLN were gracious in defeat. In his concession speech of February 26, 1990—the day after the vote—Daniel announced that, while he and his party had lost, the Nicaraguans had won something much more important—a historic, democratic transition of power, which Daniel would guarantee by stepping down in light of the results. Daniel declared,

> As President of the Nicaraguan people and as a Sandinista leader, I take pride—and all Sandinista militants can take pride—in the greatest victory.... Today, February 26, opens a new path for Nicaragua like that which we opened on July 19, 1979.... In this new path the war and the contras will disappear, and national interests will prevail over interventionist policies.[270]

Daniel himself understood that the war could only end, and national reconciliation occur, with the Sandinistas out of power. The U.S. would make sure that there was no other way. But what Daniel was wrong about was that the U.S. "interventionist policies" would somehow end with his electoral defeat. The truth is these policies would never end.

The Carter Center went out of its way to acknowledge the uniqueness of what the FSLN had achieved through the 1990 elections and its willingness to turn over the reins of government peacefully, stating:

> For the first time in the history of Nicaragua, power was transferred peacefully from an incumbent government to its rival as a result of an election that was judged by all Nicaraguans as free and fair. For the first time in the history of the world, a revolutionary government that had come to power as a result of a 20-year armed struggle voluntarily gave up the reins of power to its adversary.[271]

While credit is undoubtedly due to the Sandinista government which made this historic transition, the statement cannot be regarded as one hundred percent true. In point of fact, it was the 1984 election which was the first truly free and fair election in Nicaraguan history, despite the fact that it was held in the middle of a brutal war imposed from outside. The fact that the hardcore opposition did not recognize it as such in defeat is simply a testament to its recalcitrance—a recalcitrance bolstered by the U.S.— and not a reflection on the nature of the elections themselves. And indeed, it is debatable whether the Sandinistas' surrender of power could be regarded as voluntary, any more than when a person with a gun to their head agrees to hand over their wallet.

Nonetheless, the fact that the Sandinistas accepted their defeat in 1990, despite how unfair that election was to them, rather than carrying on their military struggle, and thereby establishing the electoral process as a norm in Nicaragua, proved once again that they are revolutionaries of a very different type than any before them or since. Theirs was a particularly benevolent revolution, and Uncle Sam made sure that they paid dearly for their magnanimity.

Daniel and the FSLN were now cast into the political wilderness. While they accepted their defeat, they certainly did not accept it as a permanent state of affairs. Now, they had to rebuild and try to claw their way back to power, but this would not be easy. One of the reasons that made a political come-back difficult was that, unsurprisingly, rifts in the FSLN, which were painted over while it held power and while it fought as a unified force against the Contras, quickly became evident. As is common in any institutional defeat, many blamed the leader—in this case, Daniel—for the loss and wanted a change. In addition, there were principled policy divisions about how to move forward to salvage the party and the Revolution itself, if this were indeed possible. With the end of the war, the time had come to fight over such lofty matters, and simply to settle old scores. As is typical of human beings, after all.

All of this came to a head at the 1994 FSLN extraordinary party Congress, a meeting which would settle the leadership and policy issues confronting the Sandinistas for years to come, and which would result in an official split in the party. As one historian, Steven Kent Smith, writing about this Congress based upon his interviews with party leaders and members on all sides, explains, "[t]he FSLN is the only party in Latin America, and perhaps the world, to have gone through a three-stage transformation from a guerrilla movement to a vanguard party in power to an opposition party searching for political meaning in a post-cold-war environment," and the pressures upon it were enormous.[272] The FSLN would not survive completely intact.

Internally, a faction had been developing over time which would become an official party in opposition to the FSLN—the Sandinista Renovation Movement (MRS), led by Daniel's former Vice-President, Sergio Ramírez—now better known as a poet than as a politician—and Dora Maria Téllez.[273] Understanding the MRS and its origin is critical to understanding ongoing debates about the current nature of the Sandinista Revolution and its leadership. In my experience many in the U.S. who used to support the Sandinistas and Daniel Ortega but who no longer do so, have been influenced by the MRS and its leaders. This is evident, for example, in the extent to which MRS leaders are relied upon by such news outlets as *Democracy Now!* and by formerly Sandinista-friendly journals such as the *North American Congress on Latin America* (NACLA) and *Latin American Perspectives*.

Indeed, it is quite fair to say that the MRS has an outsized influence in the U.S., and Europe as well, especially as compared to its size and influence in Nicaragua. As one measure of its influence in Nicaragua, in the 1996 and 2006 elections—the only elections in which the MRS ran its own candidates under the name "MRS," as opposed to not running at all or running as part of a larger coalition—it received a paltry percentage of votes. In 1996, the very first year it ran candidates, the MRS Presidential candidate, Sergio Ramírez, received fewer than 8,000 total votes, or only 0.44 percent of the vote.[274] Compare this to Daniel Ortega's winning 37.8 percent of the popular vote. The MRS did not do much better in the National Assembly elections that year, winning only 1.33 percent of the vote.[275] In 2006, the MRS Presidential candidate won 6.4 percent of the votes compared to Daniel Ortega's 38 percent and did not run any National Assembly candidates.[276]

In short, the MRS is not a politically significant force in Nicaragua, but again, this has not stopped it from being a major influence in the U.S. and Europe, largely due to personal relationships built during the 1980s between Western solidarity groups and various Sandinista leaders who would later fall away. I also believe that the fact that the MRS has such close and prominent ties with the U.S. State Department, as I detail further below, gives it an exaggerated and outsized credibility in Western circles, strangely even amongst those considering themselves "leftists." And of course, there is always the issue with U.S. NGOs, including human rights groups and even labor unions, receiving monies from the U.S. AID, NED, and other government bodies. Dependent upon such financing, they will inevitably skew their policies to please their government benefactors. Such U.S. groups relying on U.S. government funding may very well feel obligated to take an oppositional stance towards the Nicaraguan government and a more favorable position to opposition groups such as the MRS.

The AFL-CIO's international wing, formerly AIFLD (now the Solidarity Center), which receives nearly all its financing from the NED—indeed, it is one of the three NED pillars, along with the International Democratic Institute and the International Republican Institute—has been notorious for working with the CIA in helping overthrow foreign governments, like the Sandinista government. The AFL-CIO would thus earn the moniker of "AFL-CIA." I know this all too well from having worked with the United Steelworkers union, an AFL-CIO affiliate. During my tenure there, I got to know Gerald Fernandez, the USW's Director of International Affairs for many years. He regaled me with various stories about his own exploits working with AIFLD in the 1980s. Specifically, he was stationed in Costa Rica where he aided the CIA's efforts against the Sandinistas. In the course of this work, he even hosted the notorious Elliott Abrams—a prominent figure in the Iran-Contra scandal who was actually convicted of lying to Congress about the matter—for dinner in Costa Rica. In an email to then USW President Leo Gerard that was provided to me, Fernandez candidly explains how institutional work is compromised and perverted by U.S. Government financing. As Fernandez related in the February 9, 2004, email:

> In reality, the AFL-CIO has a lot to hide about the late '70s and '80s in relation to their international institutes. One has to remember the cold war, Social Democrats USA, Irving Brown etc. The AFL always fared better in getting grants from republican presidents during this period because of communist insurgencies around the world, or, at least, perceived communist insurgencies. As you may be aware, I was part of the most active period for three years in Central America and the Caribbean. Some things I can relate and some things I can't because of the potential for prosecution. I can say that there is a lot of dirty laundry. Some of the funding was related to what I would call covert

operations though this was a very small part of the total operation globally. Most of the activity was related to telling embassies and the State Department what they wanted to hear and that was the labor unions in all developing economies were under threat of communist and extreme left subversion even though in most instances it was nothing more than extreme nationalism and not communist inspired. In any event, that was how you got operating program grants and that is how the institutes built their power, with money and staff. Each country director did the same thing, money, prestige, power, influence mover and shaker.

There is obvious reasons for not dealing with the past, classified information, loss of grants, and some people are still on staff though most were cleaned out.... Some people at the AFL were co-opted by the process....

There is no doubt that other organizations could say similar things about how their work has been compromised by government funding, including how groups like the MRS have become prominent partners in their work as a result—though it is rare that organizations are so candid about such things. In his 1997 book, Smith identified three contributing factors for MRS emergence and development within Nicaragua:

(1) international (the collapse of the socialist bloc),
(2) national (the FSLN's 1990 electoral defeat), and, to a lesser extent,
(3) personal (rivalries and power struggles). These three factors (in varying combinations and degrees) have created what some party affiliates have called an ideological void or identity crisis within the FSLN; the MRS is both a manifestation of and a response to that crisis.

I have covered the first two factors above. The third factor is of less interest but suffice it to say that the rivalry between Daniel Ortega and Sergio Ramírez was certainly significant. It appeared that Ramírez no longer wanted to play second fiddle to Daniel, or anyone else for that matter. He, along with some other Sandinistas, expressed concern about what they saw as Daniel's authoritarianism and insistence to be the unquestioned leader of the Sandinistas.[277] Those who resented Daniel for this reason, and believed that the FSLN could not succeed in elections again with Daniel at the helm, even made moves to oust him from his role as FSLN Chair and from certain Party functions.[278]

All of this is understandable, but the key question is, what was the MRS, then, as a political entity? As Smith explains, no one he interviewed, including MRS leaders themselves, could really say. In short, they may have known what they were against, but they did not know what they were really for, which may explain their anemic showing in the electoral process.

As Smith explains,

> My interviews did not point toward any single description of the MRS, but they did indicate why the MRS emerged and developed into a political party. Although some said that the movement had strong ties with the Sandinista base, others described it as a small intellectual clique devoid of a political platform. "MRS is a name to sell a product," one former National Assembly member and Baptist minister said, "but it doesn't know what the product is" (Sixto Ulloa, interview, 1994)....
>
> Bayardo Arce, a member of the national directorate, argued ... that the FSLN had not suffered a crisis of identity—that the MRS had created whatever crisis existed within the party. The MRS was a sect in search of a new model, he noted, but it wanted to do away with all past models (interview, 1994). Miguel Angel Casco, a Protestant minister and member of the Sandinista Ethics Commission, described the MRS as a confluence of personal resentment and power seeking that did

not want to work within the FSLN. He considered it an intellectual elite willing to make concessions to the "dominant powers" (interview, 1994).[279]

The claim about the MRS leaders wanting "to make concessions to the 'dominant powers'" is a simple statement of fact. As Smith explains, the Sandinistas' 1994 extraordinary Congress ultimately "decided that the FSLN should develop a 'clear, open policy of opposition toward the government and reject the idea of co-government'—a decision opposed by the MRS," which wanted a closer working relationship with the Chamorro Administration. And this was not just a question of mere political tactics. As discussed further below, Chamorro and her successors would embark on policies which would attempt, and in some cases successfully, to destroy many of the gains of the Sandinista Revolution itself, such as progressive social programs and land redistribution.

During the 1994 Extraordinary Congress, Sergio Ramírez was expelled from the FSLN's National Directorate and from his role as the FSLN's leader in the National Assembly, and he would soon voluntarily leave the party entirely. His expulsion from the leadership was in part because of his position of wanting a less adversarial relationship with Chamorro and also because he and other MRS National Assembly Deputies had tried to pass legislation which would have prevented any former president from serving another term in office.[280] This was clearly aimed at preventing Daniel from running for president again. Another contributing factor for Ramírez's ouster from leadership was a longstanding and immutable one. Smith rightly explains, "[s]ome saw Ramírez only as an intellectual who had never participated in the armed struggle that led to the Sandinista Revolution in 1979. Lack of military experience appeared to be a liability for leaders in a country and region whose political history has often been violent," and in a party whose chief inspiration, Augusto César Sandino, had been an active guerilla fighter.[281]

As José Adán Rivera Castillo—long-time Sandinista, historic combatant and a leader of the Agricultural Workers Confederation (ATC)—told me, "[t]he sons and grandsons of the Conquistadors, who might have supported the Revolution at one time, became afraid that what they had would be taken away." Castillo would put Sergio Ramírez, whom he says was trained by the oligarchy, in this category. Castillo says that while he likes Sergio's writings, Ramírez was never sincere with the people in his support for their revolutionary aspirations. While this judgment may seem harsh, it is not an uncommon one in Nicaragua.

Ramírez was not the only child of the oligarchy who was once within the Sandinista fold, only to jump ship when the going got tough. The truth is that "[i]n the 1980s, many of the Sandinista Front's top-level cadre were in fact the children of some of the famous oligarchic families, such as the Cardenal brothers and part of the Chamorro family, in charge of the revolutionary government's ministries of Culture and Education and its media, respectively."[282] And it is these children of the oligarchy who went on to become the core of the leadership of the MRS, which then went on to renounce socialism and to develop an ever-increasingly close relationship with right-wing Republicans, such as Marco Rubio.[283] Notably, this hasn't stopped many in the Western left, such as Amy Goodman, from relying heavily upon the MRS for the source of their views and coverage of Nicaragua.[284]

Indeed, in my view, it is the very intellectualism and more bourgeois presentation of the MRS leaders, such as Sergio Ramírez, that makes them so attractive to so many amongst the Western Left, who are themselves intellectuals and who therefore relate to them better than to other Sandinista figures.

In the end, it was the faction of the FSLN known as the Democratic Left which came out on top in the Extraordinary Congress over the likes of Sergio Ramírez. This faction, which called for "belligerent opposition" to Chamorro and her counter-revolutionary reforms and demanded "greater and a more active commitment on the part of the FSLN toward the poor, its revolutionary vocation and vanguard nature," was led by "commanders Tomás Borge and, above all, Daniel Ortega."[285] History would quickly show the FSLN to have acted prudently in siding with this leadership. The fact that Ramírez, in the 1996 Presidential elections, did not even receive one half of one percent of the votes—a figure which does not even rise to the level of a rounding error—compared to Daniel's nearly 38 percent, demonstrated that the Nicaraguan people were not with Ramírez, to say the least. Indeed, as some commentators have correctly explained, the MRS's "poor results in the 1996 elections gave the Sandinistas' entire symbolic legacy to the FSLN."[286] In addition, the fact that Daniel would ultimately be elected President again in 2006 proved wrong the naysayers who believed the party would never win again under his leadership.

Returning to the nature of the MRS, Smith also cites a Sandinista National Assembly deputy, Herty Lewites, who told him in a 1994 interview "that the MRS was driven by a small group of intellectuals that had not yet touched the heart of the campesinos but was beginning to do so." This statement by Herty Lewites is important, for he later became a main leader of the MRS and indeed was its presidential candidate in 2006 until his untimely death before the election. In the above quote, Lewites himself acknowledges the MRS's initial failure to find support among the campesinos of Nicaragua—the major engine of the Revolution itself. And, while Lewites claimed back in 1994 that this connection with the campesinos was progressing, the truth is that it never really did happen. Nor did the MRS ever really try to make it happen.

As Lola del Carmen Esquivel González—a leader of a women's campesina collective—explained to me in an interview in March of 2022, under President Violeta Chamorro and her successor, President Arnoldo Alemán, there was an attempt to undo the Sandinistas' Agrarian Reform which had given land to her community, and so many others like it. She and other comrades, most of them women, organized and protested to defend the Reform—and more to the point, the land they lived upon —and they did so successfully. Lola, who engaged in acts of civil disobedience with others to try to save their land, ended up being thrown in jail four times under the administrations of Chamorro and her successor, Arnoldo Alemán. Lola explained that it was Daniel Ortega who had provided her with support during her times in jail, including by organizing international backing for her. She received no help from MRS leaders, including Sergio Ramírez, whom she views as out-of-touch intellectuals. "We would die for Daniel," she explains, because he never stopped fighting for her and the rights of campesinos, even during the 1990s when he was out of power.

There is little attention given in the West to the lost years of the 1990s in Nicaragua. With the election defeat in 1990, and the collapse of the Soviet Union in 1991, many Western Leftists appeared to lose interest in the very idea of revolution. That is, they lost the revolutionary imagination. And so, few paid attention to what Daniel Ortega was doing in Nicaragua at this time. However, the fact is that he never gave up on the Revolution or the idea of the FSLN returning to power. He was active throughout the 1990s, trying to defend the Revolution and to pave a path towards FSLN electoral victory. In a Nicaraguan documentary entitled "*El Imprecindible*" ("The Essential"), Daniel's efforts during this time are highlighted. As the film verifies, he continued to lead big, public rallies in support of the FSLN, as well as against the reactionary policies of the neoliberal governments, during these years.

In addition to these public political demonstrations, Daniel also worked quietly to rebuild support for the FSLN. Thus, he traveled throughout the country, meeting with workers and campesinos in their homes, sharing with them the simple food they offered him and just chatting, often late into the night. As Carlos Fonseca Terán, the son of legendary FSLN founder Carlos Fonseca Amador and a steadfast supporter of Daniel, opines in the film, it was these very personal and very private efforts of Daniel, which made all the difference in the ability of the FSLN to return to power. It is these efforts, indeed, which have made Daniel "essential" to the party and the Revolution and it is why he is so beloved by so many in Nicaragua to this very day. This is the Daniel whom we rarely see in the mainstream or even alternative press.

This idea of Daniel as the "essential" leader is commonly held in Nicaragua. Thus, in a November, 2021 interview I had with legendary Sandinista guerilla, Omar Cabezas—the author of the influential book about the armed struggle against Somoza, *Fire From the Mountain*—Cabezas opined that Daniel is "condemned" to lead the Revolution until he dies because that is what the people have decided; that he would not, indeed, be the leader unless that is what the Nicaraguan people wanted.[287] And, Cabezas explains, they have chosen him because he is "noble" and "obsessed" with making the lives of the poor and the hungry happy. It is worth noting that, when I asked whether Western media ever reached out to him to get his take on events in Nicaragua, Cabezas simply laughed and said, "no." This may seem odd given Cabezas' legendary status and his credibility as a guerilla who lost three of his brothers to the struggle against Somoza, but Cabezas himself attributed this to the fact that the media was only interested in

Omar Cabezas shows me the original manuscript of
Fire from the Mountain
DANIEL KOVALIK, NOVEMBER, 2021

giving one side of the Nicaraguan story—the side that favored the anti-Sandinista narrative.

I have heard from others who believe, in addition to Cabezas, that Daniel is by now a reluctant leader—that he is old, not in good health, and would prefer to just spend time with his family. However, he keeps going because there is no one else who can keep the country united and the struggle continuing. To outside observers, this may seem strange and even crazy, and certainly not desirable by the standards we have in the West for our leaders. However, I would submit that there are historical reasons for why this is so, and a lot has to do with the unremitting interference and aggression of the United States. Such foreign intervention has required a leadership in Nicaragua which is strong, relentless and steady. It has required a leader who is as much a military leader as a political one. Daniel has been this leader his entire life, and Nicaraguans recognize this. He is one of the last guerilla leaders left who endured the struggle against Somoza, against the Contras, against the neoliberal leaders and against the violent insurrectionists in 2018. Almost all of the other Sandinista leaders dating back to the struggle against Somoza are either dead or they retired, some long ago.

Indeed, most of the original Sandinista top leadership voluntarily ceded the leadership of the party in the mid-1990s to Daniel Ortega. As researchers Puig and Wright explain, "[a]s of 1995, five of the nine Revolutionary Commanders stopped attending [National Directorate meetings]: Víctor Tirado, Luis Carrion, Henry Ruiz, Jaime Wheelock (who did so of their own free will), and Humberto Ortega (Daniel's brother), because his role as maximum authority of the armed forces was incompatible with political militancy."[288] And this was before the Party began to be more consolidated around the person of Daniel Ortega. That is to say, these individuals decided to abandon the struggle, leaving it to people like Daniel to carry on this hard work. Some of these leaders, moreover, such as Jaime Wheelock and Daniel's brother Humberto, even moved to Costa Rica where they have lived very comfortable lives and abandoned their country completely. That is not necessarily to blame them for their decisions, but rather, to give due credit to Daniel Ortega who has been willing to lead when others have not been. Daniel has been the one constant in the lives of the people of Nicaragua, and he has stood up, and indeed won, against impossible odds.

Like Omar Cabezas, I see this as noble, and not selfish. Indeed, Daniel's is a quite selfless struggle. I am simply perplexed why more in the West seem not to understand this. And, as Michael Parenti explains, if Daniel resembles similar leaders that have gone before, like Fidel Castro, Ho Chi Minh or Vladimir Lenin, it is because historical circumstances, and especially the demands of continually fighting the U.S. Empire, have made him this way.[289]

Meanwhile, despite the best efforts of Daniel and the FSLN to defend the gains of the Revolution, the new neoliberal government of Violeta Chamorro, pursuant to the demands of the United States and the IMF, moved quickly to roll back much of the progress of the prior 11 years of Sandinista rule.

The first and major blow struck by the new neoliberal government was against the Sandinistas' signature achievements of granting land to the peasants and factory ownership to the workers. As one historian notes:

> The fundamentally conservative and anti-Sandinista strategy [of Chamorro] was evidenced by the government's headlong drive to re-privatize the economy. Within weeks after taking power, Chamorro and her advisors moved to privatize virtually all state-run property from farms to factories against the strong resistance of the labor movement. In many instances the properties were returned to former owners, including persons who had been closely associated with the Somoza dictatorship. The privatization occurred within the framework of a neoliberal policy of "structural adjustment." Such a policy was not unique to Nicaragua but rather was part of a worldwide initiative of the U.S. and international lending agencies like the International Monetary [Fund].[290]

Indeed, the neoliberal policy adjustments were first introduced in Chile by the United States after the U.S.-backed coup against Salvador Allende in 1973 and were quickly exported throughout the hemisphere and to much of the world. The Sandinistas had largely resisted these policies, but now Chamorro would impose them with all due haste upon the Nicaraguan people.

The attack on the agrarian reform was demanded by the United States which used aid as a weapon, even against the Chamorro government. Thus, U.S. officials, including right-wing Senator Jesse Helms, made it clear that U.S. aid would be withheld if confiscated land were not given back to former Somocistas, including those who had left Nicaragua after the Triumph and had abandoned their properties; if Nicaragua did not comply with all IMF demands—demands which ensured that, by 1994, 96 percent of all foreign aid went out the door anyway to service debt payments.[291]

Another part of the economic restructuring under Chamorro—again demanded by the U.S. and the IMF—was the privatizing of banks, which had been nationalized by the Sandinistas and which had been operating in the interests of poor workers and farmers, granting them financing on very favorable terms to allow them to maintain and develop their land and properties.[292] Access to such loans now was largely denied, meaning that many who had received land during the Agrarian reform, and who were lucky enough not to have it stolen from them outright under Chamorro, were nonetheless forced to sell due to their desperate economic circumstances.

In addition, the new government moved quickly to restore the old trade relations in which Nicaragua, like most developing countries in what used to be termed the Third World, would again export raw materials to the wealthy First World countries at cheap prices and import them back in the form of refined and manufactured products at exorbitant rates. This was devastating to the Nicaraguan working class which had already suffered great setbacks as a result of the Contra War. As Gary Prevost at the Department of Government at St. John's University explained back in 1996:

The new economic policies . . . seek to reverse Sandinista efforts for Nicaragua to become more self-sufficient as part of a Central American common market. In 1990 Chamorro cut import duties from an average of 80% to 30%. As a result, there was a flood of imported textiles, shoes, and metal goods with which domestic producers could not compete. The subsequent closing of plants has only made worse the country's staggering unemployment. Some 50% of the economically active population was underemployed in 1992 and 1993 and figures rose to nearly 52% in 1994. Open unemployment also grew considerably in 1994, reaching almost 24% of the labor force. The job cuts in the formal sector have been dramatic. The number of people paying social security dropped 23% between 1990 and 1994 in absolute terms, without even factoring in the growth of the employable population. According to a UN study 70% of the population is living in poverty, with 40% in acute poverty.[293]

As unemployment and poverty rose, so did consumer prices as the result of Chamorro's regressive policies, which favored foreign companies and the local bourgeoise to the detriment of the poor, whose purchasing power diminished. As Prevost continues,

Virtually all government controls of the economy have been lifted. Food prices are now almost entirely market driven with all remaining government food subsidies eliminated. Supermarkets have sprung up all over Managua with well-stocked shelves of primarily imported foodstuffs. The price of goods is comparable to North American standards and is, therefore, out of the reach of ordinary Nicaraguans. Because the stores are stocked with imported goods, local producers are not the ones to benefit from this revival of commerce. The beneficiaries are primarily the private commercial intermediaries who have reemerged."[294]

In addition, USAID funded an effort to destroy the public sector and push people into the private, many times "informal," economy which, for many, meant selling food or providing services from their homes or on the streets.[295] Thus, USAID funded the Occupational Conversion Plan which enticed public workers, with a mere $2000 severance payment, to leave their jobs.[296] Thirty thousand public workers (equivalent to 25 percent of the total), saddled with debt and desperate for quick cash, took this deal and left their jobs.

Within a few short years of Chamorro's governance, Nicaragua was suffering the worst depression in its history, "with levels of unemployment and poverty unprecedented in the country's history."[297] Meanwhile, its external debt rose to over $11 billion, "the highest per capita debt in the world."[298] Seven hundred thousand Nicaraguans (or 20 percent of the entire population) ended up fleeing the dismal situation in their country to work elsewhere and send back remittances to their families.[299]

Another huge roll-back of the Chamorro government was ideological:

> Chamorro and many of her advisers were members of a right-wing fundamentalist Catholic cult called "The City of God." Chamorro's conservatism manifested itself very well in the appointment of fundamentalist Humberto Belli to the Ministry of Education. Belli, working closely with the U.S. Agency for International Development (USAID), moved quickly to marginalize Sandinista influence from the schools on the grounds that the previous government had promoted an "atheist humanist view of life." With USAID funding, the Ministry quickly replaced Sandinista-era text with books imported from the United States.[300]

These textbooks taught students "subservience and obedience to church and state authorities." To ensure that the new curriculum was taught in the face of resistance by the Sandinista teachers' union, within the first four months of the Administration the Chamorro government dismissed or transferred over 400 teachers far from their homes. As Prevost relates, "[m]ost teachers, including Sandinistas and their sympathizers, have been forced to implement the new curriculum in order to retain their employment in very desperate economic circumstances."

The new, reactionary curriculum would endure until Daniel finally took office again in 2007, meaning that an entire generation in Nicaragua had been schooled in a way that would make them more receptive to U.S. and anti-Sandinista propaganda. The seeds for the anti-government violence that would later take place in 2018 (more on that below)—violence which the Catholic Church played a big role in organizing and instigating—had already been planted.

In addition, the Chamorro administration—with the help of Managua mayor Arnold Alemán who would later succeed her as president—went out of its way to do such things as destroying Sandinista murals, removing the FSLN letters from a mountain overlooking Managua after first replacing them with the word "FIN" (End), removing portraits of the heroes of the Revolution from public buildings, and putting out the eternal flame marking the tomb of Carlos Fonseca.[301]

In addition to the assault on the Sandinista curriculum, the Chamorro government attacked education itself, privatizing the schools, which then charged fees that many families could not afford, and slashing monies for education. Within three years, the illiteracy rate was back to where it was in 1980. As Prevost explains, "[t]he combined impact of the years of the war and the further cutbacks in education spending ... almost totally reversed any gains that may have been accomplished in the early 1980s."[302]

Similarly, the Chamorro government attacked the public health system, privatizing many of the hospitals and clinics, which now charged for everything except the doctor's visit itself. At the same time, the government reduced spending on healthcare by almost one-half, from $130 million in 1989 to $70 million by 1994.[303] Not only did this compromise the health of the public, but, as a number of health centers were shuttered, it also resulted in the layoff of numerous public health doctors and staff. Public daycare centers which had provided nutritional service to children were also defunded, and almost totally closed. The result of all this was a rise in anemia, malnutrition and the resulting permanent intellectual disability of thousands of children. [304]

The Chamorro government also attacked women's and gay rights. For example, while abortion, unlawful under Somoza, had not been legalized by the Sandinistas who did not want to take on the Catholic Church—especially during war-time—the Sandinista government had not enforced the anti-abortion law, making it all but de facto permissible.[305] However, this changed with the deeply conservative Chamorro government, which began prosecuting women for abortions, thereby driving abortions underground as they had been before the Revolution.[306] The Chamorro government also successfully opposed legislation proposed by the Women's Commission of the National Assembly, which was heavily Sandinista, for a progressive family code and a law prohibiting violence against women. In addition, over the objections of the FSLN deputies in the National Assembly, the conservative forces passed anti-sodomy legislation aimed at homosexuals.

While the CIA had started the Contra War in the Miskitu Coast and had used the plight of the Miskitu as one of their chief propaganda vehicles, the Chamorro government turned on the Miskitus with nary a protest from the U.S. Unable to reverse the Miskitus' legal status of autonomy granted by the Sandinistas, the new government simply ignored the Autonomy Statute.[307] Thus, while this Statute required that the regional Miskitu government control the resources of the Miskitu people, this mandate was simply circumvented, with control over fishing, mining and forestry sold off to private enterprises—the main beneficiary being a company run by the brother of the Presidential adviser—which exploited and destroyed these valuable resources and the environment along with them.

For good measure, Chamorro also gave up on the Sandinistas' efforts in the 1980s to win back the disputed islands ceded to Colombia in 1928 for no particular reason, therefore dooming the Sandinistas' case before the ICJ, and she sold off the assets of Nicaragua's train system, resulting in that system's demise. Nicaragua was now open again for wholesale looting.

In short, while the United States and its Contra mercenaries were never able to defeat the Sandinistas militarily, they were nonetheless able to achieve the counterrevolution by wearing down the Nicaraguan people and coercing the electorate in the 1990 elections. The biggest losers were the Nicaraguan people themselves. In his 2005 Nobel Prize Speech, Harold Pinter paints the bleak picture of the shadow that fell over Nicaragua after the 1990 election and into the new century:

> The United States finally brought down the Sandinista government. It took some years and considerable resistance but relentless economic persecution and 30,000 dead finally undermined the spirit of the Nicaraguan people. They were exhausted and poverty stricken once again. The casinos moved back into the country. Free health and free education were over. Big business returned with a vengeance. "Democracy" had prevailed.[308]

The Sandinistas would find a way, through cunning and popular organizing, to return to power and to restart what they had begun in 1979. But the United States would never cease trying to destroy them and their Revolution.

Family at the Puerta Salvador Allende, a beautiful park in Managua along the Xolotlan Lake with restaurants and playgrounds. During the 1990s, this site was a garbage dump where drug users and prostitutes gathered. After Daniel was re-elected in 2006, it was converted to a park and the adjoining lake, in which garbage and sewage had been dumped into, was cleaned.

CHAPTER 6
THE SANDINISTAS RETURN

The title of this chapter, referring to the Sandinistas' return to power in 2007, is a bit misleading because, while not in power from 1990 until 2007, the Sandinistas had not really gone anywhere. Indeed, they continued to organize and mobilize during the neoliberal years to both resist the policies of the three preceding reactionary governments and to find ways to adjust to the policies they could not prevent. Some of this work was certainly carried out on the national, party level, but much of it was also at the grass roots and more local level.

As Florence E. Babb pointed out in her book, *After Revolution: Mapping Gender and Cultural Politics in Neoliberal Nicaragua*—a book written in 2001, well before the electoral comeback of Daniel Ortega—while many of the gains of the Revolution were lost to the Contra War and years of neoliberal onslaught,

> Nevertheless, much of the revolution has endured and even deepened since the FSLN lost power, including forms of democratic participation and respect for political pluralism. Thus when I say *after* revolution, I do not intend to present the revolution as something static and now consigned to history but rather as something that has been in process and has undergone change—sometimes for better, other times for worse—and that continues to give shape to local and national politics.[309]

As she explains, "[o]ften the very groups disfavored by current policy"—e.g., the poor, working class and women—"have taken advantage of new openings for political mobilization."[310]

Prevost corroborates this conclusion, especially in regard to the enduring vitality of women's organizations after the Sandinista electoral defeat. As he explained in 1996, six years into neoliberal rule,

> the greater involvement of women in the public life of Nicaragua, an important advancement of the 80s, remains strong. The women's movement is probably stronger today than 10 years ago with the Nicaraguan Women's Association (AMNLAE) strengthened and many new organisations on the scene, including several which have clearly labelled themselves as feminist. AMNLAE operates 57 centres throughout Nicaragua that promote programmes in health, economic development, gender consciousness, political involvement, the environment, and legal rights. In 1994 the programmes reached 108,000 women.[311]

Undoubtedly, the continued and even permanent grassroots efforts of women's, peasants' and workers' organizations have been essential for keeping the Revolution alive, honest and moving in a forward direction.

However, as Babb rightly recognizes, focusing again on the grassroots work of women's groups, "even the best strategies women have devised to confront the economic crisis are not sufficient to withstand the impact of structural adjustment measures and ... more thorough-going transformation may be needed once again in Nicaragua."[312] And, while she does not say so, it should be obvious that such a truly "thorough-going transformation" was possible only by the re-taking of state power by those dedicated to the Revolution. The only group with the will and capability of doing this was and remains the FSLN. What's more, it is apparent that the only figure capable of leading the FSLN in this effort was

Daniel Ortega. He would have to make difficult choices, compromises, and deals to achieve this.

As commentators Salvador Marti Puig and Claire Wright explain, "While Violeta Barrios de Chamorro was president, the FSLN mobilized its grassroots members against the policies the government was implementing to dismantle the social achievements of the Revolution .... This logic of mobilization gave the FSLN an aggressive and popular image, on which Daniel Ortega capitalized."[313] However, after losing to Chamorro twice and then to her successor Arnoldo Alemán and failing to achieve 40 percent of the vote in any of these three elections, Daniel Ortega and the FSLN began negotiating changes with the government in order to find a path to return to power. The result was "The Pact" in 2000 between Daniel and Alemán, which many have criticized, but which would help return Daniel to the presidency. The most important part of "The Pact" was electoral reform, which, among other things,

> included a striking change in the criteria for the necessary conditions to win the presidency. The reform lowered from 45 percent to 40 percent the percentage of votes necessary to win without going to a second round, and if the difference in votes between the first and second candidate was more than 5 percent, only 35 percent of the votes. This change was an explicit demand by Ortega, since it was a necessary condition for him to be able to win the presidency, given the FSLN's electoral limit.[314]

"The Pact" also included a power-sharing arrangement which gave control over major institutions of the government to the FSLN and Alemán's Liberal Party.

Daniel lost the election that was held in the fall of 2001. I was an election observer for that election along with 35 others from the United States, who were all invited by the FSLN to serve as observers. We named our delegation the "Ben Linder Brigade" in honor of the engineer murdered by the Contras in 1987. Along with several others, I had the honor of having dinner with Daniel Ortega the very night before the election at a modest steak house in Managua. This was the first time I saw Daniel since my first meeting with him back in 1988 as part of the Veterans Peace Convoy. I was struck by the fact that, for an event with a man running for president the next day, the dinner was a relatively small and subdued one with no cameras and frankly minimal security. Back then, and until relatively recently, Daniel insisted upon driving himself around in an SUV.

At the dinner, Daniel was suffering from a cold and seemed a bit tired. Still, he was quietly friendly and listened very attentively to anyone who wanted to talk to him. He struck me as a man of few words who indeed seems happier to listen than he is to talk. He lacks the bombast of a Fidel Castro or Hugo Chavez—both of whom I have had the chance to hear speak in person. But then, Daniel has suffered so much more than Fidel or Chavez ever did. His seven years of brutal incarceration sets him apart from almost all other revolutionary leaders, with the notable exception of Nelson Mandela who was in jail for much longer but in less tortuous conditions. And this experience has molded Daniel into the person he remains today. These observations of Daniel ring true to me:

> "I felt tense in freedom, claustrophobic," Ortega recalled about his release after seven years in the Somoza prison. "I just had a hard time.... If I entered a room, I would want to get out quickly. If I got into a car, I would start feeling desperate. It was as if the cell were always with me." Although Ortega went on to say that he "overcame this" after a few months, the truth appears to be more complicated. Sergio Ramírez, who later served as Ortega's vice president, for example, believes that Ortega still retains a "prison personality"—"lonely, solitary, mistrustful, hard." Ortega also continued to display eccentric characteristics consistent with long-term incarceration. When he became head of state and hosted dinner parties in his home—which is a

private compound rather than a state structure, guarded by private security forces—he did not dine with his guests. Instead, he would slip into the kitchen and eat with his staff.[315]

To me, Daniel exhibits a certain sadness that makes me feel very sympathetic towards him, especially being aware that what he has suffered in his lifetime is equivalent to that of ten mere mortals.

In 2001, Daniel ran a very different campaign than he had done in the past. The colors used in his campaign materials were no longer the militant red and black colors of the Sandinista flag, but rather, soft, pastel colors such as pink and baby blue. He was now trying to emphasize the values and goals of peace, reconciliation and Christian love. Indeed, his very first platform item—as listed in a small, pink campaign booklet I have kept from that time—was: "The people of Nicaragua deserve, believe and develop in peace. The government of the FSLN guarantees the stability, security and peace for the country. Never more shall there be war, nor military service, nor confrontation in Nicaragua."

While many leftists in the U.S. seemed confounded by what they saw as Daniel's conciliatory and even non-revolutionary tone, Daniel—always a pragmatist and always someone very attuned to the mood of the people—was responding to what he perceived as the continuing anxiety of the country about the war which had only ended a little more than 10 years before and the fears that such a war could be sparked again. He wanted to assure the people that, under his leadership, no such war would ever come again to Nicaragua. I myself do not see anything somehow "unrevolutionary" about Daniel's campaign tactics in 2001—tactics which have continued in one form or another till the present time.

When I interviewed one former Comandante who still strongly backs Daniel—Doris Tijerino –she said to me that one must look past the rhetoric and symbols used by Daniel and the FSLN, which may not look so revolutionary or militant to the outside observer, and instead look at what they actually do for the people. This, she stated, is how one can adequately assess their true revolutionary nature. This seems correct to me. As she confirmed to me, Doris Tijerino is never interviewed by the Western press, including the alternative press. She wasn't even interviewed for a recent documentary called, *"La Sandinistas,"* about the role of women in the Sandinista Revolution. Apparently, her views are not convenient to the anti-FSLN narrative most in the West seem so dedicated to presenting.

Meanwhile, the United States, as it had done in the past, tried to convince the electorate that voting for Daniel would lead again to war. And as all were aware, the U.S. had the power to guarantee that it would. In a very real way then, the U.S. also had a big role in influencing how Daniel campaigned, for he knew all too well that he was running as much against the United States as against his Nicaraguan opponent, Enrique Bolaños.

As I wrote back in 2001 shortly after the elections, the mechanics of the polling in Nicaragua was very good from what I and other observers witnessed. Thus, as I explained,

> As an election observer, I had the honor of watching Nicaraguans, many elderly, poor and infirm, stand in line for hours in the hot sun to cast their vote. Simply put, I received a class in democracy. Seventy-five percent of the eligible voters participated in the elections, and those on the grass-roots level in charge of meticulously checking voter credentials and in distributing, collecting and counting the ballots took pride in making sure that the election was fair.[316]

However, as with the 1990 election, the 2001 election could not be characterized as free and fair, not because of FSLN interference, but because of the interference of the United States and the actions of then-president of Nicaragua, Arnoldo Alemán.

As I explained at the time,

> For many months, the U.S. had placed great pressure on the Nicaraguan voters to vote a certain way— namely, against the Sandinistas and for the Liberal

Party candidate. Thus, as early as last year, U.S. officials publicly stated that a Sandinista victory could lead to a discontinuation of U.S. aid to Nicaragua as well as a return to the "oppositional policy" of the 1980s. This threat was a clear reference to the support, at times in violation of U.S. law, for the Contra war.[317]

The George W. Bush Administration further took advantage of the 911 attacks to try to vilify the FSLN. Thus, as I wrote, "the State Department took advantage of the tense climate to state publicly that it had 'grave reservations' about a Sandinista victory, claiming that the Sandinistas had a history of 'ties to supporters of terrorism.'" Of course, everyone knew at the time what the U.S. was doing to groups and countries it designated as "terrorists" or as havens for terrorists—it was attacking and waging war against them in what the U.S. dubbed the "War on Terror." Needless to say, this amounted to not-so-veiled threats of military action against Nicaragua in the event of a Sandinista victory.

Lest there was any doubt about President Bush's posture towards Daniel Ortega, just days before the November 2001 election in Nicaragua,

> Florida Gov. Jeb Bush took out a full-page ad in a prominent Nicaraguan newspaper, *La Prensa*, in which he stated that President George W. Bush supports the Liberal Party presidential candidate, Enrique Bolaños. In this ad Gov. Bush claimed that Sandinista candidate Daniel Ortega does not understand or accept "the basic principles of freedom [and] democracy"; that Ortega "is an enemy of everything the United States represents" and that Ortega has a long-standing relationship "with states and individuals who shelter and condone international terrorism."[318]

This is the kind of language Governor Bush reserved for countries like Afghanistan that the U.S. had invaded just a few short months before the Nicaraguan elections. Nicaraguans could only interpret this as a threat that they too could be invaded if they voted for Daniel Ortega.

Taking a plan out of the Somoza playbook, President Alemán made serious threats against the Nicaraguan population shortly before the elections. As I detailed back then,

> Nicaragua's ruling Liberal Party president, Arnoldo Alemán, added to the state of fear created by these statements by threatening, up to the very eve of elections, to declare a state of emergency in Nicaragua. In so doing, Alemán implicitly threatened to cancel the elections. He issued these threats—which he enforced by the placement of troops throughout the streets of Managua on Nov. 2—claiming that he anticipated violence from Sandinista supporters. No such violence ever materialized."[319]

I ultimately concluded, in agreement with my fellow observers, that these actions of Alemán, combined with the statements and threats by the U.S. government, "had a great impact upon the Nicaragua elections. Indeed, they may have been decisive in the Liberal Party's narrow victory over the Sandinistas and Daniel Ortega." And so, democracy was again thwarted by the U.S. in the name of defending freedom and democracy.

However, Daniel, though bowed, was not broken. He used the intervening time during the new administration of Enrique Bolaños to engage in shrewd political maneuvers that would usher the FSLN back into power. Daniel was able to play one faction of the Liberal Party against the other, helping to successfully divide the Party in half. Puig and Wright explain that

> during the administration of Bolaños, Ortega negotiated with both factions of liberalism, which came face to face as the result of the clash between Bolaños and his predecessor, Alemán. As a result, the liberal bloc split between Alemánistas and Bolañistas, and the division extended to liberals who held top posts in all the state

institutions. The FSLN thus became the political force in the National Assembly, with the highest representation, controlling the rest of the public institutions, including the judicial system. It also thereby became the key player in Nicaraguan politics.[320]

The division in the Liberal Party, now split almost equally between two new parties (the PLC and the ALN), combined with the new electoral law negotiated between Daniel and Alemán through "The Pact" paved the way for Daniel to win the 2006 Presidential election with 38 percent of the vote to the PLC's 26 percent and the ALN's 29 percent.[321] The discipline of the FSLN also contributed to the win. As Puig and Wright explain, a key factor

> was the solidity of the FSLN's party machine which, in the end, was the political group with highest levels of party cohesion, obedient to its leader and spread throughout the country. Furthermore, the party showed an absolute flexibility in elaborating its discourses and strategies according to the political context.[322]

In terms of "flexibility" in "discourses and strategies," Daniel's victory could also be attributed to his again running a campaign emphasizing peace and reconciliation over class and other conflicts. To that end, he set about to work with former Contras, including Jaime Morales Carazo who served as his Vice-Presidential candidate; and successfully woo conservative elements of the Catholic Church to his side, including the powerful Bishop Obando y Bravo who had plagued the FSLN during the 1980s as an oppositional political figure.[323]

While such a victory may have seemed compromising to many leftists, it was a victory achieved in point of fact by compromise—as is the norm in modern democratic states, inevitable and necessary in order to hold the diverse elements of the state together. And, as Comandante Doris urges, the important question was what Daniel and the FSLN actually then went on to do for the people of Nicaragua with this victory. And it was in the actions of the new administration that Daniel and the FSLN really proved not just their commitment to their values, but the wisdom of the route they chose to achieve them, given the realities they faced.

The first order of business of President Daniel Ortega 2.0 was to restore the progressive social programs of the FSLN, which had been systematically destroyed during the neoliberal years. As Puig and Wright relate,

> The about-face on social issues was based on two axes. The first was making primary and secondary schools, as well as access to health and hospitals, completely free. The second was the launching of focused social policies in order to alleviate poverty through programs such as Hambre Cero [Zero Hunger], Usura Cero [Zero Usury], Desempleo Cero [Zero Unemployment], and Calles para el Pueblo [Streets for the People].[324]

In 2007, just after taking office, Daniel created Councils of People's Power (CPCs), which "were platforms designed to represent citizens in different areas of the country and to implement most of the focused social policies designed to combat poverty."[325] As Puig and Wright explain,

> According to the presidency, these groups were based on the direct participation of citizens. Their functions were to "design policy, plans, programs and actions to promote the formation of citizenship and guarantee it in practice throughout the national territory via the neighborhood, district, municipal, departmental and regional Consejos de Ciudadanos [Citizen Councils] ...with the aim of creating a democracy of citizens by means of direct democracy."[326]

Curiously, Puig and Wright simply mention the policies of the Sandinista government after 2007, without discussing whether or to what extent they advanced the interests of the people.

Instead, similar to many other researchers, they focus on the internal dynamics of the FSLN, and in particular on the increasingly ad hoc and personal nature of the leadership of Daniel as contrasted with the more formal, collectivist party structure of the FSLN of the 1980s, which they suggest was more democratic. And, while acknowledging that Daniel's leadership has come to resemble the leadership of Rafael Correa in Ecuador and Hugo Chavez in Venezuela—and to this, I would certainly add Fidel Castro in Cuba, Ho Chi Minh in Vietnam, Mao in China and Lenin in Russia—they ultimately throw up their hands, after reviewing all of the relevant literature, and conclude that this "can only be understood taking into account the political culture in Nicaragua which extols a strong, caudillo-type figure and perpetuates weakness of state."[327]

This type of racist trope, strangely put forward by people calling themselves academics, simply ignores the historic pressures on Nicaragua and the FSLN, and in particular the pressures of constant U.S. intervention, which, as Michael Parenti tells us, lead almost all modern revolutionary leaders—even those well beyond Nicaragua and Latin America—to the same place. Such pressures, I would submit, force such leaders to become as much military leaders as political ones in order to navigate the dangerous shoals of U.S. imperialism. The events of 2018 would prove that, in a very real way, Nicaragua continues to be a nation at war, and this has demanded a decisive and resolute leadership to meet this challenge.

However, the claim that Daniel is a "strong, caudillo-type figure," is clearly off base. I have heard Daniel speak publicly many times. He speaks quietly, even when speaking to thousands of people. He doesn't wave his hands around or point his fingers or make other histrionic gestures like some other truly "caudillo-type" figures. Rather, most of his speeches resemble history lessons which are delivered in a calm, conversational and reasoned style, contrary to most political speeches. Long-gone are the military fatigues he used to wear. Instead, he invariably wears a baseball cap and a wind-breaker—hardly the grandeur-promoting attire typical of some "great dictator." I actually joked once with a member of the Nicaraguan diplomatic corps that, even at his inauguration, Daniel dressed like someone who was going out to the grocery store. While the joke did not go over too well, my observation was nonetheless accurate—and not intended as a detraction.

The other observation which I and many others have made is how little security surrounds Daniel, even at big events. I have attended numerous such events, and I and the other international guests are never required to go through a metal detector. Nor are we searched or frisked, even though we end up in close proximity to Daniel. In addition, there are few armed security figures in sight. At the last event I attended—the July 19 celebrations in 2022—Daniel's path from the stage to his vehicle was guarded by unarmed Sandinista youth linked arm-in-arm. Notably, it took a

Author's friend, Scarleth Escorcia, takes a selfie with Daniel Ortega in his car after the July 19 celebration in 2022
SCARLETH ESCORCIA, 2022 [(REPRODUCED WITH PERMISSION OF MS. ESCORCIA]

long time for Daniel to reach his car because many people broke through the Sandinista youth chain to greet and hug him. Some even managed to jump into the car with him. Daniel simply waits patiently as his many supporters get their chance to say hello.

While the figure of Daniel Ortega as party and national leader became more solidified and important as the years passed, Daniel has maintained a permanent dialogue with various civil society groups in Nicaragua, and in particular with mass organizations (OMs), which have always been a key component of the Sandinistas. As Puig and Wright explain, a

> pillar of the Sandinista apparatus was its organic links with the OMs, which included trade unions and social organizations made up of neighbors, youth, children, or women. The FSLN always considered that "the masses" had to join social organizations that, although not part of the party structure, were nevertheless organically linked to it. These organizations had a very important role in bringing together large groups for revolutionary tasks. Their functions were never clearly defined, although the party statutes said that their task was to "protect and encourage the strengthening of the revolution and to become real instruments for the expression and channeling of the most pressing needs of the masses."[328]

The OMs have always had real, practical input into the decision-making of Daniel and the FSLN, and that is true to this day. As Carlos Fonseca Terán, the son of legendary Comandante Carlos Fonseca, the co-founder of the FSLN, explained recently,

> Our socioeconomic and political model has its fundamental base in popular power.... The expression of that in politics is citizens' power as an organized expression of popular influence on public affairs, the "protagonism" of social movements in the mechanisms for decision-making, the participation of social movement leaders in institutional spaces of the state.[329]

For his part, José Adán Rivera Castillo, leader of a key mass organization, the Agricultural Workers Confederation (ATC), explained to me in March of 2022, the Sandinista base became concerned when, initially after the 2006 election victory, Daniel, to be conciliatory, signed off on a lot of the laws which the bourgeoisie proposed. He explained that the base, through the OMs, went to Daniel and expressed their opposition to this, and Daniel changed course. When asked about the claims of Daniel turning into another Somoza, Rivera counters with the simple observation that

> the difference is that Somoza did not have popular support, but Daniel does. That's why we are working on advancing the Revolution rather than fighting a war. In just 15 years of government, we have been able to implement a wide range of social and economic programs like never before. In the past, the governments just stole, and stole and stole, and they told us about democracy only when they won.

Rivera further asserts,

> When they say Daniel is bad, that reaffirms that he is a good person for us. We would worry if the enemies of the Revolution began to speak well of him. Daniel also has a strong ability to interact with the rich and the poor. In the 1980s, a lot of the leaders of the military were still from the Oligarchy, but Daniel heard us, and now, the vast majority of the leaders of the military and police are workers and peasants. Now if you look at today's government, it is different from before when the leaders were trained in the U.S. Now, workers and peasants, both men and women, are leading the government.

The revamping and reconstitution of the police forces which Rivera alludes to resulted in quite impressive results, which have been recognized throughout the hemisphere. For years, the

National Police as re-constituted has been one of the most trusted institutions in Nicaragua, known throughout the region as exemplary in its use of pro-active community policing. Its focus has been on rehabilitating, rather than punishing, particularly with adolescents and children engaged in criminal activity.

As J. Thomas Ratchford III explained in a peer-reviewed *Emory International Law Review* journal article from 2017,

> In the face of surging regional violence, processes and techniques developed by the Nicaraguan National Police yield the lowest violent crime rates in the region in spite of Nicaragua's ranking as the poorest country in Central America. Bucking the trend towards militarization in regional police forces, mirroring U.S. policy, Nicaragua has developed community-centered programs that prioritize restorative justice.... This concept is codified in legislation aimed at prioritizing citizen security through programs emphasizing constant reform of security apparatuses in partnership with the population.[330]

Ratchford explained that, at the time of his writing the journal article, statistics

> place Nicaragua's homicide rates at eight per 100,000 inhabitants, the lowest such statistic in the region. Another indicator, which can be related more directly to youth gangs, is the astounding statistic that in a country of over six million inhabitants there were only seventy juveniles in custody.[331]

The low level of youth incarceration is a function of "Nicaragua's juvenile justice program ... [which] relies on: (1) political commitment to reform, (2) community involvement, (3) restorative justice through education and rehabilitation, and (4) public legitimacy."[332]

Meanwhile, Nicaragua's neighbors, which have adopted a heavy-handed, militaristic approach to dealing with gang violence and youth crimes—an approach known as *mano duro* (literally, "strong hand")—have had much worse outcomes. As Ratchford explains,

> Guatemala, El Salvador, and Honduras have seen spiking homicide rates that have oscillated between twenty-four and eighty homicides per 100,000 inhabitants over the last decade, with El Salvador's surging past one hundred homicides per 100,000 inhabitants in 2015.[333]

This accounts for the large migration to the U.S. from these three countries while Nicaragua has contributed nominally to this phenomenon. Indeed, a May 12, 2016, press release from U.S. House Democrats explains,

> Our neighbors in the Northern Triangle countries of El Salvador, Honduras, and Guatemala are in a crisis of uncontrolled violence. Women and children from these countries are coming to our Southwest border in search of refuge. Essentially, no one is coming from Nicaragua....[334]

Ratchford explains that while the current Nicaraguan National Police "traces its origins to the 1979 Fundamental Statute of the Republic (EFR), which created the first security institution distinct from the Army following the Sandinista transition from the Somoza dictatorship." the neoliberal governments attempted to sever the relationship between the FSLN and the Revolution.[335] However, they were not entirely successful at this, and the police have regained their more revolutionary nature through constant revamping, including after the return of the Sandinistas to power in 2007.

Ratchford explains that,

Throughout this continuous transformation, Nicaragua's police force has gained a reputation for being, in the words of its former director Aminta Granera, "the smallest police force in Central America, with the lowest salaries, but with the best results ...." Granera, a militant Sandinista and feminist, was previously Chief of Staff for the Interior Ministry during the first Sandinista regime and credits her decision to participate in the police force as one made after deciding "not [to hand] my rifle over to someone who will use it against my people."[336]

Not surprisingly, as of 2017, Granera —who also brought many women into the police force, and who helped create "102 women's police stations, special units that include protecting women and children from sexual and domestic violence and abuse"[337]—"sat atop the list of twenty-six Nicaraguan public officials with an approval rating of eighty-seven percent."[338] Ratchford concludes that Nicaragua's "holistic" and "rehabilitative" approach to policing resulted in the "public perception of 'fairness of police behavior' as opposed to 'the fear of police force and the threat of punishment,'" and to an overall high level of "legitimacy."

Bear in mind, the 2007 Ortega government was faced with a country which had been horribly neglected and plundered for 17 years. As José Adán Rivera Castillo told me, "[i]n the three neoliberal governments, they showed us they didn't care for us at all. They didn't want to educate us, give us jobs or give us electricity or water. They even wanted us to pay for meals in the school. We therefore realized they did not care about us." Ortega moved quickly to reverse this situation.

As Kevin Zeese, a long-time American activist and writer, and Nils McCune, an American now living and raising a family in Nicaragua, explain, in words sounding a lot like those of Rivera:

> This is the first government since Nicaraguan independence that does not include the oligarchy. Since the

1830s through the 1990s, all Nicaraguan governments—even during the Sandinista Revolution—included people from the elite with "last names" of Chamorro, Cardenal, Belli, Pellas, Lacayo, Montealegre, Gurdián. The government since 2007 does not, which is why these families are supporting the [2018] coup.

Ortega detractors claim his three-part dialogue including labor unions, capitalists and the State is an alliance with big business. In fact, that process has yielded the highest growth rate in Central America and annual minimum wage increases 5–7% above inflation, improving workers' living conditions and lifting people out of poverty. The anti-poverty Borgen project reports poverty fell by 30 percent between 2005 and 2014.

The Ortega economy is the opposite of neoliberalism, it is based on public investment and strengthening the safety net for the poor. The government invests in infrastructure, transit, maintains water and electricity within the public sector, and moved privatized services, e.g., health care and primary education, into the public sector. This has ensured a stable economic structure that favors the real economy over the speculative economy.[339]

In terms of electricity, the preceding neoliberal governments did little to provide this necessary service to the population, particularly in the rural and indigenous areas, which were almost entirely neglected. By the end of the neoliberal period, only 54 percent of Nicaraguans had any access to electricity.[340] And, by 2005, even the electricity which had been provided was by then being rationed at extreme levels, with "recurrent 8- to 12-hour-long interruptions to the electricity supply" throughout the country, in part due to the rise in the price of oil which the government depended upon almost exclusively for power generation.[341] This changed with the new 2007 administration of Daniel Ortega, which immediately began a major overhaul of the electrical system, prioritizing a conversion from fossil fuels to renewable energy sources—such as wind, solar, hydro, geo-thermal and biofuels—and the electrification of the rural areas.[342]

As the *Christian Science Monitor* explained in a 2012 article:

> Years of energy shortages debilitated the country, as its power grid aged and energy plants were unable to meet demand. Daily power-rationing blackouts lasting 6–10 hours were the norm in 2006, but in 2007 things began to change when the Sandinista government, led by Daniel Ortega, returned to power.
>
> Switching to renewable energy has become a linchpin in the Sandinistas' national development plan....
>
> Ortega worked with Nicaragua's private sector and Venezuela's Hugo Chávez to fix its immediate energy problem by installing an additional capacity of 343 megawatts of power—41 percent more power than Nicaragua was producing five years ago.[343]

As the *Christian Science Monitor* elaborated, Ortega's initiative has been universally supported within Nicaragua, and his "push for a renewable energy revolution has united the country like few other issues,"[344] pointing out that even the U.S. government applauded this effort, with William Cobb, the U.S. Embassy's energy and environment officer stating, "'[i]n keeping with United States international policies and goals, the U.S. government recognizes ambitious efforts in Nicaragua to address climate change by radically shifting its electricity generation from petroleum-based to renewable sources within a short window of time.'"[345]

By now, Nicaragua is approaching 100 percent electrification, as well as 100 percent access to mobile phone connectivity and 85 percent access to the internet.[346]

In addition, the 2007 Sandinista government began to bring water and sewage to hitherto neglected communities. By 2021, 92 percent of the urban population and 55 percent of the rural population had potable drinking water, up from 65 percent and 28 percent in 2006, respectively.[347] Meanwhile, homes connected to sewage disposal systems grew from 30 percent in 2007 to 57 percent in 2021.[348]

The Sandinista government has also "funded the building or renovation of 290,000 homes since 2007, free of charge for those in extreme poverty, or with interest free long-term loans."[349] This housing program has benefitted over one million Nicaraguans, or about one-sixth of the total population.

Education has also been prioritized by the Sandinista government, which picked up where they left off in the 1980s. The FSLN made child education free again after 2007, allowing 100,000 children to return to school while opening 265 free day care centers for preschoolers.[350] And, the government now provides a hot meal to 1.5 million school and pre-school children, and free backpacks, glasses and uniforms to those children who need it.[351]

Journalist Ben Norton, who has now moved permanently to Nicaragua and even bought a home there, wrote in 2020, "[i]n the past 13 years of Sandinista rule, overall poverty in Nicaragua has been reduced from 48.3 percent to 24.9 percent, and extreme poverty from 17.2 percent to 6.9 percent. Illiteracy has fallen from 35 percent to 3 percent."[352] Norton also quotes Carlos Fonseca Terán for the proposition that, since the return of Daniel Ortega to the presidency, Nicaragua has generally gone from the fourth most unequal country in Latin America to the fourth least unequal.[353]

There have also been huge leaps forward in terms of healthcare for the population since the Sandinista return, with life expectancy jumping from 72 in 2006 to 77 years today (equivalent to that of the United States) as a result.[354] The healthcare measures of the government have included reinstituting free health care, building over 25 world-class hospitals and over 1700 health care units, and providing 178 maternity homes near medical centers for women with high-risk pregnancies or for expecting mothers who live in areas located far from a hospital.[355] Indeed, "[w]hen Ortega was re-elected in 2006, the maternal mortality rate—a key marker of a country's well-being—was 92.8 deaths per 100,000 live births. By 2020, that number dropped 60 percent to 37.5 deaths per 100,000 live births because of programs that include [these] 'maternity homes' to monitor pregnant women close to their due date."[356]

Women's health in general has become a priority of the government, with 66 new mobile units set up throughout the country which, among other procedures, now provide screenings for breast cancer and cervical cancer, as well as Pap tests, to hundreds of thousands of women who never had access to such services before.[357]

There have also been many other advances specifically for women since the Sandinistas came back to power—advances which rarely get a mention even in the left-wing press of the U.S. which often looks down on Nicaragua and the Sandinistas as retrograde entities. As a recent *Monthly Review* article, entitled, "The gains of Nicaraguan women during the second Sandinista Government," explains, some of these advances have come from anti-poverty programs (merely mentioned in passing by Puig and Wright) which are specifically aimed at benefitting women. Thus,

> These programs, launched in 2007, raise the socio-economic position of women. Zero Hunger furnishes pigs, a pregnant cow, chickens, plants, seeds, fertilizers, and building materials to women in rural areas to diversify their production, upgrade the family diet, and strengthen women-run household economies. The agricultural assets provided are put in the woman's name, equipping women to become more self-sufficient producers; it gives them more direct control and security over food for their children. This breaks women's historic dependency on male breadwinners and encourages their self-confidence. The program has aided 275,000 poor families, over one million people (of a total of 6.6 million Nicaraguans), and has increased both their own food security and the nation's food sovereignty.[358]

There is also The Zero Usury program which is a "microcredit mechanism that now charges 0.5% annual interest, not the world microcredit average of 35%." As the *Monthly Review*

Article explains, "[o]ver 445,000 women have received these low interest loans, typically three loans each. The program not only empowers women but is a key factor reducing poverty, unlocking pools of talent, and driving diversified and sustainable growth. Many women receiving loans have turned their businesses into cooperatives, providing jobs to other women. Since 2007, about 5,900 cooperatives have formed, with 300 being women's cooperatives." The same article notes that the decrease in overall poverty "from 48% in 2007 to 25% and extreme poverty from 17.5% to 7%" has similarly "benefited women in particular, since single mother households suffered more from poverty." What's more, "[t]he Zero Hunger and Zero Usury programs have lessened the traditional domestic violence, given that women in poverty suffer greater risk of violence and abuse than others."

Similarly, the revived Sandinista land reform program also especially benefitted women, with 55 percent of the over 451 thousand land titles given out by the government to small farmers between 2007 and 2021 going to women.[359]

And, while the anti-abortion law in Nicaragua has become a controversial issue among the Western left, it is not controversial in Nicaragua where over 80 percent of the population support it in this deeply religious country. In addition, there is important context to understanding this law and its enforcement. As noted above, the law, which was on the books when the Sandinistas took power in 1979, and which became even stricter in 2006 just before Daniel Ortega was re-elected, was not enforced under the Sandinistas in the 1980s, and it is no longer enforced now that they are back in power.[360] As the *Monthly Review* article explains, "[s]ince the return to power of the Sandinistas in 2007 no woman nor governmental or private health professional has ever been prosecuted for any action related to abortion. Any woman whose life is in danger receives an abortion in government health centers or hospitals. Many places exist for women to get abortions; none have been closed nor attacked, nor are clandestine. The morning after pill and contraceptive services are widely available."[361]

Meanwhile, the Sandinista government has made huge strides in women's participation, indeed mandating by law, as of 2007, that "at least 50% of public offices be filled by women, from the national level to the municipal."[362] And, this law is fully enforced and complied with.

As the result of all of the above measures, Nicaragua is now one of the most gender equal societies in the world, going from a rank of 90 in terms of gender quality as ranked by the United Nations in 2007 to the rank today of number 5, only behind Iceland, Norway, Finland, and Sweden.[363] This marks astounding progress, especially for a developing country, but this is often overlooked by those in Western countries, like the U.S., UK and Canada, with much worse problems with gender equality.

The other incredible achievement of the Ortega government, alluded to above, has been the creation of food sovereignty in the country. Thanks to the support of the peasantry, Nicaragua is now around 90 percent food sovereign, meaning that it produces nearly all the food it consumes—an amazing advance for a developing nation, and an advance which even Cuba and Venezuela (both of which import around 70 percent of their food, meaning that they are about 30 percent food sovereign) have not achieved.[364] This food sovereignty has helped Nicaragua fight hunger and malnutrition in the country and improve the environment. As one report on Nicaragua's food sovereignty success explains:

> Nicaragua is a case study in how pursuing food sovereignty can help to reduce hunger levels within society. Food sovereignty is a system that ensures people have continual access to plentiful, healthy, and affordable food locally produced. Marlen Sánchez of the global peasant movement La Via Campesina in Nicaragua, suggests food sovereignty is a "historical process", based on indigenous rights and protection of land, water, and life. She describes it as an inherently anti-capitalist food production system. While providing sufficient food for everyone is at the core of food sovereignty movements, Fanny Boeraeve of the University of Liege and others have suggested that for food sovereignty to be effective it must be prioritize sustainable agricultural farming

methods. That is, methods that ensure a harmonious relationship with the planet.³⁶⁵

This same report details the improvements in combating hunger brought about the Sandinistas' agricultural policies. As the report relates, "[t]he Global Hunger Index (GHI) uses data from the United Nations and other multilateral agencies to determine hunger levels in countries around the world. There are five hunger levels, ranging from low (level one) to extremely alarming (level five). Nicaragua's hunger score is currently at a level two, 'moderate hunger levels,' on their index. In 2000, at the height of neoliberal governance in Nicaragua, the country was at a level three, 'alarming hunger levels.' Since the FSLN was elected in 2006, hunger has been declining rapidly. Overall, there has been a 40.8% reduction in hunger according to the index. Nicaragua is one of only 38 countries to reach the UN Millennium Development Goal of cutting malnutrition by half."

It is Nicaragua's food sovereignty, I would urge, which makes it particularly dangerous to the U.S.'s economic aims in the Americas, and indeed in the world. Thus, the U.S. government actively attempts to undermine other countries' ability to grow food for themselves so that they will be dependent upon food imports from the United States, many of the imports being heavily processed foods which are quite unhealthful. Indeed, as economist Michael Hudson explains in his book, *Super Imperialism: The Economic Strategy of American Empire*, a key pillar of U.S. international policy since WWII has been one of fostering food dependency amongst countries in the developing world, a phenomenon Hudson refers to as "food imperialism."³⁶⁶ And, those countries who resisted this policy were deemed as a threat. As he writes, "the congressional hearings on the Bretton Woods agreements [the agreements which set post-WWII economic policies] reveal a fear of Latin American and other countries underselling U.S. farmers or displacing U.S. agricultural exports, instead of the hope that these countries might evolve toward agricultural self-sufficiency." The view of U.S. policymakers, then and now, was for "industrialization of these countries to be accompanied by growing food deficits and hence higher import dependency." As Hudson explains, the policy has been one of "free-trade imperialism in its classic form. Progress of less developed countries toward agricultural and industrial self-sufficiency, which had gained momentum during their years of war-enforced isolationism, was halted and reversed" through lending policies, foreign aid, and, when necessary, through military intervention.

Modern examples of U.S. "food imperialism" abound. As former President Bill Clinton admitted to a Senate foreign Relations Committee on March 10, 2010, his agricultural policies in Haiti, for example, undermined rice production in Haiti and destroyed the ability of Haitians to feed themselves.[367] However, as he also explained, this was to the advantage of "some of my farmers in Arkansas" who were able to sell food—subsidized by the U.S. government—to Haitians into the breach left by their extinct rice crop.[368] The same policies were pursued in Mexico through NAFTA which forbids Mexico from subsidizing its crops, but which allows the U.S. to dump subsidized food products into Mexico. The result has been the destruction of the livelihood of around 1.3 million small farmers in Mexico, a significant number of whom were pushed to emigrate to the U.S. or to enter the drug trade.[369] Similar policies are being applied to Colombia under the Colombia Free Trade Agreement.[370]

Nicaragua simply does not fit into such plans the U.S. has for countries of the Global South, making it a continued "danger of a good example."

Daniel Ortega also gained antipathy from the U.S. by exhibiting too much independence in the field foreign relations. As an initial matter, Ortega stopped sending Nicaraguan troops to be trained at the U.S. Army School of the Americas in Columbus, Georgia, given its history of training brutal military forces who tortured their own people.[371]

In addition, when the U.S. helped overthrow and forcibly expel the populist President of Honduras, Manuel Zelaya, in 2009, it was Ortega who provided Zelaya safe haven in Nicaragua. The 2009 coup, carried out by a general trained by the U.S. at the U.S. School of the Americas—General Romeo Orlando Vásquez

Velásquez[372]—was an important event in Central America, and indeed a warning to countries like Nicaragua, for it demonstrated that the U.S., even under a liberal President like Barack Obama, was continuing to engage in regime-change operations in that region against leaders like Zelaya for simply engaging in moderately progressive social policy such as increasing the minimum wage.

Hillary Clinton, who was Obama's Secretary of State at the time, even bragged in the hardcover version of her book, *Hard Choices*, how she maneuvered to make sure that Zelaya was never returned to power.[373] Hillary later removed this passage in the paperback version after receiving backlash from the admission.[374] Before her murder by forces linked to the Honduran coup government, acclaimed environmental and indigenous activist, Berta Cáceras, publicly blamed Hillary Clinton for solidifying the coup and guaranteeing the violence which followed—violence that would ultimately claim Berta's very life. As she stated in an interview:

> The Clinton-brokered election [after Zelaya's ouster] did indeed install and legitimate a militarized regime based on repression. In the interview, Cáceres says that Clinton's coup-government, under pressure from Washington, passed terrorist and intelligence laws that criminalized political protest. Cáceres called it "counterinsurgency," carried out on behalf of "international capital"—mostly resource extractors—that has terrorized the population, murdering political activists by the high hundreds. "Every day," Cáceres said elsewhere, "people are killed."[375]

I visited Honduras less than two weeks after the coup on a small fact-finding delegation with the School of the Americas Watch (SOAW)—a group dedicated to shutting down the infamous School of the Americas. By this time, President Obama had announced that the U.S. had suspended all joint operations with the Honduran military as a result of the ouster of Zelaya—an event that Hillary Clinton refused to call a "military coup."

However, when we asked a Sergeant Reyes at the U.S. military base outside Tegucigalpa if this were true, he said, "no," that this was just something that Obama was telling everyone, but that nothing had changed in terms of the relationship between the two armed forces.

Another bold move Ortega made in foreign policy was in relation to Libya during the months-long bombing campaign of NATO against that country. Early on in this campaign, Muammar Gaddaffi's New York-based UN Ambassador resigned, and Gaddafi, whose country was being bombed to smithereens, was unable to send a Libyan to the U.S. to represent Libya's interests at the UN. In the breach, Daniel Ortega, with Gaddafi's assent, appointed former Nicaraguan Foreign Minister Father Miguel D'Escoto—who was in New York at the time after serving as the President of the UN General Assembly—to represent Libya at the UN.[376] In his letter to the UN, Ortega stated that Father D'Escoto would "support the Libyan brothers in their battle to ensure respect for sovereignty and self-determination—both of which are being violated by the powerful, who once again threaten the independence and peace of the people."[377] This was an incredible act of solidarity for a small country like Nicaragua to show for a country then under brutal attack by Western powers, and the act certainly did not endear Nicaragua or Ortega to the United States.

However, it was such policies of the Nicaraguan government which have endeared it to the Nicaraguan population. And thus, by October of 2017, polls showed Daniel Ortega with an incredible 80 percent approval rating.[378] But a serious challenge would be posed to the Ortega government within several months, with the country being brought nearly to civil war in another attempt to destroy the good example.

CHAPTER 7

THE APRIL 2018 CRISIS
ANOTHER COUNTER-REVOLUTIONARY INSURRECTION

When examining the events of the spring and summer of 2018 in Nicaragua and their aftermath, it is first worthwhile to put them in context by comparing them to an analogous event in the United States and how the U.S. government, media and public reacted to it. That event is what the Democratic Party and the mainstream media have dubbed the "insurrection" of January 6, 2021, in which hundreds of people, almost invariably Trump supporters, stormed the U.S. Capitol in an apparent attempt to stop the counting of the Electoral College votes, which they believed had been ultimately procured through fraudulent elections. And indeed, Daniel Ortega himself mentioned this event as comparable at his January 2022 Inauguration, which I had the honor of attending.

The January 6 insurrection was an action of a short, finite duration of several hours, which ended with property damage within the Capitol building, the injury of 150 police officers, and a total of 7 deaths directly attributable to the riot.[379] Around 725 individuals who were personally involved in the invasion of the Capitol on January 6—including some who merely entered the Capitol premises, behaving somewhat like tourists, shooting selfies and committing no acts of violence—have been arrested and charged for their role in the riot, and some have already been tried, convicted and sentenced to anywhere from a few days to over a year in jail.[380]

In addition, there have been calls to arrest and try others, though not involved directly in the Capitol riot, and who weren't even near the Capitol at the time of the insurrection, but who were considered the intellectual authors and instigators of the action. Indeed, the January 6 House Committee, referring to such individuals, argued in a federal court filing that, after investigation, the Committee "has a good-faith basis for concluding that the President [Donald Trump] and members of his Campaign engaged in a criminal conspiracy" which culminated in the insurrection."[381] The Judge who considered the evidence filed in support of this claim concluded that Donald Trump and his lawyer—two individuals who were not even present at the Capitol when the events in question occurred—were parties to a plan which "spurred violent attacks on the seat of our nation's government, led to the deaths of several law enforcement officers, and deepened public distrust in our political process."[382] That said, the deaths of the "several law enforcement officers" were not the direct result of attacks, but rather, by heart attack and suicide after the event. A slight majority of Americans polled agree that Trump should be charged for his role in helping provoke the January 6 riot, according to a poll by the *Washington Post*.[383]

The extent of the U.S. response to events of January 6th, 2021, is relevant when considering the events in the long spring and summer of 2018 in Nicaragua in which the country was brought to the verge of civil war, with hundreds killed and many more injured, and in considering how the Ortega Administration responded to these events and to those who both participated directly in them and to those who helped instigate them.

* * *

As indicated above, Daniel Ortega was wildly popular going into 2018 and the elections scheduled for that year, with a whopping 80 percent approval rating. As the *New York Times*, writing in April of 2018, explained, Ortega was especially popular among the poor "who receive housing and other government benefits support."[384] As far as the U.S. government was concerned, something had to be done about Ortega's strong popular support, and so, Congress began initiating legislation targeted at destroying his popular social programs.

Thus, in October of 2017, the U.S. House of Representatives voted unanimously in favor of the Nicaraguan Investment Conditionality Act of 2017 (NICA Act), which would cut Nicaragua off from loans offered by international financial institutions.[385] As *Telesur* reported at the time, "The Nicaraguan government uses foreign assistance from the international financial institutions to support social spending on health and education which have become an ever larger proportion of the national budget."[386]

Therefore, the NICA Act, according to *Telesur*, "pose[d] a serious danger to the Central American nation's economy and could result in a humanitarian crisis and waves of economic refugees that would flee toward the U.S. border, joining waves of migrants from Honduras, Guatemala and El Salvador."[387] Indeed, even before the NICA Act was passed by the Senate and signed into law by President Trump, the mere passage by the House "[had] already put a chill on foreign direct investment into the Nicaraguan economy, having a knock-on effect on local lending activity and private investments."[388]

It must be emphasized that, just as the Reagan administration was so determined to destroy the Sandinistas that it was willing to have the CIA sell cocaine on the city streets of the U.S. to fund the Contras, the U.S. government under President Donald Trump, even as it was building a wall to keep out migrants from crossing the southern border, was willing to risk promoting a new wave of migrants from Nicaragua which, up to that point, was not a significant source of migration. Indeed, President Trump's Secretary of State, Mike Pompeo, "openly declared that the objective of the U.S. is to destabilize and change the government" in Nicaragua, along with the governments in Cuba and Venezuela—"the countries he deems to be the axis of evil in the hemisphere. In order to achieve this objective, for years the U.S. has been funding the local media and a network of human rights agencies to construct their version of the truth."[389]

And it was not only economic coercion and propaganda the U.S. used to try to again disrupt the progress of the Sandinistas. As in the 1980s, the U.S. resorted to violence—the kind of violence which it had helped foment for years before the terrible events which broke out in April of 2018.

The National Endowment for Democracy (NED) served as the mechanism to instigate such violence. In his book, *Faustian Bargain*, William Robinson describes well the creation and purposes of the NED. As he relates, up until the early 1980s, it was the CIA alone that carried out covert operations around the world to, amongst other things, implement regime change, successfully achieving this end in such countries as Iran in 1953, Guatemala in 1954 and Chile in 1973. In each of these instances, the CIA helped overthrow democratically elected governments, which were attempting to break free from the prevailing capitalist economic order, replacing them with right-wing, repressive regimes which did the bidding of the U.S. However, after the Senate hearings led by Senator Frank Church in the 1970s—hearings which exposed the CIA's misdeeds and made its continued role in such black ops more embarrassing for the U.S.—another institution was created to augment the CIA's covert operations function and put a benevolent face on that function. This institution was the NED. As Robinson relates, the idea was that the NED, created in 1983,

> would not only play the role of skillful political surgeon; it would also overcome the taint associated with the covert operations that the CIA had been carrying out abroad. Specifically, the NED would take over much of the funding and political guidance for political parties, trade unions, business groups, news media, and civic organizations that the CIA traditionally supplied.
>
> The idea was to create a further division of labor within the organs of U.S. foreign policy. The NED would not replace the CIA but would specialize in the overt development of political and civic formations, supplementing CIA covert activities and synchronizing with overall U.S. policy toward the country or region in question. Moreover, the seemingly public nature of the

NED would allow the use of public relations techniques to an extent unprecedented in U.S. foreign policy. The NED, with its ideological underpinning of "promoting democracy," would be well equipped for rebuilding U.S. domestic consensus for political operations abroad.[390]

While William Robinson understands the nature and functions of the NED and then goes on in his book to describe how the NED carried out these functions well from 1983 to 1990, working hand-in-glove with the CIA to help undermine support for the Sandinistas, he, along with many progressives, appears to have fully bought into the claims that the uprising of 2018 was somehow a purely home-grown and spontaneous movement, rather than one brought about the same machinations used by the NED in the 1980s.

However, the role of the NED in the 2018 events in Nicaragua is not something merely implied due to its earlier role. Indeed, a publication funded by the NED,[391] *Global Americans,* carefully explained how this was the case in a May 2018 article, entitled "Laying the groundwork for insurrection: A closer look at the U.S. role in Nicaragua's social unrest." Mincing no words, *Global Americans* explained how those who believed the uprising in 2018 was somehow "spontaneous" and locally inspired were wrong:

> Nicaragua is on the brink of a civic insurrection. For two weeks, hundreds of thousands of citizens have occupied the streets protesting president [sic.] Daniel Ortega and his wife and vice-president, Rosario Murillo. The demonstrations and marches began following the government's slow response to a massive forest fire inside the Indio Maiz bio reserve. A week later, the movements quickly escalated when Ortega's government announced a series of austerity measures designed to rescue the country's social security system from the brink of bankruptcy....
>
> On the ground in Nicaragua, one gets the sense that Ortega's government is on the ropes....[392]

Global Americans explained that while the "international press has depicted the rapid escalation of civil unrest in Nicaragua as a spontaneous explosion of collective discontent... it's becoming more and more clear that the U.S. support has helped play a role in nurturing the current uprisings." The article goes on to detail that, "[s]ince 2014, the National Endowment for Democracy (NED) ... has spent $4.1 million on [54] projects in Nicaragua," which bore fruit in the violence of 2018. As *Global Americans* explained, the projects funded included those by a number of civic organizations, including youth groups, which participated in the uprising. The $4.1 million, moreover, does not even take into account the additional monies funneled into Nicaragua during this period by the NED's sister organization, the USAID.

As S. Brian Willson and Nils McCune, both of whom live in Nicaragua and lived through the insurrection of 2018, explain,

> Since at least 2010, examining Wikileaks cables, Department of State memos, NED, USAID budgets and documents seized in arrests of 2018 coup suspects, it is clear the U.S. has expended perhaps as much as $200 million to oust the Ortega-led Sandinista government. Depressed over the 2006 Sandinista electoral victory, the U.S. has had as its explicit goal "the achievement in an immediate future of a government akin to the interest of the U.S. government," ... and the "creation of conditions for regime change." An NDI (National Democratic Institute, one of four core entities of the NED) 2013 memorandum, identified four lines of attack in a strategy to destabilize and change the Nicaraguan "regime": (1) training young political leaders; (2) media war; (3) unification of the opposition; and (4) strengthening civil society organizations, preparing a "coup d'état against Daniel Ortega." The U.S. Embassy and USAID have been preparing the conditions for a coup from since at least 2013. Their efforts culminated in the April-July 2018 coup attempt....[393]

Barbara Larcom, a long-time Nicaragua solidarity activist who has been traveling regularly to Nicaragua for years, further addresses the magnitude of the funding operations of the NED and USAID in Nicaragua:

> Over a period of years, the United States has funded training for "democracy and human rights promotion" in Nicaragua, targeted at groups opposed to the Sandinista government. In 2017 alone, Nicaraguan civil society organizations and media companies received over $31 million from USAID, of which $14.5 million was focused on two categories of spending—"government and civil society" and "conflict, peace and security". Imagine the impact of this spending in a small, poor country of only 6.2 million people: the U.S. population is over 52 times its size, and the average salary in the United States is about 5.5 times higher than in Nicaragua. Taking those two multiples into account, $14.5 million would be the equivalent of over $4.1 billion if it were targeted at groups in the U.S. But even those multiples understate the impact, as many Nicaraguans don't have a salary to compare.[394]

The *Global Americans* article shamelessly linked this 2018 effort with work done by the NED in the 1980s in concert with the violent actions of the Contras, to try to overthrow the Sandinista government. As *Global Americans* proudly admitted,

> This is not the first time that NED funds have made an appearance in Central America's largest country. U.S. Congress created the NED—as a non-profit, private NGO—in 1983 at the height of the Cold War. The NED was designed to promote democracy overseas, and it was funded through the U.S. congress.... From 1984 to 1990, the U.S. NED spent roughly $15.8 million dollars to fund civil society groups and to political parties, most of them opposed to the Sandinista

government. In 1990, against all odds, Chamorro defeated Daniel Ortega, and ushered in three consecutive terms of conservative leadership.

Clearly, the goal of the NED was to repeat such a feat once more, and, at least at one point, it seemed close to doing so.

All of this must be viewed in light of the recent admission of John Bolton, President Trump's National Security Adviser from April of 2018 to September of 2019, that he was involved in attempting to overthrow foreign governments. Thus, in July of 2022, John Bolton opined that the January 6, 2021 Capitol riots did not in fact constitute a coup attempt, and that he should know, given his own actual coup plotting in foreign lands. As Bolton boasted, he himself was "somebody who has helped plan coups d'état, not here, but you know, other places. It takes a lot of work and that's not what [Trump] did. It was just stumbling around from one idea to another."[395] In other words, while many in the U.S. deride Daniel Ortega's claim that the events in 2018 were the result of a coup attempt aided and abetted by the U.S. as the rantings of a paranoid leader, and that the days of U.S.-backed coups are over, Bolton's admission gives credence to Daniel's claims. Furthermore, with regards to Nicaragua, the facts show that a lot of the coup planning work that Bolton refers to was done by the NED and USAID, quite possibly with a little help from John Bolton himself.

In April of 2018, the hard work of the NED and the USAID to incite an insurrection paid off. But there were strange aspects to this uprising from the very start. First of all, the narrative was put out that the troubles began because of modest changes to social security benefits that Daniel Ortega had announced to try to keep the social security system solvent. There is no question that something had to be done to keep the social security system funded in light of shortfalls and as noted above, the U.S. House passage of the NICA Act "ha[d] already put a chill on foreign direct investment into the Nicaraguan economy, having a knock-on effect on local lending activity and private investments." In short, this action by the U.S. Congress was giving the Nicaraguan government fewer options to make up the shortfall, which everyone acknowledged existed. However, what we were not told in the mainstream press is that Daniel announced his modest social security changes—slightly increasing the amount workers would pay from their paychecks into social security in order to sustain their payouts, and requiring an even greater contribution from employers—after he was unable to come to terms with Nicaragua's chamber of commerce (COSEP), which was in fact demanding even more draconian cuts to social security in order to comply with IMF demands.[396]

What also was strange about all this was that it was students, or at least young people posing as students, who led the revolts against the proposed social security reforms. Why would students be that worked up by changes to benefits which they did not stand to receive until decades later or even to a small increase in employee contributions which, students, qua students, themselves do not have to make? Why, indeed, would COSEP and many members of the bourgeoisie quickly line up in support of the protesters, despite the fact that the proposed reforms were less severe than the very ones being demanded by COSEP in the first place? What's more, the protests only intensified after Daniel Ortega announced, very swiftly after the protests began, that he would not go forward with the announced social security changes.[397]

All of this points to the fact that the protests had little to do with their proclaimed issue but rather concerned what quickly became the demands of the protests' leaders—that Daniel Ortega, a president up to that point with stunningly high approval ratings—"must go." Indeed, one of the prominent student leaders of the insurrection, Lesther Alemán, at the very outset of the national dialogue made it clear that this was what the protests and indeed the dialogue, at least in the view of most of the opposition forces, were about. Thus, he told Daniel Ortega to his face: "[t]his is not a table of dialogue. This is a table to negotiate your exit and you know it well. Give up!"[398]

In other words, this was all about regime change, and not a progressive or revolutionary change as we have been led to believe. (Needless to say, it is difficult to see how protests against changes intended to protect social security, even if requiring present raises in contributions from workers—and indeed, greater ones from employers—could be billed as progressive…) Surely, as one Nicaraguan explained at the time, this was a reactionary, counter-revolutionary movement that was trying to unseat a president bent on protecting the people's interests. Thus, in her April 29, 2018, article, entitled "My Contra Parents Are Marching For a New 'Old' Nicaragua: Are We, Too?", Melissa Castillo wrote:

> Another suspicious aspect of this opposition is that it claims to include former Sandinistas who have now turned against Ortega because of his corruption. This is confusing because the opposition's social media platform does not seem to consist of any socialist groups. The Sandinistas were built on socialism and the leaders at the time of the revolution were largely Marxists. A group involved in the opposition, for instance, is the Sandinista Renovation Movement (MRS). The MRS are Social Democrats who have partnered with a right-wing coalition in recent years in order to expand their base. By now, the MRS seems to have grown more centrist and devotes much of its platform to anti-Ortega rhetoric.
>
> Leftists and Sandinista supporters may have legitimate concerns about Ortega, but that does not mean these are the same people joining forces with right-wingers and the U.S. government or appealing to the American public to "share" images of unrest on social media. I believe true leftist concerns include the concessions Ortega has made to the private sector in his economic policy, the power he has ceded to the church, his softening towards capitalist policies, and the increasing influence of Western international entities in public sector decision-making. It would not rationally be in the interest of leftists to join a coalition led by a private sector interested in pulling Nicaragua further to the right.[399]

Kenneth E. Morris, in his book about Daniel Ortega and the Sandinista Revolution, makes a similar point which cannot be impressed upon the reader enough. First, Morris, while very critical of Daniel, recognizes his important contributions to the Revolution, his sincere concern for the poor of Nicaragua, his lack of any desire for personal financial gain and the fact that his desire to continue leading the FSLN and the nation is not about any lust for personal power, but rather comes from his dedication to the Revolution.[400] In addition, Morris recognizes a fact which is obvious to any honest observer of Nicaraguan politics—that the only real, viable opposition to Daniel would, if in power, pull Nicaragua to the right, ignoring the needs of the poor and bringing Nicaragua back into the orbit of the U.S., which has at best ignored Nicaragua, and at worst terrorized it, for well over a century. This is not, in either Morris's opinion or mine, what any decent person should be rooting for.

Acclaimed Argentine writer and winner of UNESCO's International José Martí Prize, Atilio Boron, made this very point at the time of the unrest in 2018. He wrote at the time that:

> the fall of Sandinismo would weaken the geopolitical environment of the brutally attacked Venezuela and increase the chances for the generalization of violence throughout the region.
>
> While in the Forum of Sao Paulo that just took place in Havana, I was able to delight in the contemplation of the Caribbean. There I saw, in the distance, a fragile little boat. It was handled by a robust sailor and, at the other end, there was a young girl. The helmsman looked confused and struggled to keep his course in the middle of a threatening swell. And it occurred to me that this image could eloquently represent the revolutionary process in Nicaragua, in Venezuela, Bolivia or anywhere.
>
> The revolution is like that girl, and the helmsman is the revolutionary government. There is no human work safe from error; mistakes can be made that leave

the helmsman at the mercy of the waves and endanger the life of the girl. To top it all, not far away was the ominous silhouette of a U.S. warship, loaded with lethal weapons, death squads and mercenary soldiers. How to save the girl? The helmsman could jump into the sea letting the boat sink, and with it the girl, delivering it to the mob of criminals thirsty for blood and ready to plunder the country, steal its resources and rape and then kill the young girl.

I do not see that as the solution. More productive would be that some of the other boats that are in the area approach the one in danger and make the helmsman stay on course. Sinking the boat that carries the girl of the revolution, or surrendering her to the U.S. ship, could hardly be considered revolutionary solutions.[401]

In the case of Nicaragua, Daniel has been the helmsman who continues to refuse to jump ship and abandon his people even in the case of great adversity, and this included during the 2018 crisis when the pressures led many to believe at the time that his government could very well fall.

As for the specific concern about pulling Nicaragua closer to the U.S., it should be noted as ATC leader José Adán Rivera Castillo explains, that the opposition leading the protests in 2018 were *openly calling for U.S. intervention* to overthrow the Sandinista government—hardly the call of true patriots or indeed, leftists. In fact, a number of the student leaders (or at least, ostensible student leaders) toured the U.S. at the time of the unrest, meeting with unsavory U.S. politicians such as Marco Rubio, who openly call for regime change in Nicaragua and allied nations like Venezuela and Cuba. And again, it was these leaders that U.S. "progressives" and Latin American studies professors were hosting to speak to the public. I attended just such an event hosted by the Center for Latin American Studies (CLAS) at the University of Pittsburgh in the later summer of 2018. I was taken aback by how academics who had once supported the Sandinistas took the words of these student opposition leaders who had just been meeting with right-wing interventionist Congress people at face value, seemingly unconcerned that they were thereby cozying up to U.S. imperialism. And no alternative voices were given a platform to speak.

As *The Grayzone* noted, at least one U.S. "progressive," Daniel La Botz of the Democratic Socialists of America (DSA), was clever enough to have the same "students" appear at a public event with bandanas covering their faces so that the left-wing audience wouldn't be able to determine that they were listening to people "who were junketed to meet with Republican lawmakers in Washington by the U.S. government-funded right-wing organization Freedom House."[402] LeBotz quite disingenuously claimed the masks were necessary for the speakers to safely return to Nicaragua when in fact they had already been publicly posing in photos with Republican Congressmen like Marcio Rubio.

In addition, as *The Grayzone* also pointed out, "La Botz has admitted in leaked emails obtained by *The Grayzone* that 'there is virtually no left among the opposition' to Nicaragua's democratically elected socialist government." But this has not stopped similar elements from supporting this opposition in Nicaragua and publicly claiming that they somehow represented a progressive alternative to the Sandinistas.

An understanding of the initial days of the protests, and how they were presented is critical to grasping the true nature of the months-long crisis that enveloped Nicaragua in 2018. The claim that many in the U.S., but few in Nicaragua, continue to believe to this day was that there had been a massacre by police of students peacefully protesting the social security reforms at the outset of the crisis, and that this was the spark of the major protests against the Ortega government. While it is indeed true that the wide-publicized claim that such a massacre had occurred was a catalyst for major demonstrations, the massacre claim itself is false. There was not then, nor was there ever, a massacre of students by the police—forces which, as described above, had been lauded up to this point for their peaceful, community-oriented policing, which included trying to rehabilitate youth involved in crime rather than incarcerate them. Indeed, the first individual killed in the protests, which were far from peaceful, was a police officer, not a student.

As Nan McCurdy and Stephon Sefton, both residents and citizens of Nicaragua, who were in-country at the time, detail:

> On Wednesday April 18 private university students held marches against the social security reforms claiming they threatened the rights of workers and pensioners. There were clashes between members of the Sandinista Youth and the student marchers. Police tried to restore order. An intense social media campaign targeted students in other cities like León and Estelí with unsubstantiated allegations of police violence, including a report that a student from the private Central American University (UCA) had been killed. This was later proven to be false, but on April 18th it fanned the flames of violence as it went viral on social media.
> The following day, Thursday the 19th, many students continued to protest, but by this time they were infiltrated by armed opposition supporters and paid criminals who killed police officer Hilton Manzanares Alvarado. Two other young men were also killed: 1) Richard Antonio Pavon Hernandez, 17-year-old Sandinista Youth member who was shot in the abdomen near the Mayor's Office in Tipitapa. His parents are historic combatants. There are reports that he shot himself in the abdomen accidentally. 2) Twenty-nine-year-old supermarket worker Darwin Manuel Urbina, who was shot near the UPOLI [another private university] on his way home from work by someone with a shotgun, most likely part of or paid by the opposition. He was not on any side so the person who shot him was not specifically going after him but killing in order to have deaths to assign to the government.[403]

There were similar instances as these at the very same time in various other cities, suggesting that the uprising that was occurring was far from spontaneous, but rather had been carefully orchestrated. Suddenly the protests were no longer peaceful, with the protesters firing mortar rounds and lobbing Molotov cocktails. Again, McCurdy and Sefton explain:

> Similar attacks occurred in other cities, including Managua and the northern town of Estelí where municipal workers occupied their offices to defend them against possible attacks by opposition activists. Estelí's municipal offices were attacked on the night of Friday April 20 by over 500 people, most of whom local police identified as outsiders brought in from other areas but including both some local students and a number of local criminals. With police trying to keep order, the attackers fired over 1000 mortar rounds and threw at least 17 Molotov cocktails in an attempt to destroy the municipal offices and other targets nearby. 18 police officers and 16 municipal workers were wounded. Among the protesters, two young students were shot dead and numerous people injured. The fighting lasted for five hours, covering an area of around 16 blocks with the attackers using firearms and knives....
>
> Nationally, most estimates, including the opposition online media outlet *Confidencial*, as of April 23 estimate around 20 people killed in the violence. Among the dead were two police officers and a journalist with a Sandinista TV channel, while other fatalities include Sandinista and opposition activists as well as bystanders caught up in the violence. The pattern of the attacks suggests a well-formulated plan with preparations already in place before the protests started. For example, outside Managua there was no violence reported in large towns like Matagalpa, Jinotega and Ocotal. By focusing on Managua, Masaya, León and Estelí, the opposition extremists tried to create a comparison between their violent offensive and the centers of insurrection against the Somoza dictatorship in 1979.

As the above description of events makes clear, there was no massacre of students here, either. Indeed, there was political violence which claimed lives on both sides of the conflict as well as bystanders. And, to the extent students, or young people posing as students, were involved, they gave at least as good as they got in terms of violence, and indeed showed up to the demonstration with arms already at hand and ready to be used. In other words, these were never the "peaceful demonstrators" we were being led to believe they were by the mainstream press in Nicaragua and the U.S. But again, the disinformation around these events sent Nicaraguan society into a tailspin of protest and violence and won over much of the U.S. Left, which turned on the Ortega government, even though this meant aligning with reactionary forces attempting to overturn that government and roll back the Sandinista Revolution itself.

The other fact that needs emphasized, as seen in the description of events in Estelí where municipal workers were attacked, was that this was not a rebellion by working class people, but rather, an attack against them. Nor was this an uprising by the peasantry—the backbone of the Revolution. To the contrary, it was the working class and peasantry, and the unions which represent them, that stood firm against the violence in 2018 and helped to defend the government and the economy, which the opposition was trying to undermine and destroy in its effort at regime change, just as the Contras had done in the 1980s. Thus, as a *Monthly Review* article from 2018 noted,

> La Vía Campesina, the National Union of Farmers and Ranchers, the Association of Rural Workers, the National Workers' Front, the indigenous Mayangna Nation and other movements and organizations have been unequivocal in their demands for an end to the violence and their support for the Ortega government.[404]

José Adán Rivera Castillo, a leader of the Rural Workers Association (ATC), explained to me in an interview in March of 2022,

> Big business called for work stoppages, but the people kept the buses and small businesses and farms going. The food sovereignty was never interrupted. The popular economy continued to function, and that is now a big area of focus. All of the union movement made sure that the economy kept going, including the unions in the free trade zone. In the fincas [plantations] also, the unions, including ATC, made sure that production continued. The workers kept production going.
>
> With the big landowners, we told them that if they didn't want to keep producing, we would engage in another big land reform which might impact them. Ultimately, this threat did not have to made good on. The peasantry was not as bombarded by the misinformation, and they were more in touch with the popular organizations and Daniel.

Rivera's comment about the peasantry not being "as bombarded by misinformation" is an apt one. The countryside was much more peaceful during the disturbances of 2018 because (1) as Rivera also alludes, the peasantry was and is more connected to the revolutionary process than any other sector of society; and (2) they are not as reliant on the technology being used to manipulate the population—for example, through smart phones and computers which barraged the population with sophisticated and manipulative "news" and social media posts. Ironically, it was the very advances which the Ortega government had made in providing electricity and internet service to the Nicaraguan people that ended up being used against the government by the opposition. And, as one friend of mine in Nicaragua commented to me, because this technology was relatively new for many people in Nicaragua, they had yet to learn how this technology could let them down and even be used to manipulate them. As he explained, "[w]e trusted our cell phones." But again, the peasanty was a bit more insulated from this phenomenon.

Rivera participated in the National Dialogue that was set up by Daniel Ortega to try to find an end to the violence. He was there representing the peasant and workers sector, such as those working in the markets and transportation services. Workers and peasant representatives, such as Rivera, were consulting with Daniel daily on the events of the day, and on how to keep the peace and maintain the functioning of the economy. Rivera explained to me how, on April 18 when reports were being made about a student massacre at the UCA, he called his contacts at the UCA to verify these reports. He relates that he confirmed that the reports were false but that many were fooled by the propaganda. As he explained to me, "[w]e were dominated by the right-wing press. It was total media invasion. They threw out all these things that made people motivated, even using the Sandinista songs," to try to undermine support for the government. As for this comment about domination by the right-wing press, it is important to emphasize that, while we are told that Nicaragua is a dictatorship that censors free speech, most of the press in Nicaragua is in strong opposition to the government, is very open about this opposition and in fact was not prohibited from openly calling for the overthrow of the Sandinista government, especially during this period.

Yorlis Gabriela Luna, a grassroots educator and researcher in Nicaragua, explains in detail how social media was used to manipulate public opinion among much of Nicaraguan society and to stir up the turmoil that quickly embroiled the country:

> During the first few days of turmoil, Facebook became the main source of fake and real news in Nicaragua. Hundreds of accounts purchased ad pages with very disturbing scenes of violence, many which were later determined to have come from El Salvador, Honduras, and even countries as far away as Paraguay. But the impact was that young Nicaraguans shared these Facebook ads which, once shared on Facebook, no longer appear as paid advertisements and looked like all other shared content. This is how a lot of false news reports were disseminated throughout the country, such as reporting deaths that had not occurred and even

accusing the government of installing snipers to kill civilians.

This explosion of digital information stirred up a sense of solidarity among the youth and society for the "defenseless protesters" and against the government, which had been denominated as "the dictatorship" on Facebook. This kind of narrative holds a lot of sway in Nicaraguan society, because of the long and heroic struggle of students against the Somoza dictatorship. It did not matter so much that it was untrue; what mattered was that they had achieved the capacity to repeat such messages hundreds of thousands of times, through all media outlets available to the Nicaraguan people.... Among the scenes posted there were fake photographs and photos from other countries and other times, along with manipulated videos and still shots, and a very sophisticated campaign spread them through Facebook ads....

Social media was used on such an overwhelming scale to create a state of shock, panic, and paranoia that absurd reports—hard to believe for the Nicaraguan context—became "the truth." For example, they said that cities were being bombed and that small planes were spraying the major cities with agrochemicals; that Cuban snipers had come to Nicaragua; that Russian drones were attacking young protesters, among other messages which both before and after were and are patently absurd, but at that time managed to mobilize a certain segment of the youth to protest.[405]

As Luna and many other Nicaraguans I spoke with explained, in a short amount of time, social media users, many quite unsophisticated with regard to this new media, were inundated by fake news messages which successfully "provoked violent protests in two dozen cities."

I remember how disorienting these events were to everyone, given how they were being portrayed at the time. For example, when I talked at the time about these events to my Nicaraguan friends Sandra and Gerardo—die-hard Sandinistas and Danielistas who now live in Pittsburgh after leaving Nicaragua during the neoliberal period and who still have family in Nicaragua—their faith in the Nicaraguan government was visibly shaken. Seeming to support the protests, Sandra, who once worked for Comandante Omar Cabezas, simply exclaimed, "What about the students?!," of course referring to the students who were claimed to have been massacred. By the end of the summer, Sandra and Gerardo, along with many other Nicaraguans, were back on board with Daniel and the FSLN, when they finally realized what had truly happened. But it was remarkable to observe how the propaganda initially achieved its intended function of inspiring loyal supporters, overnight, to question the very government they had believed in for so long.

Meanwhile, trouble continued to brew at the universities—ground zero for the protests allegedly over benefits for retired workers. Upon visiting Nicaragua in July of 2018, I was introduced to a UPOLI student who was on campus during the early days of the protests. At the time of our meeting, Verónica Gutiérrez, a Nicaraguan of African descent, was hidden away in a safe house run by Sandinista adherents. As Verónica explained to us, she initially supported the protests on campus. However, she was shocked when criminal elements were brought into the campus and took over the demonstrations. According to Verónica, these individuals were engaging in violence, including trashing the university, and were doing drugs as well. They were well-supplied from the outside with food, cash, arms and drugs. This was not what she signed up for. She quickly turned against the protests and wanted out. But this was not an option as far as the demonstrators were concerned. They threatened her to try to keep her on board with the anti-government activities. She was eventually able to escape and went into hiding with the help of Sandinistas. While she remained physically safe, the insurgents deployed psychological tactics, including posting a sophisticated video over all of social media. She showed us the video. It was of a naked woman with Verónica's face writhing in a sexual manner. It was a deep fake of

Verónica, and it was, as intended, quite humiliating to her. This was not the work of amateurs, but of sophisticated people who knew how to manipulate images as desired using computer technology. It was obvious to her that the demonstrators were getting trained help.

As Nicaraguan researcher Enrique Hernández explains, outside the universities, the country remained relatively peaceful for the two-week period between April 23 and May 10, 2018, and peaceful, opposition demonstrations went ahead without incident. As he relates,

> Between April 23 and May 10, in a period of 15 days, three major protests took place: April 23, 'Walk for Peace and Dialogue' convened by *COSEP*; April 28, 'Pilgrimage and consecration of Nicaragua to the heart of Mary' convened by the *Catholic Church*; and, May 9, 'National March for Justice and Democratization of Nicaragua' convened by the Movement for Nicaragua and the April 19 Student Movement. Fortunately, none of the three demonstrations reported clashes or deaths.[406]

At the same time, according to Hernández, turmoil continued to brew in the universities. As he relates,

> During the 15 days referred to, there was no decrease in violence in the vicinity of some university campuses, especially the Polytechnic University of Nicaragua (UPOLI), the sector where on May 8 a man returning from his job was killed by a hand-made weapon, shot in the neck. However, it was after May 10 that there was an increase [generally] in the number of Nicaraguan brothers and sisters killed.

Hernández then tries to answer the question of why there was this relative calm for two weeks, and why this calm was then broken. In short, he concludes that the extreme opposition used this 15-day period to plan and organize themselves into carrying out additional acts which would provoke violence and even deaths that they could then try to blame on the police and the government, for without such violence, Hernández argues, the opposition would be unable to win over the international support necessary to overthrow the government. To put a finer point on it, it was not the Nicaraguan government or police who broke the peace in May of 2018, but rather the extreme opposition, who did so with grave intention.

Hernández focuses on what was happening at the UPOLI and the stories of those like Verónica Hernandez. As he writes,

> In the UPOLI, which was already taken over (by April 23), there was recruitment and regrouping of young people, of whom very few really had a clear vision of their socio-political objective, and who, after a short time, defected for reasons of conscience, and like the UNEN (Nicaraguan National Union of Students), affirmed that groups that were in the UPOLI were being financed and armed by the MRS (Sandinista Renovation Party). However, by then those who dominated the UPOLI were mostly criminals, drug addicts, gang members and delinquents.
>
> The 15 days signified the organization of those in the UPOLI into a base of criminal operations, establishing an internal hierarchy and strengthening the roadblocks and checkpoints within the security perimeter around the UPOLI that affected more than ten neighborhoods of District VI of Managua.[407]

In addition, as Hernández explains, various other groups involved in the demonstrations between April 23 and May 10 who were intent on overthrowing the government, including COSEP, used this period to organize their coup plans. A necessary part of the coup plot was to "be able to identify/create 'university student leaders' to be presented as the face of the university community." The Catholic Church played a key role in helping these coup efforts, as Hernández relates, by accepting Daniel's invitation to mediate a National Dialogue on April 24, but by then insisting on delaying the start of the Dialogue for another 20 days. Again, this delay was intended to enable the organization of the forces which would begin the terror in Nicaragua in earnest, and for the opposition to therefore be able to go to the bargaining table with violence they could point to, to justify their demand for Daniel Ortega to step down.

Just after the Dialogue began, major events took place which were meant to accelerate Daniel's removal. These events, which are still the stuff of legend and much controversy, took place at and around the Mother's Day marches organized in the center of Managua on May 30, 2018. As José Adán Rivera Castillo, who was participating in the Dialogue as a representative of rural workers at the time, explained to me, the opposition protesters made

> an attempt to get to El Carmen [the Presidential residence] to kill Daniel. That day the protesters were given permission to march all the way from Managua to Masaya if they wanted. When they saw that the marchers were headed to the [Denis Martínez] stadium, warning shots were made, but no one was hurt. There were deaths later that day. There were snipers (mercenaries) brought in by the golpistas [coup leaders]. Some were neutralized, others were not.

Concerning the snipers, Barbara Moore, a resident of Nicaragua who lived there during the terrible events of 2018, writing at the time in an open letter defending the Sandinista government against the mainstream media attacks, relies on the forensics described in a report by the Nicaraguan Center for Human Rights to argue that the known evidence appears to support the claim that it was opposition snipers who were doing most of the killing at events such as the Mother's Day march:

> The opposition claimed and continues to claim the National Police had used lethal and deadly force, firing indiscriminately into crowds with live ammunition. Yet

that seems impossible given the forensics; nearly every fatality occurred in a precise, specific, even clean shot to the head, neck or chest. Not exactly what one would expect given the street battles filled with heightened levels of chaos or that, when police do shoot to kill, they are trained to aim for the mid-section.

The public, deceived by press reports by the international mainstream media and rightfully outraged over the killings, continued over the following weeks to take to the streets. Almost always the same pattern repeated itself; more killed—always a male, despite the fact the early protests were well attended by females. The victims continued to be shot with incredible precision always in the head or neck, sometimes in the chest. These facts, incidentally, corroborate government claims that snipers were responsible for the killings. As the death toll continues to rise this pattern has remained entirely constant.[408]

Meanwhile, Sandinista adherents also organized a Mother's Day march and clashes ensued between the two sets of marchers. As one detailed account of the events of that day explains,

> Large pro- and anti-government marches were planned for Managua on May 30, Mother's Day. Authorities set the routes to keep them apart. Despite police efforts, at the end of the opposition march, violent groups headed towards the rival demonstration. In the resultant clashes two pro-government marchers and seven antigovernment protesters were killed, while 20 police were injured and there were two deaths among bystanders."[409]

This was not the end of the mayhem on Mother's Day. Thus,

> At the end of the opposition march, protesters got into the new Denis Martínez Baseball Stadium and vandalized it.... Nearby, antigovernment protesters burned down [the pro-Sandinista] Radio Station "Tu Nuevo Radio Ya" with over 20 workers inside. Opposition protesters attacked the police and firefighters trying to save the besieged radio workers. Protesters also burned down the offices of ALBA Caruna near the Central American University UCA."[410]

True to form, the mainstream media and most human rights groups have portrayed the events of Mother's Day as one of the Nicaraguan police savagely attacking and killing opposition protesters—though it is not clear the police killed anyone—while the violence of the opposition, some deadly, has been completely ignored.[411]

Meanwhile, a big part of the opposition's efforts, beginning in May of 2018, was focused on setting up and maintaining roadblocks, known as *"tranques,"* throughout a number of major cities in order to block transportation routes, molest the population and prevent economic activity. Indeed, there were a number of truckers from other countries with vehicles loaded with goods, including perishables, who were traversing through Nicaragua on the Pan-American Highway from one Central American country to another and who were trapped by these roadblocks in Nicaragua for weeks. This was obviously devastating to these truckers and their families, but the protesters, indifferent to the needs of working-class people, were unconcerned by this fact.

Yorlis Gabriela Luna details well the significance and the function of the *tranques:*

> Another tactic the opposition used throughout Nicaragua was roadblocks, which also served the purpose of conquering tangible territory. The idea was to

mimic the barricades used during the popular uprising against Somoza in 1979....

It was a well-designed, planned, and organized physical and ideological attack in which physical spaces, objects, systems, and power relations remained immersed in tangible and intangible territories.... The roadblocks converted public spaces into areas in which the opposition used violence to control the circulation of people, vehicles, and supplies. They paralyzed international commerce, made it possible to burn and loot public and historic buildings, and torture, burn, and publicly murder people known historically to be Sandinista. This resulted in the weakening of the national and local economies, the loss of 100,000 jobs, and the loss of US$182 million worth of government infrastructure, schools, hospitals, and historic sites that were burned, looted, and completely destroyed.... It also led to a reduction of the national government budget and left people dead, wounded, and psychologically traumatized. It left thousands of Nicaraguan families divided and broken.[412]

Quite symbolically, one of the historic buildings the opposition forces set on fire and severely damaged was the historic Palacio Municipal in Grenada which dates back to the 1500s. Even William Walker, who had torched Grenada when defeat was near, had not managed to damage this building. The Sandinista government has subsequently restored the building after the 2018 fire.

The roadblocks set up and manned by the protesters, and the criminal gangs they partnered with, were places of great danger. At these *tranques*, people trying to drive or walk past them were invariably questioned, often shaken down for money or outright robbed, sometimes assaulted and in some cases killed. Interestingly, one person robbed at a *tranque* was a young woman from Pittsburgh named Rosa De Ferrari. I know her parents, Mel and Emily, well as they are fellow activists in Pittsburgh. As

Emily told me, Rosa went to Nicaragua in 2018 to support her friends who were involved in the anti-government protests. Emily explained to me that she thought Rosa was misguided in supporting the protesters but hoped she might have a change of heart. One incident that happened in Nicaragua, Emily hoped, might be a catalyst for such a change. While there, Rosa's backpack was stolen by some of the protesters manning the *tranques* who then drove off with it on a motorcycle. Some members of the Sandinista Youth then jumped on a motorcycle to chase down the thieves and retrieve the backpack for Rosa. Hopefully, Emily related, this was an education to Rosa about who was who in Nicaragua. Apparently, this real-life experience did not in fact impact Rosa very much as she would go on to help organize the above-described pro-insurrection event at the Center for Latin American Studies at the University of Pittsburgh.

When I arrived in Nicaragua for the July 19 celebrations in 2018, I met with my friends John Perry and his Nicaraguan wife Abigail Espinoza Muñoz (Abi for short), who had just arrived from their hometown of Monimbó, a sectioin of Masaya, which had been famous for its revolutionary militancy during the insurrection against Somoza, but which in 2018 had become a nucleus of counter-revolutionary activity. Again, as McCurdy and Sefton explained, this was not a mere coincidence. The insurrectionists in 2018 made a point of trying to convert once- revolutionary towns into hotbeds of anti-government activity, and Monimbó was one of the best examples of this. Monimbó was the very last town to be freed in 2018 from the oppression of the *tranques*—just a couple days before July 19 and before I arrived in Managua. And so, when I saw John and Abi, they had come to Managua fresh from having been liberated—and "liberated" is the word they used to describe this—from the state of siege they had been living in for months, and their emotions were raw.

Abi, who has been a Sandinista dating back to her childhood days in the late 1970s and whose brother Socrates was a guerilla killed by the National Guard shortly before the Triumph, was especially emotional. She sobbed, sometimes uncontrollably, as she detailed what they had been through in the past months in which she had to cross *tranques* every day just to get to and from work, visiting family and friends and shopping. Abi explained that, as she went through the *tranques* to go about her day, she was harassed, intimidated, and put in fear for her physical integrity. She said, "I was not afraid that they would kill me. I am not afraid of dying. What I was afraid of is that they would rape me." Here, she was referring to other incidents in which rapes were carried out by people manning the *tranques*. As just one example, a female police officer was kidnapped and raped by violent opposition forces over a three-day period. As Valeria Borge, the daughter of Tomás Borge told me, opposition forces threatened to rape her daughter during this period. At the time, her daughter was a baby of one and half years old.

Abi, like so many Nicaraguans, was shocked by the violence she witnessed in 2018—violence which seemed to come out of nowhere and from people who were neighbors and had even been friends. She explained that she confronted some of the people harassing her at the *tranques,* some she recognized as young neighbors despite the bandanas which covered their faces. She asked how they could be doing this to her and other people they knew. She wondered how people for whom she had advocated, to whom she had helped bring paved roads, running water and sewage through her direct lobbying to Daniel Ortega himself, could turn on her in this way. The anger and hatred shown by the protesters was shocking and inexplicable.

In many cases, the people who terrorized people like Abi and John, some of whom were jailed for a time, are now back in their neighborhood. It will take a long time before the wounds created in this period will be healed, if ever. Meanwhile, Abi and John took in the two daughters of one of Abi's relatives, who joined the insurrection then went into hiding after being threatened by the insurrectionists themselves when she started to question her support for them. The oldest daughter, at age 11, decided to stay with Abi and John permanently, not only because she felt abandoned by her mother, but also because she faithfully aligns herself with the FSLN and disapproved of her mother's actions. Children in

Nicaragua grow up quickly as one can see, and form sophisticated political opinions at a young age.

The presence of the ubiquitous *tranques*, just as the anti-government insurrection, had clearly been planned over a long time, and they were well-funded and supplied. As McCurdy and Sefton explain:

> Whoever funded the very widespread attacks also supplied regular firearms and a quantity of artisan made weapons produced on a semi-industrial scale. Overall the attackers fired many thousands of mortar rounds, each one costing almost a dollar. The cost of transport to move hundreds of militants between Managua, Masaya, León and Chinandega, Estelí, and towns around Granada also runs into many thousands of dollars. In Managua, impoverished young delinquents were paid US$10 to US$15 per day to participate in the attacks plus food, alcohol, cigarettes and in some cases drugs. Clearly, the opposition extremists who hijacked the student protests for their own ends were well organized, funded and prepared long before the protests even began.[413]

If the phenomenon of the *tranques* in Nicaragua during this time looks familiar to those following events in Latin America and elsewhere, it is because it resembled other U.S.-backed regime-change operations such as those in Venezuela in 2014 and 2017. Specifically, the *tranques* of Nicaragua looked much like the *garimbas* of Venezuela in which, just as in Nicaragua, masked youths set up barricades in various Venezuelan cities—armed with weapons, many home-made—to try to undermine economic activity, snarl traffic, provoke state violence and ultimately to try to overthrow the government. The fact that the events in countries like Nicaragua and Venezuela—both countries targeted for U.S. regime-change—are so similar is, I would strongly contend, the result of the fact that they were instigated, funded and supported by the same source: the government in Washington, D.C.

Several alternative Spanish-speaking news outlets, including the on-line publication *Misión Verdad,* have detailed a number of ways in which the violent demonstrations in Nicaragua look like those organized by the right-wing in Venezuela.[414] These include:

(1) the demonstrators' use of "artisanal weapons," such as mortars and rockets, designed to obscure "the line between peaceful protest and the tactics of subversion and urban warfare," and thus to provoke a government response which could then be labeled "a violation of human rights";

(2) attempts to falsely blame the government for chemical weapons use (a tried-and-true way to provoke foreign intervention, as was done, for example, in Syria)[415];

(3) the inflation of the number of those killed in clashes, combined with the downplaying of the deaths of state security forces;

(4) looting of private and public property, including memorials to left-wing revolutionary leaders;

(5) the support of the Catholic Church and various NGOs for the anti-government activities; and

(6) the use of snipers, whose kills are blamed on the government.

As for the use of snipers, one must recall how, as revealed in the extraordinary film, "The Revolution Will Not be Televised," snipers were used to great effect by the coup plotters against Hugo Chavez in 2002, provoking an uprising by firing at opposition demonstrators and successfully (at least for a time) blaming the resultant deaths on the national police forces. As John Perry and Rick Sterling note in their article about, *inter alia,* the Mother's Day march in Nicaragua, what happened there looked a lot like what had happened during the Maiden coup in Ukraine in 2014 in terms of the coup plotters' use of snipers, who in fact fired on both protesters and police.[416]

Indeed, as I noted at the time, the tactics used to try to overthrow the Sandinista government in Nicaragua were the very same as those used in various U.S.-backed regime-change operations going back as far as the CIA-backed coup in Iran in 1953—the very first CIA-backed coup operation—which deposed the government of democratically elected Prime Minister Mohammad

Mosaddegh and replaced him with the murderous Shah of Iran, Mohammad Reza Pahlavi. The Shah would rule over Iran with an iron-hand, with the use of widespread and systemic torture, and with the unfaltering support of the United States, until eventually being overthrown in a popular revolution in February of 1979, just months before the Sandinistas overthrew Somoza. Journalist Steven Kinzer details the tactics used by the CIA in Iran in 1953, which included violent demonstrations, in his acclaimed book, *All the Shah's Men: An American Coup and the Roots of Middle East Terror*. As Kinzer relates in detail:

> The riots that shook Tehran on Monday intensified on Tuesday. Thousands of demonstrators, unwittingly under CIA control, surged through the streets, looting shops, destroying pictures of the Shah, and ransacking the offices of royalist groups. Exuberant nationalists and communists joined in the mayhem. The police were still under orders from Mosaddegh not to interfere. That allowed rioters to do their jobs, which was to give the impression that Iran was sliding towards anarchy. [CIA Bureau Chief Kermit] Roosevelt caught glimpses of them during his furtive trips around the city and said that they "scared the hell out of him."

Kinzer explains that when this violence was not quite enough to provoke the desired crackdown by the government, Roosevelt sent the U.S. Ambassador to Mosaddegh to trick him into using force against the rioters by claiming that this was necessary to protect Americans allegedly under attack in Tehran. Roosevelt knew that Mosaddegh, inevitably moved by the Iranians' famous feelings of hospitality towards foreign guests, would have to act. And act he did, even going so far as to attack his own supporters in the interest of saving American lives, or so he was led to believe. The coup followed shortly thereafter.[417]

But as I noted at the time of the 2018 crisis in Nicaragua, Kinzer, a veritable expert on various U.S.-backed regime changes throughout the world, was nonetheless quick to accept the narrative of the coup plotters in Nicaragua that it was they who were the victims of a despotic government rather than the instigators of violence intended to overthrow a popular government which had been targeted by the U.S. for a coup. I remain baffled by such historical amnesia by those who should have known better—but may have been influenced by former Sandinistas.[418] This demonstrates how powerful the pro-coup propaganda of Washington and its foreign quislings has become.

The planning, organizing and funding for the insurrectionists' activities in Nicaragua, including the *tranques,* came from four major sources—Nicaraguan NGOs which, in turn, were funded by the NED and USAID; the MRS; a number of Nicaraguan businesses; and large sectors of the Roman Catholic Church in Nicaragua.

According to Lola del Carmen Esquivel González, leader of a women's coffee collective in El Crucero, Nicaragua and General Secretary of Managua Department of the ATC, "bandits" from Guatemala and Honduras were brought in to help set up and man these *tranques.* As she related, the *tranquistas* had a lot of money which they received from a number of sources. For example, according to Lola, while Daniel had a historic alliance with the business sector which was doing very well during the booming economic years of the post-2007 period, that sector, even while in constant dialogue with the Ortega administration and while prospering under it, was studying and plotting to remove Daniel from office. They supported the *tranquistas* to this end. Specifically, according to Nicaraguan journalist Jorge Capelán, the figures of the economic elite which openly supported the uprising included José Adán Aguerri, president of the Superior Council of Private Enterprise, COSEP; the Chamorro family which continued to run the anti-Sandinista and U.S.-funded *La Prensa* newspaper; The Pellas family, "which has a monopoly on liquor in the country" and which, during the Contra War, had declared an economic strike to try to bring down the Sandinista Government; the private Vivian Pellas Hospital which provided various supplies to protesters within the UPOLI; and Piero Cóen, "the richest man in Nicaragua, head of the financial group Coen and the seventh largest capitalist in Central America, according to *Forbes* magazine."[419] These are hardly the type of people who might be anticipated to bring about progressive change in Nicaragua—to the contrary, they were planning to achieve a counter-revolution. And again, the fact that they helped sponsor the uprising did not give pause to many leftists in the West who also supported the insurrection.

More must be said regarding the MRS, which openly supported the 2018 uprising, and its leaders Dora María Téllez and Sergio Ramírez—darlings of the Western left. As journalist Ben Norton, now a permanent resident of Nicaragua, explains, the MRS (Sandinista Renovation Movement) has recently changed its name to repudiate any historic connection to the Sandinistas and Sandinismo, now calling itself the Unión Democrática Renovadora (Democratic Renovation Union), or UNAMOS.[420] Furthermore, the MRS (which I'll continue to use here for sake of ease) has been colluding with the U.S. government against the Sandinistas for years. As Norton, writing for *The Grayzone*, relates:

> Under the leadership of Téllez and her colleagues, the MRS developed a close relationship with Nicaragua's rightist oligarchy. It also collaborated extensively with the United States government, working with neoconservative members of Congress and Miami's regime-change lobby, all while raking in funding from U.S. interventionist organizations.
>
> Classified State Department cables published by WikiLeaks and analyzed by The Grayzone show that Téllez and fellow leaders of her MRS party have frequently met with the U.S. embassy and served as informants for years.
>
> In regular meetings with U.S. officials, Téllez, Sergio Ramírez, Hugo Torres Jiménez, Victor Hugo Tinoco, and other top MRS figures provided the United States with intelligence about the FSLN and internal Nicaraguan politics in an attempt to prevent the Sandinistas from returning to power. They then

helped Washington try to destabilize the government of President Daniel Ortega after he won the 2006 election.

The embassy clearly stated that "the USG [U.S. government] position [is] that the MRS is a viable and constructive option, with whom the United States would maintain good relations."

The embassy added approvingly, "if the MRS can shift votes from the FSLN and garner some of the undecided vote, it is still a viable option—and could be the key to preventing an Ortega win."

The fact that the MRS is a U.S. government-approved alternative to the Sandinistas is indicative of its true nature, and specifically, that it is anything but a progressive or revolutionary organization. However, while approved by both the U.S. government and most of the U.S. Left, the MRS was not even close to winning the 2006 elections. It lost to Daniel Ortega and the FSLN, only garnering just over 6 percent of the vote. Surely the very unpopularity of the MRS in Nicaragua should demonstrate that it is not an organization one should look to as a reliable source reflecting the opinions and desires of the Nicaraguan people.

It cannot be over-emphasized how much the MRS broke, not only with the FSLN, but with Sandinismo itself. Indeed, during the uprising of 2018, numerous symbols, statues and memorials of the Sandinista Revolution were targeted by the MRS and its allies for vandalism and destruction. Meanwhile, the MRS-backed insurrectionists went around Nicaragua painting over the red and black of the Sandinistas with the blue and white colors of the historic Nicaraguan national flag[421]—the blue and white national flag being a major symbol of the protesters. Meanwhile, in a scene straight out of the Old Testament, scores of Sandinista rank-and-file members were targeted for harassment, kidnapping, torture and even murder, by means of the door frames of their dwellings being marked with paint to show that they should be attacked.

Probably the most famous Sandinista so targeted was Bismarck Martinez who is still memorialized today as a martyr. Bismarck was a life-time Sandinista militant. He joined the Sandinistas at age 15 to fight against Somoza.[422] When the Revolution triumphed, he joined the literacy brigades. He would go on to work for the office of the Mayor of Managua from 2002 until his death. At the end of June 2018, Bismarck disappeared. Then, in September, a video was put on-line showing him being tortured by insurrectionists. He was shown tied up, beaten and bruised. He was also painted blue and white. It was a typical tactic of the protesters to torture and paint their Sandinista victims blue and white, and just as jihadists in the Middle East, to videotape their crime and broadcast the crime publicly as a means of terrorizing the population.

Nearly a year after his disappearance, Bismarck's bones and clothes were found by police behind a baseball stadium, and he was pronounced dead. As an article in *Telesur* explains,

> Upon hearing about the forensic report, Vice President Rosario Murillo indicated that the remains of Bismarck Martinez, who has already become a symbol of the Nicaraguan people, will be honored at the National Palace of Culture on Wednesday.
>
> "For months all his family and our militants looked for Bismarck in the fields where they told us that the terrorists had thrown him after torturing him," Murillo said and commented that Martinez will continue to live in thousands of Nicaraguan families who are beneficiaries of a housing program named after him.[423]

The first person I met when I arrived in Nicaragua in July of 2018 was Idania Castillo, the former daughter-in-law of Daniel Ortega and Rosario Murillo and the head of Nicaragua's film institute, Cinemateca. I have come to know Idania as a strong and courageous individual who is quite confident and self-composed, but on that day, she looked tired and was quite emotional as she described what she and other Nicaraguans had been through in the prior months. Idania was the first individual whom I heard talk about the targeting of Sandinistas and Sandinista symbols and memorials for violence and destruction. I'll never forget her

The Bismarck Martinez housing project for low-income residents
DANIEL KOVALIK, 2021

telling our delegation through tears that, at one point during the insurrection, she and others wondered if they would ever be able to wave the red and black Sandinista flag again in Nicaragua. This is a quite profound statement, and shows just how much destruction—physical, psychological and ideological—had been done in such a short time. The goal of the insurrectionists, as Idania recounted, was not just to depose the government, but to destroy all vestiges and historical memory of Sandinismo itself. Again, that the MRS could be part of such a horrifying project shows just how far from the revolutionary roots of its leaders that party has fallen.

As for the Catholic Church, its open support for the insurrection and the *tranques* is well-known. Even the *New York Times* acknowledged this, but of course, the *Times* portrayed this as a good and noble thing, explaining at the time that "[o]n the streets, the church defends the rebellion's foot soldiers, including the citizens who guarded cobblestone barricades [the *tranques*]. . . ."[424] The *Times* article specifically highlighted the support of Bishop Silvio Báez, who had agreed to help mediate an end to the violence on behalf of the insurrection. The *Times* did at least note, in a clear understatement, that some Nicaraguans at the time questioned whether the Church's support for the activities of the "rebellion" conflicted with its role as mediator in the dispute between the government and the protesters—a role the Church accepted after Daniel Ortega himself invited it to perform this function. But then, the Catholic Church abandoned any role as neutral arbiter in a very public way at the mediation table itself. As Nicaraguan journalist Jorge Capelán explained at the time:

> Bishops like Msgr. Silvio Báez have acted as coup leaders, calling the insurrectionaries to arms. Bishop Abelardo Mata de Estelí, in the first session of the dialogue, practically made a declaration of war against the government. For his part, the head of the Episcopal Conference, Cardinal Jaime Brenes, shows total passivity in the face of the belligerence of his bishops. We see nuns celebrate when the vandals on the right knock down Trees of Life, 30-meter-high metal structures that light the cities that, when they are knocked down, have already caused human deaths.[425]

It's important to understand the nature of the Catholic Church in Nicaragua as it was by 2018. Long past, for the most part, were the days of Liberation Theology, which had propelled some figures like the Cardenal brothers and Miguel d'Escoto Brockmann into leadership roles in the Sandinista government in the 1980s. Liberation Theology had been largely destroyed throughout Latin America, not only through U.S.-sponsored violence against Liberation Theologians as discussed above, but also through the direct assault against Liberation Theology by the Vatican under Popes Paul VI, John Paul II (who became Pope in 1978, shortly before the Sandinista Triumph) and Pope Benedict XVI. Indeed, Paul John Paul II, when visiting Nicaragua shortly after the Triumph in 1983, famously wagged his finger in the face of Father Ernesto Cardenal when he knelt down to try to kiss the papal ring. And in turn, as the *Washington Post* detailed at the time, Nicaraguans "heckled Pope John Paul II at mass...as he called on the hundreds of thousands in the vast central plaza to reject the 'popular church' that is allied with the revolutionary government and to accept the absolute authority of his bishop," Miguel Obando y Bravo, who was a staunch critic of the Sandinista government at that time.[426] As the *Post* further related,

> As he warmed to his homily, however, with unremitting demands for obedience from radical priests who have served in this government against his wishes, the Sandinista partisans who had packed the front of the crowd of about 350,000 began chanting, "One church on the side of the poor!" and "We want peace!" The pope was forced to stop his homily and to order, "Silence!"

As the *Post* noted, "Members of the papal entourage said they had never seen anything like it on other tours." This famous episode came to be a symbol of the tension between the Sandinistas and the Church in Rome.

Ultimately, the priesthoods of the Cardenal brothers and Miguel D'Escoto were suspended by Pope John Paul II in 1985 because of their active role in the Sandinista government, which they refused to leave.

Daniel Ortega eventually made peace with Archbishop Miguel Obando y Bravo, who retired in 2005, shortly before Daniel was elected, and died in June of 2018. Meanwhile, as Lauren Smith tells us in an excellent article, entitled "Nicaragua: Imperialist snakes in holy vestments," the clerics that came to dominate the Church in Nicaragua were from the far-right Opus Dei sect of the Church, which Pope John Paul II had elevated in status in 1982.[427] As Smith explains,

> Josemaría Escrivá, a priest and ardent fan of the murderous U.S. installed right-wing military dictator Francisco Franco (1939–1975), founded Opus Dei in Spain in 1928. Franco is accused of the murder and

disappearance of 114,000 people, which consisted of Liberals, Socialists, Trotskyists, Communists, anarchists, Protestant Christians and intellectuals between the years 1936 and 1952.

Smith further relates that

> Under Popes John Paul II and Benedict XVI, proponents of the right-wing Opus Dei prelature were installed in key positions in the Vatican and deployed to Nicaragua and other socialist countries to build, though deceit and manipulation, foundations for regime change. In countries with Military dictatorships, Opus Dei's role is to keep the poor and oppressed, confused and docile. Additionally, Liberation Theologians (who believe in assisting the poor and oppressed through socio-political activism, in addition to teaching scripture) were excised from the Church.

In Nicaragua in 2018, the Opus Dei clerics brought their planned regime change operation to fruition.

The role of these clerics and the Catholic Church they came to dominate was quite disturbing. A number of them were using the churches to stir up anti-government sentiment as well as to organize and support the insurrectionists with money, weapons (caches of which were discovered in some of the churches),[428] alcohol and drugs. Some priests even oversaw the torture of government adherents within the churches. As *Monthly Review* explains,

> The Catholic Church, long allied with the oligarchs, has put its full weight behind creating and sustaining anti-government actions, including in its universities, high schools, churches, bank accounts, vehicles, tweets, Sunday sermons, and a one-sided effort to mediate the National Dialogue. Bishops have made death threats against the President and his family,

Reynaldo Urbina Cuadra, who lost his left arm to torture during the 2018 insurrection, stands in front of the wreckage of Masaya municipal vehicles, including sanitation trucks and equipment used to pave roads, which the opposition destroyed.
DANIEL KOVALIK, JULY 2021

and a priest has been filmed supervising the torture of Sandinistas.[429]

Reynaldo Urbina Cuadra, a security officer for the Mayor's office whom I met in Masaya ended up having one of his arms amputated after having been tortured in one of the Catholic churches in Masaya. As Reynaldo explained, he was kidnapped and tortured by the insurrectionists who attempted to coerce him into giving them the whereabouts of the Mayor of Masaya, who had gone into hiding at this time for fear of his life.[430] After losing consciousness from the extended torture, Reynaldo, a Roman Catholic himself, was shocked to wake up in the Church, where he found he no longer had the use of his arm.

Despite its obvious conflict of interest, the Church continued to serve as a mediator in the National Dialogue between the Sandinista government, civil society groups and representatives of the insurrectionists. In late May of 2018, the Church representatives demanded that the National Police be removed from the streets, claiming that it was the police who were committing the violence in Nicaragua and that removing them would bring about peace. It must be noted that the army never left its barracks during the entire conflict, taking the position that its role is to protect the nation from foreign invasion and not to police internal disputes.

The demand of the Church was a provocative one, given who really was stirring up and committing the violence. However, much to the shock of many Sandinista supporters, Daniel Ortega agreed to this demand, and ordered the police off the streets and contained to their barracks for over 50 days. In addition, as José Adán Rivera Castillo explained to me, Daniel ordered supporters of the government not to take matters into their own hands in trying to forcibly take down the *tranques*. As Rivera relates, while the government and its supporters certainly had the fire power to forcibly remove the *tranques* and the people manning them, Daniel wanted to minimize bloodshed, hoping that the latter would ultimately be

Police station in Masaya displays photos of police killed in Masaya in 2018
DANIEL KOVALIK, MARCH, 2022

convinced to take down the *tranques* themselves. And, according to Rivera, many ultimately were taken down peacefully.

Daniel's other motivation for agreeing to the Church's demand was to demonstrate to the Nicaraguan people who was really behind the violence. With the police off the streets, the people would know for sure that it was not they, despite opposition and media claims, who were causing all the mayhem. In this thinking, Daniel again proved himself to be a patient and brilliant strategist. As Rivera explains,

> Daniel had lots of patience.... We could have taken all the roadblocks down, but that would have cost us a lot. If we would have acted too quickly, we would have destroyed families which were already divided. Daniel said that we had to wait and have patience during these two months. We thought there was a part of the Catholic Church which would comport with their mediator role, but they fully took the side of the coup.

Meanwhile, violence continued for some time until the *tranques* were finally removed. Indeed, as was reported at the time,

> With the police off the streets, opposition violence intensified throughout May and June. As a result, a process of neighborhood self-defense developed. Families who have been displaced, young people who have been beaten, robbed or tortured, and veterans of the 1979 insurrection and/or the Contra War, held vigil around the Sandinista Front headquarters in each town.[431]

Sandinistas even ended up building roadblocks of their own to try to keep violent insurrectionists out of their communities.[432]

All told, the death and destruction in Nicaragua during the civil disturbance, which lasted from April to July of 2018, was incredible. According to *Telesur*, writing about a year after the crisis, "[a]ccording to official figures, ... the 2018 right-wing attempt at destabilization of the country left almost 200 deaths, hundreds of wounded and over US$1 billion in economic losses."[433] In the course of the anti-government protests—which we were incessantly told were "peaceful" by the mainstream press in the U.S.:

> Over 60 government buildings have been burned down, schools, hospitals, health centers attacked, 55 ambulances damaged, at least $112 million in infrastructure damage, small businesses have been closed, and 200,000 jobs lost causing devastating economic impact during the protests. Violence has included, in addition to thousands of injuries, 15 young people and 16 police officers killed, as well as over 200 Sandinistas kidnapped, many of them publicly tortured.[434]

In a classic case of misinformation, "Violent opposition atrocities were misreported as government repression" by the mainstream media.[435]

Finally, in July, it had become quite apparent to the vast majority of the Nicaraguan people that it was the opposition that was terrorizing them, and not the police in their barracks, who themselves were being attacked even while in their quarters. The calls for the Nicaraguan government and its security forces to clear the *tranques* from the streets now became deafening. Answering these calls, Daniel finally ordered the police to remove the *tranques,* but to try to do so without force. And largely, the police were able to do so peacefully.

But the police did not act alone. As many Nicaraguans explained to me, there was a force that actually acted as the vanguard ahead of the police to bring down the *tranques:* the historic combatants—now middle-age and older, who had fought Somoza's National Guard and then the Contras, who organized themselves to restore order and peace to the country. This is a detail almost always overlooked in the narrative of the events of 2018—that those who had fought for the Revolution from the beginning remained loyal to the Revolution, the FSLN and Daniel, and acted again to defend that Revolution. In addition to the historic combatants, the Sandinista Youth also played their part in defeating the coup of 2018.

Historic market in Masaya which the opposition torched, destroying nearly all of the inside of the building. The Sandinista government has subsequently restored the market.
DANIEL KOVALIK, 2021

Alfonso Guillen, himself a historic combatant and a peasant who grows coffee at the same coffee collective as Lola del Carmen Esquivel González, whom I quote herein, explained all this to me in March of 2018. Indeed, he sought me out to tell me this story, quite proudly, when I was visiting the collective. Shirtless after a long day's work, and still holding a machete in hand, he told me:

> Imperialism won't accept the reality that this was kidnappings, killings and rapes and not a civil action. The Empire funded all of this mayhem. The local bourgeoisie also put in their own money. A lot of young people, including the Sandinista youth, organized to take down the roadblocks. In addition to the police, the militants of the FSLN and the historic combatants organized to take down the *tranques*. Veterans in their homes whose candles have not burned out yet organized to do this. The historic combatants were ready. The people here are very organized. Daniel waited a while to take down the roadblocks. The goal of the *tranques* was to destroy the economy and to create terror through the torture and rapes. Institutions, parks, ambulances were burned down. A lot of gringos don't believe this, including the OAS.

When the time came, Alfonso was one of the historic combatants, who participated in helping rid his community of the *tranques*. By the time this happened, the mood of the country had shifted radically in favor of the government and Daniel. Those manning the *tranques* were demoralized and knew they had lost the hearts and minds of the people. Therefore, Alfonso and his comrades were able to remove the *tranques* peacefully, just as Daniel had wanted.

For her part, Lola also described this event to me:

> This community of Santa Julia was tasked with getting rid of the *tranques*. Twenty-eight men were assigned to do this, all of them historic combatants. Some were missing an eye or a limb. Fourteen were placed in the FSLN offices and fourteen were placed in the municipal offices to protect the property and papers. A truck of riot police came to take down the roadblocks, but everyone fled before they got here, and no one was hurt. Most of the people on the roadblocks were drunks and druggies.

When the smoke cleared, many Sandinistas recognized that the insurrection of 2018 had a silver lining. First and foremost, a number of my friends in Nicaragua have told me that the FSLN learned that it cannot be complacent; that it must be ever vigilant, and it must continue to educate and organize. The work of creating, continuing and reproducing the Revolution is one that never ends, because if it does, those bent on the Revolution's destruction will attack. The other silver lining, as José Adán Rivera Castillo told me, was that the alliance between the FSLN, business and the Church—one which Daniel and the FSLN had reluctantly made and engaged in as a matter of pragmatism—had ended with the betrayal by both business and the Church. No longer would concessions have to be made in the interest of peace and reconciliation, to the possible detriment of the peasants and the working class. Business and the Church had showed their true colors—literally—and they now could forget about having a say over government policy.

As my friend Nils McCune, who lives in Nicaragua told me, the biggest loser of all in this was the institutional Catholic Church. Its complicity and indeed leadership in the violence has brought lasting shame and disrepute upon it. The Church went for broke in 2018, and it lost. It could never again play such a treacherous role, for the people had been awakened to its true deceitfulness. Even Pope Francis seems to have recognized this, having recalled from Nicaragua one of the worst offenders during the 2018 crisis—Auxiliary Bishop Silvio Báez. I happened to run into Baez at the Augusto Cesar Sandino Airport in Managua the day he was being shipped out. I was happy to say "good riddance" to him.

Pope Francis, an Argentine cleric who lived through the brutal, fascist "Dirty War" of the 1970s, seems more inclined towards the Sandinistas than his predecessors, even pardoning and reinstating the priesthoods of both Father Miguel D'Escoto Brockmann and Father Ernesto Cardenal. Certainly, as Pope Francis seemingly recognizes, the world needs more clerics like them than the ultra-right clerics who led the coup of 2018.

When I visited Nicaragua to attend the annual July 19 celebration of the Sandinista Triumph, held that year in the Pope John Paul II Plaza (yes, despite Pope John Paul II's ill treatment of the ever-forgiving Sandinistas, they still have a Plaza and Museum dedicated to his name adjacent to the Plaza of the Revolution), I saw that while the *tranques* had been removed throughout the country, the threat of violence had not entirely passed. Therefore, Daniel called upon those who wanted to celebrate the Triumph to stay in their own towns lest they be attacked on the roads to Managua. Therefore, those who attended the celebrations in the Pope John Paul II Plaza were, unlike other years, almost exclusively from Managua.

Still, the turnout was massive, and the mood was festive and exuberant. Young and old came, some with red and black face paint, almost all waving the red and black Sandinista flag. It was a moving experience. At the celebration, they played the song "Daniel se Queda" (or "Daniel Stays") several times. As I witnessed, this song was playing everywhere in Nicaragua at this time and is still popular to this day. This song was written by a peasant mariachi band from Boaco, Nicaragua called "Mariachi Azucena" in response to the *golpistas,* who wanted Daniel gone, countering that with "Daniel here stays, Daniel, Daniel, the people are with you, Boaco is with you, Matagalpa is with you, Estelí is with you, León is with you, Managua is with you, all of Nicaragua is with you ... Daniel, Daniel, we are with you!" The song must have seemed strange to those claiming that the people had somehow turned against Daniel, and so its existence and popularity were simply ignored by the press.

As many Nicaraguans told me that day of July 19, 2018, they were not only celebrating the Triumph of 1979; they were also celebrating the new Triumph of 2018 over the violent coup plotters. Similarly, as I witnessed myself in 2022, in Masaya and Monimbó, the people now celebrate July 17—which is already designated the "Day of Joy" because it marks the departure of Somoza in 1979—as a day of joy because it was the day they were liberated from the *tranques* in 2018.

Daniel Ortega would run again for president in November of 2021, and I was there to observe the elections. As I wrote shortly after this election, "over 65 percent of voters turned out, 75 percent of whom cast their ballots on November 7 for Sandinista leader Daniel Ortega, securing him a fourth consecutive presidential term."[436] While the U.S. government and the mainstream press, along with most of the alternative press as well, attempted to demean the freeness and fairness of this election, the results were actually predicted by the independent opinion poll taken by M&R Consultants shortly before the elections. As I wrote at the time,

> 77.5% of Nicaraguans polled a few days before the election agreed "that for Nicaragua to advance socially and economically," the Sandinista National Liberation Front (FSLN) should govern the country, while 74.6% believe that the country would be better off with a Sandinista government. In addition, "91.8% of Nicaraguans agree with President Daniel Ortega's proposals on unity to be stronger and defeat poverty." The strong support for President Ortega's "proposals on unity to be stronger" is telling, for it seems to show approval of recent measures taken by the government against a number of people accused of helping orchestrate and/or support, often with U.S. financing and other support, the violent insurrection of 2018, which cost the lives of at least 200 Nicaraguans.[437]

As for the Nicaraguan people's support for the arrest and trial of various individuals involved in the coup attempt of 2018—including MRS leaders Dora Maria Téllez—my friends in Nicaragua were clear that a feeling of relief fell over the country when these arrests were made. Indeed, many Nicaraguans remained anxious until these arrests that the terror which had enveloped Nicaragua in 2018 could be repeated. According to Nicaraguan intelligence, they had indeed uncovered a plot in the summer of 2021 that various opposition leaders were planning a coup along the lines of that which took place in Bolivia in 2019 when Evo Morales was overthrown and exiled with U.S. and OAS support after claims—later debunked, as reported by the *New York Times* months later[438]—that the re-election of Morales was the product of a fraudulent electoral process.

The arrests in Nicaragua were made to forestall such a coup, and the vast majority of Nicaraguans approved of this course of action. In my view, the Sandinista government finally learned what history had taught them ever since Sandino was murdered when traveling to Managua in good faith to sign a peace accord—that the U.S. Empire and its faithful servants in Nicaragua do not reward acts of kindness and reconciliation. Rather, they take advantage of them to destroy revolutionary movements and impose their will upon the people. And, as any revolutionary worth their salt will tell you, the first duty of a Revolution is to defend itself, for if it cannot meet this most essential goal, it obviously cannot serve and defend the people as they deserve. The fact that so few on the U.S. "Left" recognize this says so much about them personally and their own failings as revolutionaries.

As I write these words, the U.S. Congress is holding hearings about the January 6 insurrection—an event of less than one day, which was nowhere near as deadly and destructive of the months-long violent insurrection in Nicaragua in 2018—and many are calling for the arrests of people like Donald Trump who is accused of helping incite the insurrection, even though he didn't participate in it.

Surely in this context, the Nicaraguan people's support for the arrest of the leaders and inciters of the coup that had wreaked such destruction on their country should be quite understandable.

The restored market in Masaya
DANIEL KOVALIK, 2021

Plaza of the Revolution, July 19, 2022
DANIEL KOVALIK

CONCLUSION

As of January of 2022, Daniel Ortega's approval rating among Nicaraguans, according to M&R Consulting, was soaring to over 70 percent.[439] In addition, "84.1% express their trust in the president," and believe in his course of action, and in his "commitment to the good of all."[440] A more recent poll in July of 2022 produced similar results, again showing Daniel Ortega with a 70% percent approval rating, the second highest approval of any leader in the Western Hemisphere.[441]

Comparatively, President Joe Biden is polling at an anemic 36 percent after approving $40 billion in Ukraine-related funding (I say Ukraine-related, because most of that money will never get to Ukraine but will stay in the coffers of the U.S. defense industry), even while there is a shortage of baby formula for our own children.

The reason Daniel's rating is so high is because he, unlike Joe Biden et al, is actually meeting his country's needs. As *Telesur* explains, breaking down the poll numbers:

> At least 94 percent of those polled agreed with Ortega's call for unity to defeat poverty, and 78 percent of them said the construction of an interoccanic canal, a project promoted by his administration, will benefit the country.
>
> The poll also revealed that about 77 percent of adult citizens considered that inter-urban transportation, road reparation, drinking water supply, education, and public health services are optimal. Another 63.3 percent of the Nicaraguans think that the FSLN government has prompted job opportunities.[442]

These approval numbers are astronomical, especially when compared to any U.S. president or party in modern history. And it is not surprising that these approval numbers are so high. Despite the troubles of 2018, U.S. sanctions, the pandemic and worldwide economic woes, Daniel Ortega has continued to lead Nicaragua on a path toward prosperity for the Nicaraguan people. As Nicaragua's Finance Minister, Ivan Acosta, explained in June of 2022,

> The year 2021 was an exceptional year in economic performance, in growth, across all the numbers. If we look at expenditure, it means that the construction of roads is accelerating, the momentum in drinking water and sanitation is continuing; more resources are being invested to make an impact on employment and above all on the welfare of the population."[443]

Describing the unprecedented growth in Gross Domestic Product (GDP) during this challenging period, Acosta related that "2021 was a year of a reactivation, a growth of 11.3%, the highest ever combined figure. During the COVID pandemic in Latin America there was 8.3% growth over the two years, 2020–21, and definitely those numbers have been the base scenario that we are acting on in 2022."[444] He estimated that Nicaragua would have economic growth of between 4 and 5 percent in 2022.

Despite these realities, there will be many in the U.S., including "progressives" and "leftists," who will sit comfortably in their armchairs and claim to know better about the nature of Daniel Ortega and the FSLN than the Nicaraguan people, themselves. They will continue to try to compare Daniel to Somoza, who looted the Nicaraguan treasury, even as Daniel has overseen the growth of Nicaragua's treasury reserves to over $4 billion and counting.[445]

Thankfully, Daniel and the Nicaraguan people have decided to go their own way in the world, and what passes for the U.S. and European Left can decide to support them or not. Having been attacked brutally by the United States for over a century and a half,

Celebration of the anniversary of the liberation of León from Somoza
DANIEL KOVALIK, 2020

Nicaragua has sought and found new allies in the world to help it with its development. Thus, around his re-election in November of 2021—an election I personally observed—Daniel announced that he was now recognizing the People's Republic of China for the first time since the neoliberals took over in 1990. Daniel announced at his inauguration, that I had the honor of attending, that he had signed up to join China's Belt and Road program. Much to the chagrin of the U.S., China will be helping Nicaragua build infrastructure projects, including a train system to replace the one Violeta Chamorro sold off and destroyed. It is also believed that

China will help Nicaragua build that canal which the U.S. has so coveted for over a century—the U.S.'s obsession with the canal being so strong that it invaded Nicaragua in 1910 because, at least it was rumored, it dared to work with Japan to build one. But this time, the strength of China may help ward off such an intervention.

Nicaragua has also pulled closer to Russia and Iran, with the latter recently shipping fuel to Nicaragua and announcing that it will help Nicaragua rebuild some of its oil refineries—the ones that, you may recall, the CIA destroyed in the 1980s.

In addition, Daniel has pulled Nicaragua out of the Organization of American States (OAS)—an entity long-dominated by the United States. As I wrote at the time this withdrawal was announced,

> This action is long overdue, and other Latin and Caribbean nations should quickly follow suit. To say the least, the OAS—appropriately headquartered in Washington, D.C. with a statue of Queen Isabella of Spain in front—has always been a problematic organization for the poorer nations of the Western Hemisphere, operating as it has as the handmaiden of the U.S. with its attempts to rule over these nations. Indeed, Fidel Castro referred to the OAS as "the ministry of United States colonies."[446]

As I noted, the OAS has played a treacherous role in paving the way for the CIA overthrow of Jacobo Árbenz in 1954; gave a legal fig leaf to the U.S. invasion of the Dominican Republic in 1964; tacitly supported the U.S. overthrow of Chilean President Salvador Allende in 1973; and played a critical role in the coup against Bolivian President Evo Morales in 2019.[447] Nicaragua, in joining Venezuela in leaving the OAS, has taken a positive step towards national independence and sovereignty.

Furthermore, the countries of Latin America and the Caribbean have rallied around Nicaragua, Venezuela and Cuba in rejecting the U.S.'s refusal to include these three countries in the June of 2022 "Summit of the Americas." Thus, Mexico, Bolivia,

Honduras, Antigua and Barbuda refused to attend this meeting in Los Angeles at the presidential or even ambassadorial level in solidarity with these three countries.[448] For its part, the tiny island nation of St. Vincent and the Grenadines, a country of about 100,000 people that obtained its independence from the UK in 1979, refused to attend the Summit at all.

At the July 19, 2022, celebrations I attended, Daniel conferred the Augusto Sandino Order upon the Prime Minister of St. Vincent, Ralph Gonsalves, for his longstanding support of Nicaragua and opposition to U.S. imperialism. Ralph, as he likes to be called, gave an amazing address at the celebration. These words from his speech are quite apt here:

> The Empire does not understand that it has a country of 350 million people, it has the largest economy in the World, it is said that they have the largest army in the World; Nicaragua has about 6.2 million people, a Central American country that only aspires to develop its country and its People.
>
> Why in the name of God, such a big country, with so many resources, with so much military force, why attack a country like Nicaragua? I ask myself that question daily, and it is difficult for everyday understanding to understand something like that. But even that which one cannot understand, we know what they are doing and we know that it is wrong.

And yet, there is no doubt that the U.S. Empire will continue to target Nicaragua for regime change, and to try to punish it for having successfully overthrown a U.S.-backed dictator. As The Grayzone reports, "the USAID's latest regime-change scheme in Nicaragua:"

> a leaked internal document revealing the agency's Responsive Assistance in Nicaragua (RAIN) program... calls openly for the overthrow of the Sandinista government, as well as imposing neoliberal reforms based

on a "market economy" and the "protection of private property rights," and purging the military, police, and all state institutions of any trace of Sandinismo.[449]

Sending a clear message to the Nicaraguan people that they would be punished if they continued to vote for the Sandinistas, the U.S. Congress approved a new round of economic sanctions against Nicaragua before the November 2021 election. And then, when the Nicaraguans overwhelmingly voted the "wrong way"— that is, for Daniel Ortega—President Joe Biden signed the new sanctions bill, known as the RENACER Act, into law just three days after the election.[450] The "punitive measures" put in place by the Act "increased coordination of such measures with the European Union and Canada, and expanded U.S. oversight of international lending to Managua," thereby making it more difficult for Nicaragua to obtain international loans which it has been using to fund its progressive social programs.

In addition, the Biden Administration, just in time for the July 19 celebrations in 2022, announced that the U.S. would stop giving Nicaragua the longstanding preferential tax rates on sugar imports, thereby all but ensuring that Nicaraguan sugar will no longer be bought in the U.S.[451]

And, even as I write these words, the U.S. is considering throwing Nicaragua out of the Central American Free Trade Agreement (CAFTA). This would follow three rounds of economic sanctions against Nicaragua in the past three years. Ousting Nicaragua from CAFTA could devastate the Nicaraguan economy and throw tens of thousands of Nicaraguans out of work. As the Associated Press reports,

> Expulsion from the Central America Free Trade Agreement, which was signed in 2004, would be a major blow, depriving Ortega's government of important export earnings and foreign investment. Nicaragua is the only nation in CAFTA to run a trade surplus with the U.S., about $2.5 billion last year, or 20% of its gross domestic product.[452]

As is usual, while the U.S. makes claims about wanting to expel Nicaragua because of alleged concerns about its democratic nature, it seems that it is indeed Nicaragua's successes under CAFTA, which is meant to work for the benefit of the U.S., which is more its concern. Still, Nicaragua remains firm.

The U.S. continues to menace Nicaragua, and Venezuela as well, militarily, conducting NATO exercises with NATO "global partner" Colombia in the Caribbean in February of 2022.[453] The U.S., reaffirming the vitality of the Monroe Doctrine, claimed these exercises were intended to counter alleged Russian interference in the region. These exercises included a nuclear submarine, thus violating the longstanding nuclear-free zone which Nicaragua and neighboring states had agreed to some time ago.

As Simon Bolivar prophetically stated two centuries ago, "[t]he United States appear to be destined by Providence to plague America with misery in the name of liberty." Sadly, these words ring even more true today than when they were uttered. However, Nicaragua, led by the Sandinistas, is one country in the Americas which has decided to reject such a fate, and it has shown the resolve to pursue another reality in which the U.S. can no longer determine its destiny.

Massive march in Masaya celebrating the July 19 anniversary
DANIEL KOVALIK, 2022

AFTERWORD

by Orlando Zelaya Olivas*

This book by Dan Kovalik cannot be more timely. United States aggression against Nicaragua continues to escalate, with the U.S. bipartisan regime even threatening to ban all trade with this country in a bid to bolster the ruling class's neocolonial interests—a throwback to the full-blown economic war against Nicaragua in the 1980s. The collusion of the western media and the political elite amplifies the demagoguery of partisan opportunists and political clerics who seek to undermine the self-determination of peoples and the creation of a multipolar world. It is therefore crucial to set the record straight about Nicaragua, the Sandinista Revolution, and President Daniel Ortega, who continues to be the focal point of the U.S.'s crusades to vilify Nicaragua and justify its hostile foreign policy towards it.

For over 169 years, from 1853 to 2022, Nicaragua has bravely resisted the devastating U.S. foreign policy of systemic state terrorism, enduring military interventions, regime change operations, coups d'état, election meddling, trade blockades, illegal sanctions, and other criminal covert operations such as secret wars, assassination programs, and illicit drugs and arms deals.

Regarding military interventions alone, in its March 2022 report on "Instances of Use of the United States Armed Forces Abroad," the Congressional Research Service (CRS), a public policy research institute of the United States Congress, briefly

---

* Orlando Zelaya Olivas was born in Jinotega, Nicaragua. The storytelling by his grandmother and his mother about General Sandino's guerrilla resistance and the savagery of U.S. interventionist soldiers and their spawn, the genocidal National Guard, made him aware of the suffering of the people at an early age. Like many other youths, he was engaged in the struggle to overthrow the Somoza dictatorship and, afterward, defend the Sandinista Revolution.

mentions eleven U.S. military interventions against Nicaragua—among the 469 overtly acknowledged U.S. military interventions in distant countries between 1798 and 2022. Of course, the report's authors use traditional euphemistic wordings to protect neocolonial exceptionalism, conceal geopolitical economic motives, and distort the historical context of such interventions.

For example, concerning the U.S. military intervention to support the "Contra War" against Nicaragua, the CRS report blatantly obscures a prolonged military intervention in Honduras between 1983 and 1989, stating that "the United States undertook a series of exercises in Honduras that some believed might lead to conflict with Nicaragua. On March 25, 1986, unarmed U.S. military helicopters and crewmen ferried Honduran troops to the Nicaraguan border to repel Nicaraguan troops." (Emphasis added) It fails to clarify that the military intervention in Honduras was designed to build the infrastructure and maintain logistics for the "covert" proxy war against Nicaragua, including the construction of three U.S. military bases as well as a handful of paramilitary headquarters and training camps for counterrevolutionaries.

The United States assault against Nicaragua did not halt in 1989 when the Sandinistas lost in the general elections held on February 25, 1990, nor has it slowed afterward, regardless of whether the Sandinistas were in power or had been defeated by the U.S.-backed presidential candidates in the 1990, 1996, and 2001 elections. That said, the U.S. hostility has become more intense after the Sandinistas democratically retook power following 17 years of neoliberal governments.

Kovalik notes that, regrettably, many in the West who were rumored to support Nicaragua and its Revolution have fallen to misinformation campaigns against Nicaragua and Daniel's revolutionary leadership. And some intellectuals and elites in Nicaragua, many of whom formerly professed loyalty to Daniel and the Revolution but now owe allegiance to the U.S. administration, have aided in these smearing tactics since 1990. As a Nicaraguan who has lived abroad for over three decades but has continued to stay in touch with my homeland, I believe I have a unique perspective on these matters. While Kovalik paints a vivid and accurate picture of Nicaragua, the incessant U.S. intervention against my motherland, and the heroic resistance of the Nicaraguan people to this hostility, I have been asked to add some color, shading and texture to this image.

As an initial matter, I want to explain why these Nicaraguan intellectuals and elites, who sadly hold tremendous influence, particularly amongst the so-called Western left, despise Daniel Ortega and the Sandinistas, as well as their unwavering anti-imperialist and socialist stances of national dignity. In short, I believe their obvious contempt is a clumsy attempt to erase Daniel's steady involvement in Nicaraguan politics for more than 60 years so as to elevate their own role by comparison. However, let us further examine the role of Daniel Ortega, who indeed is a leader of the people's resistance to the hegemonic intervention of the United States and its allies and an iconic representative of the people's victory in the struggle for peace, justice, and socioeconomic prosperity.

Commander Daniel Ortega did not rise to prominence by chance on July 17, 1979, when he was designated Head of the Junta of National Reconstruction after the Sandinistas deposed Somoza's dictatorship. He was born on November 11, 1945, in a poor family in La Libertad, Chontales. The hardships at home led to the early deaths of two of his younger siblings. Another younger brother, Camilo Ortega, born on December 13, 1950, was killed in the struggle to overthrow the Somoza regime in Monimbó, Masaya, on February 26, 1978. Camilo is regarded as the Apostle of the Sandinista Unity. Many of Daniel's relatives fought with the revolutionary guerrillas commanded by General Augusto C. Sandino against the U.S. occupation troops. His father, Daniel Ortega Cerda, and mother, Lidia Saavedra Rivas, were staunchly against Somoza's dictatorship, which brought upon them numerous prison experiences.

At the age of just 14, the young Daniel Ortega Saavedra started his political activism in January 1960 within the *Juventud Patriótica Nicaragüense* (JPN) (Nicaraguan Patriotic Youth), a civil opposition movement that adopted Sandino's ideology. Somoza's repression was not long in coming down on the JPN.

In 1962, Daniel began studying law at the private UCA university in Managua, but after a few months, he left the classroom in 1963 to dedicate himself fully to political resistance. He joined the clandestine Sandinista National Liberation Front (FSLN), a political-military organization founded in Honduras in July 1961 by Carlos Fonseca Amador, Tomás Borge Martínez, Silvio Mayorga Delgado, and Colonel Santos López (an ex-combatant of General Sandino), among others.

One of Daniel's first actions in the FSLN was the publication of the newspaper *El Estudiante* (*The Student*), a publication of the *Frente Estudiantil Revolucionario* (*FER*) (Revolutionary Student Front). He later organized some Popular Civic Committees to resist the dictatorship, as well as a network of armed commandos to carry out urban guerrilla actions, including sabotage and bank robberies to seize funds. In 1965, at just 20 years old, he was promoted to commander and member of the FSLN National Directorate. A year later, in 1966, he gained command over the Internal Front that operated in urban areas. In 1967, the year the last of the three Somozas ascended to the presidency, Daniel was captured by the National Guard during a bank robbery.

As Kovalik has described in detail, Daniel was in prison for more than seven years until, together with other Sandinista prisoners, he was exchanged for Somoza's direct collaborators captured in the house of Minister José María (a.k.a. Chema) Castillo on December 27, 1974 by the "Juan José Quezada" guerrilla command of the FSLN, a bold action, which became known worldwide. Daniel and other freed comrades traveled to Cuba, but after a few weeks, he infiltrated back into Nicaragua to rejoin the National Directorate, where he found an FSLN divided into three factions: the *Guerra Popular Prolongada* (Prolonged People's War), *Tendencia Poletaria* (Proletarian Tendency), and *Tendencia Tercerista* (or Insurrectionary Tendency). It was not until March 8, 1979, that the three Sandinista factions, with the mediation of Commander Fidel Castro, reconstituted a joint National Directorate through the reorganization of the entire opposition to Somoza by means of alliances and coalitions.

During the final insurrection, Daniel directed political-military operations throughout the different guerrilla fronts to defeat the Somoza dictatorship and its repressive National Guard. After the Triumph on July 19, 1979, as the Commander of the Revolution, Daniel Ortega Saavedra, at the age of 33, came to undertake relevant responsibilities as head of the government and the historic National Directorate of the FSLN party. He won in the presidential elections of November 1984, and on January 10, 1985, he was inaugurated as the first leftist president in the history of Nicaragua. Although, due to the war weariness of the Nicaraguan people and the fear of renewed U.S. military assault, the Sandinistas were defeated in the early elections in 1990, he continued to be engaged in the FSLN and civil struggles against three successive neoliberal regimes.

Daniel was democratically re-elected president for four successive terms in 2007–2011, 2011–2017, 2017–2022, and 2022–2026. It is these later years, the second stage of the Sandinista Revolution, which are so misunderstood and underappreciated, and it is therefore this stage upon which I focus my analysis.

Speaking at his presidential inauguration ceremony on January 10, 2007, Daniel Ortega proclaimed that "Nicaragua cannot be free with unemployed people, with people [living] in poverty. Nicaragua cannot be free with illiterate men and women. Nicaragua cannot be free with thousands of children who cannot go to school. Therefore, the challenges we have are immense."[454]

It goes without saying that the new Sandinista government in this second stage of the Revolution in 2007 immediately resumed the tasks it had begun in the first stage of the Revolution in the 1980s. Foremost amongst these tasks has been the reduction of illiteracy. Even before the 1979 Triumph, the FSLN had developed a literacy blueprint, which served as the starting point for the great National Literacy Crusade (*Campaña Nacional de Alphabetización, CNA*), dedicated to the "Heroes and Martyrs of the Liberation of Nicaragua."

Fifteen days after the Triumph, the new Government of National Reconstruction appointed Father Fernando Cardenal as coordinator of the CNA, and the planning and organization ensured a thriving inaugural ceremony and liftoff of the Ejército Popular de Alfabetización, EPA (People's Army of Literacy) in the Plaza of the Revolution on March 23, 1980. The EPA's civic mission was titanic. The illiteracy rate was 50.35%. But with the participation of 95,582 students, teachers, health workers, pedagogical advisors, drivers, office workers, and housewives, the goal to teach 406,056 Nicaraguans to read and write was achieved, reducing illiteracy to 12.96%, fulfilling the mandate of Commander Carlos Fonseca Amador in the guerrilla camps: ". . . and also teaching them to read." The CNA in Spanish officially ended on August 23, 1980, and on September 30 of the same year, literacy training in Miskito, Sumo, and Creole English to teach reading and writing to around 16,500 Nicaraguans began in the indigenous communities on the Caribbean Coast. Literacy training continued until 1990 under the responsibility of the Vice Ministry of Adult Education.[455]

Quite tragically, the successful literacy campaign of the Sandinistas was abandoned by the three consecutive neoliberal governments between 1990 and 2006. In effect, the governments of Violeta Barrios de Chamorro, Arnoldo Alemán, and Enrique Bolaños were responsible for increasing illiteracy rates, which rose to 20.5% in 2001 and 22% in 2006, according to surveys to measure the level of living conditions. Due to the efforts of the Sandinista government during the second phase of the Revolution since 2007, illiteracy has now been reduced between 4% and 6% in 2020 alone, and 98,274 youngsters and adults are integrated into the literacy and primary schooling programs.[456]

The end of the 1990–2006 neoliberal era generally saw the education system exhibit significant coverage and quality gaps, as well as low budget allocation, disconnection between educational programs, constrained institutional capacity, and degraded and inadequate infrastructure. One of the first actions of the Sandinista government in 2007 was the restitution of the right to free education at all levels, prohibiting in all public schools the tuition and monthly fees, and the sale of school supplies. In this direction, the budget allocation for investment in education went from C$4,409.8 million córdobas in 2006 to C$21,191.9 million córdobas in 2020, a 381% increase, despite the brutal economic impact of the failed coup attempt. In fact, the Sandinista government manages education (and healthcare) as a social investment and not as an expense.

In its National Plan against Poverty 2022–2025, the Nicaraguan government pointed to its achievements, as cited in a 2019 World Bank study carried out at the request of the Sandinista government:

> Nicaraguans have been reaching higher levels of education, both in urban and rural areas; likewise, young people present a better level of schooling. Already 40% of young adults report having completed secondary or some tertiary [vocational and/or university] education. Young adults, especially the 15-29 age group, are achieving better educational outcomes. In 2010, young people without any type of schooling amounted to 7%, a figure that was almost halved, to 4% in 2018; those who finished their secondary education increased from 15% to 21%, while the rate of completion of tertiary education increased from 13% to 19%.[457]

Another big issue for the Sandinistas has always been land reform and reclaiming the private holdings of the wealthy elites for the people. While the Sandinistas made great strides with such issues in the 1980s, many of the gains were reversed during the neoliberal period when many properties in the hands of the State, cooperatives, or individuals were returned or compensated multiple times to their former owners while others were irregularly occupied by new settlers. By issuing 427,434 property titles (255,818 in urban areas and 172,616 in rural regions) between 2007 and 2020, the Sandinista administration has helped to align, stabilize, and secure both private and communal property, including 23 indigenous communities in the Caribbean regions, and benefiting 235,089 women and 192,345 men, mostly from low-income households.[458]

In addition, since 2007, the Sandinista government has implemented a strategy to furnish an efficient road network and transportation service for all Nicaraguans, through the improvement and expansion of roads and bridges, emphasizing the interconnection of productive areas, in harmony with the environment. In this way, the goal is to ensure excellent coverage of essential social services (education, health, transport, etc.), recreational activities (tourism, sports, culture, etc.), and economic growth while integrating and aligning the entire country. By the end of the neoliberal period, in 2006, the road network had only 2,044 paved km, which were neglected with little or no maintenance.

From 2007 through 2020, the Sandinista government constructed and rehabilitated 3,794 km of roads, comprising 1,968 km of newly paved roads (asphalt, cobblestone, and hydraulic concrete) and 856 km of old paved roads and 970 km of unpaved roads. Likewise, the government has ensured the timely maintenance of 16,709 km of secondary roads and has built and rehabilitated 12,045 linear meters of bridges and 34,272 linear meters of drainage works. The areas in which the road infrastructure has been developed have become effective economic corridors that boost the supply chain from the production to distribution and marketing processes, substantially contributing to development and growth and influencing poverty reduction.[459] All of these accomplishments provide significant benefits to the Nicaraguan people and begin to close the gap between rich and poor. However, these achievements also exacerbate the inherent contradiction between class struggle, economic nationalism, sovereignty interests, and U.S.-led interventionism.

Among the other programs, the Zero Usury initiative aims to support and promote small, mostly women-owned enterprises in order to boost loan availability, decrease unemployment, and raise income. In order to make these businesses a tool in the battle against poverty, between 2007 and 2020, 396,394 participants (92,820 on an annual average) received 1,253,060 credits, totaling C$8,815 million, or C$653 million annually.[460]

Nicaragua's electricity coverage index went from 54% in 2006 to 98.5% in 2020. In 2006, only half of the population, mostly in the cities, had had access to inadequate electrical services. By the end of 2020, with the completion of 8,985 urban and rural electrification projects, 652,764 families now have safe and dependable access to electricity, benefiting nearly 6.4 million Nicaraguans. Similarly, the emphasis on transformation and diversification between 2007 and 2020 has significant policy consequences for the energy generation matrix, which has subsequently evolved into a dynamic element of the national economy. The installation of new power plants has increased electricity generation with renewable resources from 26% in 2006 to 75.94% in 2020. The diversification of the electricity generation matrix with renewable sources contributed in this period to the saving of 38.0 million barrels of derivatives of petroleum and ensured a reliable and clean supply of electricity to the Nicaraguan population.[461]

Alongside, between 2007 and 2020, the entire subsidies for energy, transportation, and retired workers totaled C$8,285 million córdobas, or an average of C$592 million córdobas annually. This is more than three times what the former neoliberal administrations granted in 2006.[462]

Kovalik had the opportunity to participate in a reforestation brigade in Ocotal, Nicaragua, in 1987. Since then, the Sandinista government has continued such projects during the second period of the Revolution. The government has been supporting a National Reforestation Crusade since 2007 and has now succeeded in reforesting 242,575 hectares (25.3% of the amount required). This has been accomplished despite the devastating effects of the failed coup attempt and the ongoing U.S.-led economic aggression. The government also continues to safeguard an average of 72 protected places each year, including water sources, private reserves, reserves designated as water zones, and marine and terrestrial areas. Additionally, an average of 82,980 hectares were scientifically identified, evaluated, and validated for their natural regeneration between the years 2014 and 2020.[463]

All advancement became possible once the budgetary allocation for investments in public health increased from C$3,088 million córdobas in 2006 to C$17,804 million córdobas in 2020, a rise of 476%. Thus, between 2007 and 2020, the Sandinista government carried out a social model that has harmonized a health system focused on the family and the community. In addition to policies for the promotion, prevention, education, treatment, and rehabilitation of the individual and the population, this model is strongly focused on the monitoring and evaluation of the factors that affect health through the infrastructure and network of health services.[464]

Just as in the 1980s, the U.S. has threatened to refuse to allow Nicaragua to proceed with this "dangerous example" of independent development and progressive social change. Indeed, ever since Daniel Ortega shocked the U.S. political establishment by again becoming president in 2007, the U.S. has engineered counterrevolutionary activity against Nicaragua, culminating in the violent coup attempt in 2018. At that time, with U.S. support, the right-wing coup leaders and their cadres in the *tranques* brought back, now in the cities, the terror attacks the Contras used to carry out in the countryside during the U.S. unconventional war in the 1980s. The key movers in this violent coup attempt were the big business community, represented by the Nicaraguan quasi-Chamber of Commerce (COSEP), sectors of the Roman Catholic Church and the MRS.

The troubles in 2018 were directly brought about by the demands of the U.S.-controlled IMF, which put pressure on the Nicaraguan government to cut back on its social programs and to implement measures targeting the livelihoods of the working class. Thus, the IMF asked for the doubling of worker's social security contributions, raising the statutory retirement age up to 65 years, and cutting spending on health care for insured workers, retirees, and pensioners. The government and the large workers' unions, on the other hand, wanted to improve the social security policy reforms, maintaining the retirement age at 60 years, the number of contributions to 750 weeks, a minimum on pensions, the bonus for retirees and pensioners, and the extensive healthcare programs for oncology, hemodialysis, and cardiac catheterization. These reforms would require a 3% increase in the employer's contribution quotas, a 0.75% increase in the worker's contribution quotas, and a 5% increase in deduction to existing pensions with a view to improving the quality of medical care for those insured workers, retirees, pensioners, and victims from the U.S.-backed Contra War in the 1980s who presently receive pension and medical care.

The reforms would also require removing the annual salary ceiling of C$80,000 córdobas (approximately US$2,500) to estimate the worker's pension plan contribution.[465] The National Institute of Social Security (INSS) had been used as a "petty cash" coffer during the sixteen years of neoliberal governments, and many social programs were reduced or eliminated. In 2007, the Sandinista government found that the INSS only provided 19,073 pensions for the mothers of the heroes and victims of the Contra War in the 1980s. Between 2007 and 2020, the revolutionary government increased the payment of each pension by 100% and awarded 29,611 new pensions for the mothers of heroes and victims of counterrevolutionary terrorism, despite the damages caused to the economy during the failed coup attempt in 2018.[466]

The COSEP's reaction, meanwhile, was as predictable as it was revealing. A few days before April 18, 2018, the COSEP delegation deserted the tripartite negotiation table (government, workers, and businesspeople), denouncing the government's proposal for social security reforms. It was the signal for the rest of the coup plotters to begin violent protests, mostly carried out by students and youths, paradoxically against social reforms that would not have directly affected the students.[467]

The COSEP, an NGO acting like a chamber of commerce, is easily the most antagonistic organization in Nicaragua. From its inception on February 16, 1972, the COSEP has had the ability to reshape itself quickly to fit immediate needs, from a neoconservative association of the wealthiest oligarchs and capitalists opposing Somoza's dictatorial oligopoly (1934–1979), to a reactionary entity supporting the U.S.-backed Contra terrorist war (1979–1990), to a neoliberal business organization promoting and participating in the corrupt privatization of the State assets and the dismantlement of the people's political, economic and social security rights (1990–2006). From January 2007 until April 2018, the COSEP formed part of a tripartite negotiating commission created by the Sandinista government, which was seeking to integrate peace and reconciliation into a comprehensive program to manage the disparate socioeconomic interests between the poor and the rich. Everything appeared fair. The rich were getting richer, and the poor were improving their livelihood, reflecting the most considerable poverty reduction program in Nicaragua's history.

While the mainstream press in Nicaragua and the so-called civilized West tried to portray the opposition movement in 2018 as peaceful and as a victim of Nicaraguan police repression, this portrayal was far from the truth. Indeed, the first person killed in the 2018 unrest was a police officer—Captain Hilton Rafael Manzanares Alvarado. He was killed in the line of duty by a sniper rifle bullet that impacted his chest during the self-proclaimed "peaceful protests" in Managua city at 9:00 pm on April 19, 2018. The first student killed, Cristhian Emilio Cadenas, was a member of the Sandinista Youth. He was killed at sunset on Friday, April 20, 2018, in León City, trapped and burned to death in the historic *Casa del Centro Universitario de la Universidad Nacional, CUUN* (University Center of the National University). He was a student of agroecology at the public university UNAN-León. At the National Federation of University Students (UNEN) congress in December 2018, Vice President Rosario Murillo said that the young Cristhian had already left the CUUN building, but armed protesters had started shooting at him to force him to re-enter the building. The protesters then set the building on fire.[468]

Soon, the *tranques,* or roadblocks, mentioned above, were set up throughout major cities in Nicaragua. These blockades on streets and roads made possible the burning, looting, theft, and destruction of infrastructure and vehicles in the public and private sectors and imposed high socioeconomic costs in health, trade, free movement, and education, among others. The roadblocks also interfered in the implementation of the National Dialogue because, for the elements in the trenches, the agreements reached by the negotiation table were meaningless, and the number of violent crimes continued to rise in the country. In remote places, far from journalists and cameras, people became hostages.

The opposition minions unleashed a widespread and gruesome terror through the kidnapping of bystanders, public officials, and Sandinista sympathizers to create insecurity and torture victims with beatings, whipping, rapes, broken bones, burns with chemical substances, or fire to the point of death.[469] They also forced them to witness the torture of other victims or family members, with girls and women in the *tranques,* victims of sexual abuse, degrading treatment, and torture. There were many cases of maternal and infant mortality when women, forced by the roadblocks, gave birth on the roads, or could not reach a maternity clinic.[470] Likewise, the roadblocks caused deaths by denying the circulation of vehicles and ambulances and the provision of medical assistance to chronic patients, in some cases by charging tolls[471] or destroying the vehicles and ambulances, including Red Cross ambulances.[472]

Meanwhile, from the roadblocks, the coup plotters tried to demoralize the people, terrorizing and committing horrendous crimes against thousands of citizens and police officers. On May 7, at the roadblock in *Hertylandia* near the city of Jinotepe, the coup plotters kidnapped the young police officer, Yadira Ramos, who was riding with her husband on a motorcycle. They murdered her spouse and subjected her to torture and rape for three days.[473] As in other politically motivated hate crimes, the coup plotters filmed and uploaded thousands of videos showing their terrorist acts to online platforms. Yadira was rescued, but she was never able to recover from the physical and psychological trauma.

Hundreds of other people and police were less lucky to survive the roadblocks. A 23-year-old police officer, Gabriel de Jesús Vado Ruiz, was kidnapped at the Mebasa roadblock, on the *Las Flores-Catarina* road in Masaya on July 15. Gabriel was tortured, dragged on the road and burned alive at 1:00 p.m. The putschists filmed and displayed his mutilated body, mocking the corpse. You could call it all a satanic and terrorist ritual. Priest Harvin Padilla, from San Juan Bautista parish in Masaya, led the terrorists who grossly murdered Gabriel. In audio through a well-known messaging application, he tells them, "[...] the parishioners of Pacaya told me there that the riot police have already entered that place and that they are coming to Masaya.... hold these paramilitaries, tie them down no matter what, because that's good evidence for international [organizations] ...." Concerning the murder of the police officer, Padilla adds, "find how to tie him up and how to hide him, even if it's in a shithole ... [And] don't upload that photo and video of the paramilitary that you are burning [to death] so that there is no problem .... Likewise, we must delete these photos."[474]

Francisco Ramón Aráuz Pineda and Antonio Fernández, two civilians, were also abducted, tortured, and killed by coup plotters in the early morning of June 16 at a roadblock close to the university UPOLI.[475] Francisco was a historic FSLN guerrilla who was just 16 years old in 1979, the year he saw the Revolution Triumph. One of his siblings, Armengol, barely 17 years old, had died soon before the Triumph while fighting the Somoza's National Guard in the city of Matagalpa. Francisco was the son of Amada Pineda Montenegro, a peasant of the legendary Mujeres del Cuá (Women from the Cuá county), who demanded better working conditions from landowners by organizing with their husbands and relatives into fledgling unions at a time when the National Guard was ramping up its persecution of peasant unionists in the countryside and the mountains. Amada was raped and tortured while she was detained during the Somoza dictatorship. In the coup plotters' films posted on social media, Francisco is tortured before his unconscious body is lit on fire, as some criminals gleefully jumped around him.

At a certain point in May, the coup leaders announced the "liberation" of Masaya city, claiming their seizure of power in order to create a transitional government.[476] No one could dispute anymore that the roadblocks were designed to execute a coup d'état and were carried out by an extensive network of leaders and members of NGOs sponsored by the United States and the Catholic Church. The coup plotters took advantage of the fact that the National Police remained in their barracks as part of an agreement reached at the National Dialogue table and in compliance with a presidential order. On July 17, the National Police finally unblocked streets and roads with the help of municipal workers, volunteer police, and former Sandinista combatants from the 1980s.

The coup plotters committed hundreds of politically motivated hate crimes, albeit blaming crimes on the Sandinista government: the classic propaganda scenarios where the victims are blamed or where the victims are turned into criminals. One of the worst situations occurred in the early hours of June 16 in the Carlos Marx neighborhood of Managua, when masked elements threw Molotov cocktails into the Velásquez family's three-story house. The fire spread quickly from the first floor, used for the family business of manufacturing mattresses, to the living areas upstairs where the family was beginning its day. Six people were burnt alive, including a baby and a two-year-old girl. Only two young daughters survived. This could have been a self-inflicted blow to the fake peaceful image of the protesters, but without any investigation, an executive member of the former opposition NGO CENIDH, "who happened to be on-site," immediately blamed the fire on government supporters, calling it an act of State terrorism.[477] This was deliberately deceptive disinformation, as the extremist opponents killed and blamed others. On December 19 of the same year, the National Police clarified the case against the Velásquez family, describing the criminal action as terrorism and arson, as well as presenting two detainees and a list of fugitives who had participated in the crimes.[478]

By the end of July 2018, the reports from the different municipalities indicated that the *tranques* caused 140 deaths or 55.3% of the total fatalities and hundreds more injured victims during the failed coup d'état.[479] The coup leaders, however, suffered no remorse and ordered that their cadres continue recklessly carrying out violent assaults throughout the country.

Again, sectors of the Roman Catholic Church were key organizers and participants in the 2018 violence. This is crucial to understand as some of the offending clergy are now being held responsible for their crimes—much to the relief of most Nicaraguans. For example, in one of the two high-quality audios from this period that was later revealed, Bishop Silvio Báez described the *tranques* as "an extraordinary idea" while expressing a desire for the assassination of President Daniel Ortega,[480] adding that "the government needs to be pressured again so [the Sandinistas] ask the Episcopal Conference to resume the [National] Dialogue. The option of putting the *tranques* up again has been thought about. . . ."[481] He proposes that the [so-called] Blue and White National Unity [coup group] should include all adversaries to the Sandinista government, expressing with scornful derision, "even if there is suspicion that [they are] opportunists, abortionists, homosexuals, drug traffickers [. . .] to achieve the final goal. . . ."[482] The audios were allegedly recorded during a plotting session to bring about a resurgence of the failed coup d'état—and, to no one's surprise, the anti-Sandinista media rushed to deride the authenticity of the lengthy recordings vehemently.[483] However, given the overwhelming evidence, Cardinal Leopoldo Brenes could not excuse Báez's unjustifiable and criminal activities by refusing to confirm the authenticity of the audio.[484] Bishop Báez did not challenge the recordings and on the contrary wrote without remorse of his participation in the meeting that "I will continue my struggle from Nicaragua, since it is a duty that God has entrusted to me."[485] Months after the denunciation and petition to the Pope written by a Christian community (*Comunidad eclesial de base de la Colonia 14 de septiembre*) and signed by almost 500,000 Nicaraguans, the Vatican rescinded his auxiliary bishopric of Managua. Bishop Báez left Nicaragua on April 23, 2019. He now resides in Rome and Miami, where he is actively engaged in political and social networks against the Sandinista Revolution.

On June 6, 2018, the opposition newspaper *La Prensa*[486] reported that the Bishop of Estelí, Abelardo Mata, had met with Vice President Mike Pence at the White House on May 30 to discuss "the sociopolitical crisis and the religious persecution of the Catholic Church" in Nicaragua. In "their lengthy and very deep conversation," according to Mata, he would have informed Pence "concretely the things that we are experiencing in the country." Bishop Mata has consistently held a strong anti-Sandinista political attitude since the 1980s, and his actions during the coup attempt and National Dialogue negotiations were no exception.[487]

Indeed, the Nicaraguan Episcopal Conference's most hardliner bishops—Silvio Báez, Rolando Álvarez, and Abelardo Mata—actively participated in the protests from April to July 2018, and beyond, as evidenced by the Church's full support for the self-proclaimed civic society, which Báez, according to himself, assembled from the U.S.-funded NGO network during the first round of negotiations at the National Dialogue table in May 2018. As a result, the Catholic Church abandoned its role as mediator and religious conciliator, establishing itself as party to the conflict.[488]

As a result of the coup violence, 198 civilians and 22 police officers (twenty men and two women) were murdered,[489] and over 1,846 civilians and 418 police officers were wounded.[490] In the end, the failed coup attempt's social and economic costs are comparable to those of the 1972 Managua earthquake, which left the capital city in ruins, and are more than three times more devastating than those of Hurricane Mitch in 1998. In addition to severe damage amounting to US$231 million in tourism, US$525 million in transportation, and US$63 million in social security due to lost contributions,[491] the government reported that the terrorist actions caused US$207 million in direct damage, including US$174 million in public and private buildings partially and totally destroyed; US$9.5 million in furniture and computer equipment destroyed or stolen; US$7.6 million in heavy equipment destroyed; US$9.1 million in other assets destroyed or damaged; and US$6.1 million in extraordinary expenses in materials, goods, and services. The country's municipal infrastructure suffered the most, with damages totaling US$148 million, followed by damage to main roads and other road infrastructure worth US$39.6 million, damage to the National Police infrastructure value US$5.7 million, and damage to other public institutions for US$13.4 million.[492]

Despite all of this, the Sandinista government offered amnesty to the violent coup plotters upon certain conditions. This amnesty and its conditions are crucial to understand in light of the current debate surrounding the arrests of various figures involved in the violence of 2018 who received amnesty but went on to violate the terms of the amnesty.

Following a new round of negotiations in a modified version of the National Dialogue between March and April 2019, the Sandinista government made a significant step toward peace and stability by passing three laws: Law 985 for a Culture of Dialogue, Reconciliation, Security, Work, and Peace of January 28, 2019; Law 994 of Comprehensive Attention to Victims of the coup attempt of May 31, 2019; and Amnesty Law 996 of June 10, 2019.[493] The amnesty law, in particular, granted the release of all individuals prosecuted for having allegedly participated in crimes such as homicide, murder, violation, damage, robbery, unlawful possession of firearms, and terrorism, among other acts of violence between April 18, 2018, and June 10, 2019, and extending to people who were under investigation or had not been probed. The amnesty bill was also one of the instruments for compensating victims, families, and communities harmed by the coup attempt.[494]

During the first semester of 2019, a total of 306 detainees were released under the amnesty law to help the Nicaraguan people achieve peace, reconciliation, economic recovery, development, and social well-being.[495] Enacting an amnesty law that grants an official pardon to all alleged criminals participating in the failed coup attempt in 2018 was a courageous decision, but it was unsurprising for the "most steadfast and generous in victory" Sandinistas, who took the name Government of National Reconciliation and Unity (GRUN for its Spanish abbreviation) in 2007. Needless to say, implementing amnesty was a difficult pill to swallow, particularly for the families of victims and survivors of the bloody sieges, kidnappings, tortures, rapes, robberies, homicides, and killing sprees, for whom it was exceedingly difficult to see terrorism perpetrators walk free.[496]

Moreover, the 2019 amnesty law has a caveat: Article 3 literally establishes that "[t]he persons benefited by this Law must refrain from perpetuating new acts that incur in repetitive behaviors that generate the crimes contemplated therein. The non-observance of the principle of non-repetition results in the revocation of the benefit established by this Law."[497]

Despite this quite extraordinary exercise of forgiveness and reconciliation, the coup leaders in the Nicaraguan Catholic

Church and the U.S.-supported NGOs do not regard this legal caveat to be a deterrent and take no notice of it. As anticipated, the opposition side, together with their U.S. handlers, still tries to play the political persecution card and cause by contending, notwithstanding the amnesty, that common criminals currently incarcerated in Nicaragua's jails are in fact "political prisoners." This is one of their primary fabricated justifications for seeking foreign media coverage. Additionally, they keep pushing for additional economic sanctions against Nicaragua—and the U.S. keeps paying them for these misdeeds. The opposition's lobbying has made it abundantly obvious that their sole goal is to gain power at all costs.

Since the amnesty law grants pardons to those allegedly involved in crimes between April 18, 2018, and June 10, 2019, it is not surprising that the Attorney General's Office, with the assistance of the National Police, has initiated judicial proceedings against elements who defiantly continue to carry out crimes through a network of NGOs sponsored by the United States, the United Kingdom, and the European Union. These new court cases are peculiar in that some coup middle-level leaders and cadres are finally being brought to justice and put under judicial investigation and arrest, even though they considered themselves immune and deliberately ignored the *non-repetition* proviso of the amnesty law.

The amnesty was a decisive step toward family and community reconciliation, since it was intended to lead to forgiveness and peaceful and respectful coexistence among Nicaragua's various social and political sectors. The Sandinistas' willingness to achieve peace and security by forgiving those responsible for such heinous crimes as kidnapping, torturing, and killing people, as well as burning down homes, daycare centers, universities, schools, markets, ambulances, and other public buildings and cultural heritage monuments, is consistent with their long history of pardoning their adversaries.

At the same time, the U.S., as per its usual *modus operandi*, will continue to try to exploit the Sandinistas' benevolence in an attempt to destroy them. The U.S. goal remains to eradicate the

Sandinistas as a political alternative to the old elite they back, because the Sandinistas dare to represent the needs and dreams of the people rather than the demands of U.S. transnational corporations.[498] Fortunately, thanks to Kovalik, this book is a testament to this stark reality.

Orlando Zelaya Olivas

ENDNOTES

1. Jon Lee Anderson, "Oscar Romero Becomes a Saint," *The New Yorker*, October 22, 2018. https://www.newyorker.com/news/daily-comment/archbishop-oscar-romero-becomes-a-saint-but-his-death-still-haunts-el-salvador.
2. Zinn Information Project, https://www.zinnedproject.org/news/tdih/ben-linder-murdered-nicaragua/
3. Zinn Information Project.
4 Erika Takeo, "Remembering Ben Linder's legacy through the Ben Linder Solidarity School," *Tortilla con Sal* (July 21, 2021). https://tortillaconsal.com/tortilla/node/12478.
5. *See*, https://blog.pmpress.org/authors-artists-comrades/s-brian-willson/
6. Michael J. Schroeder, "Social Memory and Tactical Doctrine: The Air War in Nicaragua during the Sandino Rebellion, 1927–1932," *The International History Review* 29, no. 3 (Sep., 2007): 508–549. https://www.jstor.org/stable/40110855.
7. Schroeder, "Social Memory and Tactical Doctrine."
8. Aleynes Palacios Hurtado, "Latin America and the Caribbean are nobody's yard, Cuba says," Prensa Latina News, last modified January 22, 2022, https://www.plenglish.com/news/2022/01/22/latin-america-and-the-caribbean-are-nobodys-yard-cuba-says/.
9. *See*, "Harold Pinter—Lecture: 'Art, Truth & Politics'" (pre-recorded and shown on video December 7, 2005), The Nobel Prize in Literature 2005, https://www.nobelprize.org/prizes/literature/2005/pinter/lecture/. [Excerpts reprinted herein with permission of the Nobel Committee.
10. U.S. State Department, Office of the Historian, "Monroe Doctrine, 1823," *Milestones: 1801–1829,* https://history.state.gov/milestones/1801-1829/monroe.
11. "Monroe Doctrine, 1823."
12. "Monroe Doctrine, 1823."
13. Richard W. van Alstyne, "The Panama Canal: A Classical Case of an Imperial Hangover," *Journal of Contemporary History* 15, no. 2 (Apr., 1980): 301.
14. *See*, Text of the Clayton-Bulwer Treaty, Organization of American States, https://www.oas.org/sap/peacefund/belizeandguatemala/timelinedocuments/TheClayton-BulwerTreaty-English.pdf.
15. Kinzer, *Overthrow.*
16. U.S. Department of State, Office of the Historian, "Message from the president of the United States, transmitting a convention between the United States and Great Britain, to facilitate the construction of a ship canal to connect the Atlantic and Pacific Oceans, signed at Washington, November 18, 1901,"

Papers Relating to the Foreign Relations of the United States, With the Annual Message of the President Transmitted to Congress December 3, 1901, https://history.state.gov/historicaldocuments/frus1901/d233.

17. U.S. State Department, Office of the Historian, "Milestones, 1899–1913: Building the Panama Canal, 1903–1914," *Milestones: 1899–1913,* https://history.state.gov/milestones/1899-1913/panama-canal.

18. Eduardo Galeano, *The Open Veins of Latin America: Five Centuries of the Pillage of a Continent* (New York: Monthly Review Press, 1997), 107.

19. Suzanne Daley, "Lost in Nicaragua: A Chinese Tycoon's Canal Project," *The New York Times,* April 3, 2016, https://www.nytimes.com/2016/04/04/world/americas/nicaragua-canal-chinese-tycoon.html.

20. Howard Zinn, *The Politics of History,* Second Ed. (Urbana and Chicago: University of Illinois Press, 1990), xvi.

21. *See,* Benjamin J. Swenson, "The Obits of William Walker, Filibustering President of Nicaragua," *The History Avenue,* April 9, 2022, https://the-history-avenue.eu/2022/04/09/the-obits-of-william-walker-filibustering-president-of-nicaragua/.

22. Swenson, "The Obits of William Walker."

23. Galeano, *The Open Veins of Latin America.*

24. Galeano, *The Open Veins of Latin America.*

25. Kinzer, *Overthrow.*

26. Jonathan M. Katz, *Gangsters of Capitalism: Smedley Butler, The Marines, and the Making and Breaking of America's Empire* (New York: Saint Martin's Press, 2021), 133.

27. Kinzer, *Overthrow.*

28. Kinzer, *Overthrow.*

29. Galeano, *The Open Veins of Latin America.*

30. Galeano, *The Open Veins of Latin America.*

31. Katz, *Gangsters of Capitalism,* 134.

32. Katz.

33. Katz, 137.

34. Katz, 143.

35. Katz, 144.

36. Chomsky, Noam. *Turning The Tide, U.S. Intervention in Central America and the Struggle for Peace.* (Chicago: Haymarket Books, 2015) 6–7.

37. U.S. Department of State, Office of the Historian, "Dollar Diplomacy, 1909–1913," *Milestones: 1899–1913,* https://history.state.gov/milestones/1899-1913/dollar-diplo.

38. Katz, 143.

39. Katz, 143.

40. Smedley D. Butler, *War is a Racket* (Feral House, August 1, 2003; first published November 1935).

41. Samuel Clemens, as quoted in Anri Ichimura, "'Let Men Die to Make Us Rich': How Mark Twain Used Poetry to Oppose the U.S.–Philippine War," *Esquire Magazine,* January 4, 2020, https://www.esquiremag.ph/long-reads/features/mark-twain-philippines-a00304-20200104.

42. Samuel Clemens, "Comments on the Moro Massacre," March 12, 1906, as quoted in "History as a Weapon," https://www.historyisaweapon.com/defcon1/clemensmoromassacre.html.

43. British Frank, "The Philippines Genocide: 3 million Filipinos Killed," *Pan-Asian Blogspot* (blog), April 25, 2017, updated July 2, 2019, http://pan-asian.blogspot.com/2019/07/the-philippines-genocide-3-million.html. *Also see,* E. Ahmed, "The Theory and Fallacies of Counter-Insurgency," *The Nation,* August 2, 1971.

44. *See,* John Perkins, *The New Confessions of an Economic Hitman* (New York: Berett-Koeler Publishers, Inc., 2016).

45. Katz, *Gangsters of Capitalism.*

46. Katz.

47. Scott Mobley, "'By the Force of Our Arms': William D. Leahy and the U.S. Intervention in Nicaragua, 1912," *Federal History* (2019): 45–47, http://www.shfg.org/resources/Documents/4-Mobley.pdf.

48. Mobley.

49. Mobley, 52.

50. Mobley, 54.

51. Katz, 157.

52. Katz.

53. U.S. Library of Congress, "U.S. Intervention: 1909–1933," *Country Studies – Nicaragua,* http://countrystudies.us/nicaragua/10.htm.

54. Emma Thomasson, "World Court Upholds 1928 treaty on Colombian Islands," *Reuters,* December 13, 2007, https://www.reuters.com/article/us-colombia-nicaragua-court-idUSN1323732520071214.

55. Stephanie van den Berg, "World Court Rules Colombia Must Cease Activities in Nicaraguan Maritime Zone," *USA Today,* April 21, 2022, https://www.usnews.com/news/world/articles/2022-04-21/world-court-rules-colombia-must-cease-activities-in-nicaraguan-maritime-zone.

56. Schroeder, "Social Memory and Tactical Doctrine."

57. U.S. Library of Congress, "U.S. Intervention: 1909–1933."

58. U.S. Library of Congress, "U.S. Intervention: 1909–1933."

59. Schroeder, "Social Memory and Tactical Doctrine."

60. U.S. Library of Congress, "U.S. Intervention: 1909–1933."

61. U.S. Library of Congress, "U.S. Intervention: 1909–1933."

62. U.S. Library of Congress, "U.S. Intervention: 1909–1933."

63. Schroeder, "Social Memory and Tactical Doctrine."

64. Schroeder, Michael. "The Sandino Rebellion, Nicaragua 1927–1934, a documentary history," http://www.sandinorebellion.com/.

65. Schroeder, "The Sandino Rebellion, Nicaragua 1927–1934."

66. Schroeder, "Social Memory and Tactical Doctrine."

67. Schroeder, "Social Memory and Tactical Doctrine."

68. Schroeder, "Social Memory and Tactical Doctrine."

69. Schroeder, "Social Memory and Tactical Doctrine."

70. Schroeder, "Social Memory and Tactical Doctrine."

71. Schroeder, "Social Memory and Tactical Doctrine."

72. U.S. Library of Congress, "U.S. Intervention: 1909–1933."

73. Galeano, *The Open Veins of Latin America,* 110–111.

74. U.S. Library of Congress, "The Somoza Era: 1936–1974," *Country Studies – Nicaragua,* http://countrystudies.us/nicaragua/11.htm.

75. U.S. Library of Congress, *Country Studies – Nicaragua.*

76. Dianna Melrose, *Nicaragua: The Danger of a Good Example* (Oxfam, 1985), https://oxfamilibrary.openrepository.com/bitstream/10546/121188/5/bk-threat-good-example-nicaragua-010189-en.pdf.

77. Noam Chomsky and Edward S. Herman, *The Washington Connection and Third World Fascism (The Political Economy of Human Rights – Volume I)* (South End Press, 1979), 284.

78. Melrose, *Nicaragua*.

79. "Company of U.S.-backed Somoza sucked Nicaraguan Bloody, literally," *Telesur*, July 19, 2016, https://www.telesurenglish.net/news/Company-of-US-backed-Somoza-Sucked-Nicaraguan-Blood--Literally-20160719-0022.html.

80. "Company of U.S.-backed Somoza sucked Nicaraguan Bloody, literally,"

81. "Company of U.S.-backed Somoza sucked Nicaraguan Bloody, literally,"

82. Rose George, "The Problem with the Plasma," *Science Friday*, October 25, 2018, https://www.sciencefriday.com/articles/the-problem-with-the-plasma/.

83. Jorge Castillo, "Remembering Roberto Clemente as a Black man who fought against racial injustice," *L.A. Times*, September 8, 2020, https://www.latimes.com/sports/dodgers/story/2020-09-08/roberto-clemente-fought-racial-injustice.

84. Castillo, "Remembering Roberto Clemente."

85. "Beyond Baseball: The Life of Roberto Clemente," http://www.robertoclemente.si.edu/english/virtual_story_nicaragua_09.htm.

86. Gerald K. Haines, "CIA and Guatemala Assassination Proposals, 1952–1954", CIA History Staff Analysis, June 1995, National Security Archives, https://nsarchive2.gwu.edu/NSAEBB/NSAEBB4/docs/doc01.pdf.

87. U.S. State Department, Office of the Historian, "154. Editorial Note," *Foreign Relations of the United States, 1950–1955, The Intelligence Community, 1950–1955,* https://history.state.gov/historicaldocuments/frus1950-55Intel/d154.

88. USC Shoah Foundation, "Guatemalan Genocide," https://sfi.usc.edu/collections/guatemalan.

89. CIA, *Official History of the Bay of Pigs Operation, Volume II: Participation in the Conduct of Foreign Policy,* National Security Archives, https://nsarchive2.gwu.edu/NSAEBB/NSAEBB353/bop-vol2-part1.pdf.

90. CIA, *Official History of the Bay of Pigs Operation, Volume II.*

91. CIA, *Official History of the Bay of Pigs Operation, Volume III: Evolution of CIA's Anti-Castro Policies, 1951–January 1961,* National Security Archives, https://nsarchive2.gwu.edu/NSAEBB/NSAEBB353/BayOfPigsHistory_Vol3.pdf.

92. Wikileaks, "Department of State, 1976 regarding $600,000 military proposal for Nicaragua in year 1977," Cable: 1976MANAGU00867_b (wikileaks.org).

93. Programa Histórico del FSLN, May 11, 2011, http://revolucionsandinista.blogspot.com/search/label/Programa%20Hist%C3%B3rico%20del%20FSLN. Translated with www.DeepL.com/Translator (free version).

94. Programa Histórico del FSLN.

95. Wikileaks, "1976 Memo on agricultural loan to Nicaragua in light of Somoza's human rights abuses," Cable: 1976STATE288351_b (wikileaks.org).

96. Stephen Sefton, "Remembering Carlos Fonseca, Architect of the Sandinista Revolution," *Telesur*, November 5, 2015, https://www.telesurenglish.net/bloggers/Remembering-Carlos-Fonseca-Architect-of-the-Sandinista-Revolution-20151105-0001.html.

97. Stephen Sefton.
98. U.S. Department of State, [unclassified] Memorandum of Conversation of June 8, 1976 in Santiago, Chile (President Pinochet's Office), *Homeland Security Digital Library,* https://www.hsdl.org/?view&did=438484.
99. "Pinochet held on Murder and Torture Charges," *The Guardian,* October 30, 2006, https://www.theguardian.com/world/2006/oct/30/chile.pinochet.
100. Jonathan Franklin, "Pinochet directly ordered killing on U.S. soil of Chilean diplomat, papers reveal," *The Guardian,* October 8, 2015, https://www.theguardian.com/world/2015/oct/08/pinochet-directly-ordered-washington-killing-diplomat-documents-orlando-letelier-declassified.
101. Jonathan Franklin.
102. Julian Borger, "Kissinger backed Dirty War in Argentina against the Left," *The Guardian,* August 27, 2004, https://www.theguardian.com/world/2004/aug/28/argentina.julianborger.
103. Julian Borger.
104. David B. Rivkin, Jr., and Darin R. Bartram, "Wanted: Henry Kissinger," *Wall Street Journal,* April 22, 2002, https://www.wsj.com/articles/SB1019423836817291120.
105. George Evans, "The Deaths of Somoza," *World Literature Today,* May 2007, https://www.worldliteraturetoday.org/deaths-somoza-george-evans.
106. Inter-American Commission on Human Rights (IACHR), "Report on the Situation of Human Rights in Nicaragua," November 17, 1978, http://cidh.org/countryrep/Nicaragua78eng/intro.htm.
107. George Evans, "The Deaths of Somoza."
108. IACHR.
109. IACHR.
110. IACHR.
111. IACHR.
112. IACHR.
113. IACHR.
114. IACHR.
115. Chomsky and Herman, 286–287.
116. Chomsky and Herman, 286–287.
117. Dana Priest, "U.S. Instructed Latins on Executions, Torture," *Washington Post,* September 21, 1996, https://www.washingtonpost.com/archive/politics/1996/09/21/us-instructed-latins-on-executions-torture/f7d86816-5ab3-4cf0-9df6-f430c209392f/.
118. Anastasia Maloney, "Silence Surrounds Colombia's 92,000 Disappeared: ICRC," *Reuters,* August 29, 2014, https://www.reuters.com/article/us-foundation-colombia-missing/silence-surrounds-colombias-92000-disappeared-icrc-idUSKBN0GT22520140829.
119. Oscar Lopez, "GONE: Nearly 100,000 people have disappeared in Mexico. Their families now search for clues among the dead," *The New York Times,* October 3, 2021, https://www.nytimes.com/interactive/2021/10/03/world/americas/mexico-missing-people.html.
120. IAHCR.
121. V.G. Kiernan, *America: The New Imperialism, From White Settlement to World Hegemony* (London, New York: Verso, 2005), 330–331.

122. IAHCR.

123. Barbara Myers, "The Secret Origins of the CIA's Torture Program and the Forgotten Man Who Tried to Expose It," *The Nation*, June 1, 2015, https://www.thenation.com/article/archive/secret-origins-cias-torture-program-and-forgotten-man-who-tried-expose-it/.

124. Barbara Myers.

125. Kenneth E. Morris, *Unfinished Revolution: Daniel Ortega and Nicaragua's Struggle for Liberation* (Lawrence Hill Books, 2010), 48–57.

126. Kenneth E. Morris, *Unfinished Revolution*.

127. Morris.

128. Morris.

129. Morris.

130. Katz, *Gangsters of Capitalism*, 138–143.

131. Morris.

132. Philip Davidson, "Tomás Borge: Last Surviving Founder of the Sandinistas," *The Independent*, May 1, 2012, https://www.independent.co.uk/news/obituaries/tomas-borge-last-surviving-founder-of-the-sandinistas-7704217.html.

133. Noam Chomsky, "The Responsibility of Intellectuals, Redux," *Boston Review*, September 11, 2011, https://bostonreview.net/articles/noam-chomsky-responsibility-of-intellectuals-redux/.

134. Tomás Borge, *Christianity and Revolution: Tomás Borge's Theology of Life* (Orbis Books, 1987).

135. *Report of the Amnesty International Missions to the Republic of Nicaragua, August 1979, January 1980 and August 1980* (Amnesty International Publications, 1982).

136. Salman Rushdie, *The Jaguar Smile: A Nicaraguan Journey.* (New York: Viking Press, 1987), 35–36.

137. Carlos M. Vilas, *The Sandinista Revolution: National Liberation and Social Transformation in Central America* (Monthly Review Press, 1986), 137–143.

138. Vilas.

139. Chomsky and Herman, 283–285.

140. Chomsky and Herman, 283–285.

141. Chomsky and Herman, 283–285.

142. Chomsky and Herman, 283–285.

143. Vilas.

144. Chomsky and Herman, 291–294.

145. Chomsky and Herman, 291–294.

146. Chomsky and Herman, 291–294.

147. Chomsky and Herman, 291–294.

148. Chomsky and Herman, 291–294.

149. Vilas, 138–143.

150. Vilas, 138–143.

151. Vilas, 138–143.

152. Vilas.

153. Morris, 74–75.

154. Matilde Zimmerman, *Sandinista: Carlos Fonseca and the Nicaraguan Revolution* (Duke University Press Books, 2001), 209.

155. Kenneth E. Morris, *Unfinished Revolution*, 97–101.
156. Morris, 97–101.
157. Chomsky and Herman, 294–296.
158. Chomsky and Herman, 294–296.
159. Chomsky and Herman, 294–296.
160. Chomsky and Herman, 294–296.
161. Matilde Zimmerman, *Sandinista*, 209.
162. Morris, 105.
163. Morris, 110.
164. Tomás Borge, *Christianity and Revolution*, 2.
165. Borge, 2.
166. *See*, Noam Chomsky, "The Responsibility of Intellectuals, Redux," *Boston Review*, September 1, 2011.
167. Ken Klippenstein, "America's dirty history exposed: FBI investigated US-backed assassination of Salvadoran Archbishop Oscar Romero," *The Grayzone*, October 12, 2016, https://thegrayzone.com/2016/10/12/fbi-us-assassination-oscar-romero/.
168. Stephanie M. Huezo, "The Murdered Churchwomen in El Salvador," *Origins*, December 2020, https://origins.osu.edu/milestones/murdered-churchwomen-el-salvador.
169. The Center for Justice and Accountability, "Where We Work: El Salvador," https://cja.org/where-we-work/el-salvador/.
170. The Center for Justice and Accountability.
171. Tomás Borge, *Christianity and Revolution*, 1.
172. Walter LaFeber, William, *Inevitable Revolutions: The United States in Central America* (W. W. Norton & Co., 1983; 2nd. ed., 1993).
173. Peter R. Mitchell and John Schoeffel (Eds.), *Understanding Power: The Indispensable Chomsky*, 1st Edition, 9th printing (The New Press, 2002).
174. *Live From Nicaragua: Uprising or Coup? A Reader* (The Alliance for Global Justice, updated June 2019), 22, https://www.tortillaconsal.com/live_from_nicaragua_june_2019.pdf.
175. Melrose, *Nicaragua*, 15.
176. Melrose, *Nicaragua*, 21.
177. Gary Prevost, "The Nicaraguan Revolution: Six Years after the Sandinista Electoral Defeat," *Third World Quarterly* 17, no. 2 (June 1996): 307–308, https://www.jstor.org/stable/3993095.
178. Melrose, *Nicaragua*, 11.
179. Rushdie, *The Jaguar Smile*, 27.
180. Melrose, *Nicaragua*, 12.
181. Melrose, *Nicaragua*, 13.
182. Melrose, *Nicaragua*, 14.
183. Melrose, *Nicaragua*, 15–26.
184. Prevost, 308.
185. Erika Takeo and Rohan Rice, "Women's struggle in Nicaragua: From liberation fighters to building an alternative society," *People's Dispatch*, November 4, 2021, https://peoplesdispatch.org/2021/11/04/womens-struggle-in-nicaragua-from-liberation-fighters-to-building-an-alternative-society/?eType=EmailBlastContent&eId=e5e7ac9e-db64-4b8d-bd6f-5e892debb268.

186. Takeo and Rice.
187. Helen Collinson et al., *Women and Revolution in Nicaragua* (Zed Books, 1990), cited in Rohan.
188. Takeo and Rice.
189. Takeo and Rice.
190. Melrose, *Nicaragua*, 19.
191. Melrose, *Nicaragua*, 19.
192. Melrose, *Nicaragua*, 19.
193. Vilas, 145.
194. Vilas, 146.
195. Vilas, 146.
196. Fairness & Accuracy in Reporting (FAIR), "Lie: The Sandinistas Won't Submit to Fair Elections," October 1, 1987, https://fair.org/extra/lie-the-sandinistas-wont-submit-to-free-elections/.
197. FAIR.
198. FAIR.
199. FAIR.
200. Michael Parenti, "Left anti-communism: The Unkindest Cut," *Blackshirts and Reds: Rational Fascism and the Overthrow of Communism* (San Francisco: City Lights Publishers, 1997); posted online by Connolly Youth Movement on April 1, 2020, https://cym.ie/2020/04/01/left-anti-communism-the-unkindest-cut-by-michael-parenti/.
201. "Throwback Thursday: Che Guevara on U.S.-Cuba relations in 1964," video posted on CBS *Face the Nation* YouTube, January 22, 2015 (RT 3:07), https://www.youtube.com/watch?v=xELHGR_ur0Q.
202. Office of the Historian, U.S. State Department. "Central America, 1981–1988," *Milestones: 1981–1988,* https://history.state.gov/milestones/1981-1988/central-america.
203. "The Counterrevolutionaries ('The Contras')," *Understanding the Iran-Contra Affairs,* Brown University, https://www.brown.edu/Research/Understanding_the_Iran_Contra_Affair/n-contras.php.
204. "The Counterrevolutionaries."
205. "The Counterrevolutionaries."
206. "The Counterrevolutionaries."
207. "The Counterrevolutionaries."
208. Michael Shapiro, "Bilingual-Bicultural Education in Nicaragua's Atlantic Coast Region," *Latin American Perspectives* 14, no. 1, *On the Revolutionary Transformation of Nicaragua* (Winter 1987), 67–86, https://www.jstor.org/stable/2633674; and, Richard L. Harris, "The Revolutionary Transformation of Nicaragua," *Latin American Perspectives* 14, no. 1, 3–18, https://www.jstor.org/stable/2633671.
209. Roxanne Dunbar-Ortiz, "Red Christmas," *Counterpunch,* July 20, 2005, https://www.counterpunch.org/2005/07/20/red-christmas/.
210. Michael Fredette, *Contemporary American Print Media Coverage of Nicaragua's Miskitu People during the Contra War,* Senior Honors Thesis (SUNY, September 15, 2020), 17–25, https://soar.suny.edu/handle/20.500.12648/6823.
211. Melrose, *Nicaragua*, 29.
212. Fredette.

213. Fredette.
214. Fredette.
215. "The Miskitu conflict: CIA incompetence matched by Sandinista reforms and indian pragmatism," *Journal de la Société des Américanistes* 74 (1988), 209–212, https://www.persee.fr/doc/jsa_0037-9174_1988_num_74_1_2733.
216. Lulu Garcia-Navarro, "Ortega is likely Winner of Nicaraguan Vote," *NPR,* November 6, 2006, https://www.npr.org/2006/11/06/6444204/ortega-is-likely-winner-of-nicaraguan-vote.
217. Lulu Garcia-Navarro.
218. Phil Davison, "Edén Pastora, Nicaraguan guerrilla and politician, dies at 83," *Washington Post*, June 16, 2020, https://www.washingtonpost.com/local/obituaries/eden-pastora-nicaraguan-guerrilla-and-politician-dies-at-83/2020/06/16/c775b89e-af11-11ea-8758-bfd1d045525a_story.html
219. Doralisa Pilarte, "Commander Zero Claims Opposition Did Not Want Him Back," *Associated Press,* December 4, 1989, https://apnews.com/article/f04df4c77ffdee5b245d214413064e70.
220. John Stockwell, "The Secret Wars of the CIA" (1987 lecture), posted on *libcom.org* December 11, 2012, https://libcom.org/article/secret-wars-cia-john-stockwell.
221. Melrose, *Nicaragua*, 27.
222. John Stockwell.
223. Robert Shephard, "Report: Contras Responsible for Most Human Rights Abuses," *UPI,* February 20, 1986, https://www.upi.com/Archives/1986/02/20/Report-Contras-responsible-for-most-human-rights-abuses/1214509259600/.
224. Robert Shephard.
225. *Nicaragua v. United States of America, Case Concerning Military and Paramilitary Activities in and against Nicaragua*, International Court of Justice, Judgment of June 27, 1986, https://www.icj-cij.org/public/files/case-related/70/070-19860627-JUD-01-00-EN.pdf.
226. Philip Taubman, "Recanter's Tale: Lesson in Humility for State Department." *The New York Times,* April 2, 1982, https://www.nytimes.com/1982/04/02/world/recanter-s-tale-lesson-in-humility-for-state-dept.html.
227. Noam Chomsky, *Turning the Tide: U.S. Intervention in Central America and the Struggle for Peace* (New York: Haymarket Books, 2015), 178–179.
228. Chomsky, *Turning the Tide.*
229. Latin American Studies Association (LASA), *The Electoral Process in Nicaragua: Domestic and Foreign Influences,* The Report of the Latin American Studies Association Delegation to Observe the Nicaraguan Election of November 4, 1984 (November 19, 1984), https://lasaweb.org/uploads/reports/ElectoralProcessNicaragua.pdf
230. LASA, *The Electoral Process in Nicaragua.*
231. LASA, *The Electoral Process in Nicaragua.*
232. LASA, *The Electoral Process in Nicaragua.*
233. LASA, *The Electoral Process in Nicaragua.*
234. LASA, *The Electoral Process in Nicaragua.*
235. LASA, *The Electoral Process in Nicaragua.*

236. Chomsky, *Turning the Tide*, 371.
237. "The Iran-Contra Affair," *American Experience*, PBS, https://www.pbs.org/wgbh/americanexperience/features/reagan-iran/.
238. "Iran: The Iran-Contra Affair, 1985–1987," *Jewish Virtual Library*, https://www.jewishvirtuallibrary.org/the-iran-contra-affair.
239. "Iran: The Iran-Contra Affair, 1985–1987," *Jewish Virtual Library*.
240. Christopher Davidson, *Shadow Wars: The Secret Struggle for the Middle East* (One World Publications, 2016).
241. Ian Black, "Iran and Iraq Remember War that cost more than One Million Lives," *The Guardian*, September 23, 2010, https://www.theguardian.com/world/2010/sep/23/iran-iraq-war-anniversary.
242. William Blum, "The CIA, Contras, Gangs, and Crack," *Foreign Policy in Focus*, November 1, 1996, https://fpif.org/the_cia_contras_gangs_and_crack/.
243. Steve Maas, "The Lingering, Lethal Toll of America's Crack Crisis," *NBER Digest* no. 10 (October 2018), https://www.nber.org/digest/oct18/lingering-lethal-toll-americas-crack-crisis.
244. "The History of the War on Drugs: Reagan Era and Beyond," *Landmark Recovery*, February 13, 2019, https://landmarkrecovery.com/history-of-the-war-on-drugs-reagan-beyond/.
245. Dr. Wassim Daghrir, "The United States' 'Realist' Foreign Policy: Operation Just Cause in Panama as a Case Study," *Journal of Arts & Humanities* (2016), https://www.theartsjournal.org/index.php/site/article/download/941/472.
246. Daghrir.
247. Daghrir.
248. Daghrir.
249. "The Contra War 1981–1990," *The New York Times*, June 29, 1990, https://www.nytimes.com/1990/06/29/opinion/the-contra-war-1981-1990.html.
250. Melrose, *Nicaragua*, 31.
251. Melrose, *Nicaragua*, 35.
252. Chomsky, *Turning the Tide*, 179–180.
253. William I. Robinson, *Faustian Bargain: U.S. Intervention in the Nicaraguan Elections and American Foreign Policy in the Post-Cold War Era* (New York: Routledge, 1992), 1–2.
254. William I. Robinson, *Faustian Bargain*.
255. The Carter Center, "Observing Nicaragua's Elections—1989–1990," May 1990, https://www.cartercenter.org/documents/1153.pdf.
256. "George Lucas Reveals How Star Wars Was Influenced by the Vietnam War," *AMC Talk* (blog), May 9, 2018, https://www.amc.com/blogs/george-lucas-reveals-how-star-wars-was-influenced-by-the-vietnam-war--1005548.
257. Flora Drury, "The story behind Princess Leia's hairstyle," *BBC News*, December 28, 2016, https://www.bbc.com/news/world-us-canada-38452953.
258. John Pilger, *Freedom Next Time: Resisting the Empire* (London: Bold Type Books, 2007).
259. John Pilger, *Freedom Next Time*.
260. The Carter Center.
261. William I. Robinson, *Faustian Bargain*, 148.
262. S. Brian Willson, "How the U.S. Purchased the 1990 Nicaragua Elections," *Brian Willson blog*, July 1, 1990, http://www.brianwillson.com/how-the-u-s-purchased-the-1990-nicaragua-elections/.

263. S. Brian Willson.
264. William I. Robinson, *Faustian Bargain*, 60.
265. "Nicaragua's GNP 1962–2022," Macro Trends: Nicaragua, https://www.macrotrends.net/countries/NIC/nicaragua/gnp-gross-national-product.
266. S. Brian Willson.
267. S. Brian Willson.
268. S. Brian Willson.
269. Charles Litkey, et al., "U.S.-waged 'Low Intensity' Warfare in Nicaragua: Excerpt from Report of Veterans Peace Action Team Pre-election Observation Delegation to Nicaragua, November 30 to December 14, 1989," December 1, 1989, http://www.brianwillson.com/u-s-waged-low-intensity-warfare-in-nicaragua/.
270. William I. Robinson, *Faustian Bargain*, 1.
271. The Carter Center.
272. Steven Kent Smith, "Renovation and Orthodoxy: Debate and Transition within the Sandinista National Liberation," *Latin American Perspectives* 24, no. 2, *Communal Strategies and Intellectual Transitions: Central America Prepares for the 21st Century* (March 1997), 102–116, https://www.jstor.org/stable/2634074.
273. Steven Kent Smith, "Renovation and Orthodoxy."
274. Salvador Marti Puig and Claire Wright, "The Adaptation of the FSLN: Daniel Ortega's Leadership and Democracy in Nicaragua," *Latin American Politics and Society* 52, no. 4 (Winter 2010), 101, fn. 24. Distributed by Cambridge University Press on behalf of the Center for Latin American Studies at the University of Miami Stable, https://www.jstor.org/stable/40925837.
275. Puig and Wright.
276. *Democracy Assistance and Election Guide*, https://www.electionguide.org/elections/id/2027/.
277. Steven Kent Smith, 110–112.
278. Steven Kent Smith, 110–112.
279. Steven Kent Smith, 103–104.
280. Gary Prevost, "The Nicaraguan Revolution," 110–112.
281. Prevost, 110–112.
282. Nils McCune and Kevin Zeese, "Correcting the Record: What Is Really Happening in Nicaragua?" *Counterpunch*, July 13, 2018, https://www.counterpunch.org/2018/07/13/correcting-the-record-what-is-really-happening-in-nicaragua/.
283. McCune and Zeese.
284. McCune and Zeese.
285. Puig and Wright, 88 (citing *Barricada*, 1993), https://www.jstor.org/stable/40925837
286. Puig and Wright, 88.
287. "Fire from the Mountain, In Search of Omar Cabezas," *Mint Press News*, May 3, 2022, https://www.mintpressnews.com/sandinistas-omar-cabezas-interview-daniel-kovalik/280362/.
288. Puig and Wright, 201, fn. 25.
289. Michael Parenti.
290. Prevost, 310–311.

291. Prevost, 311–312.
292. Prevost, 315.
293. Prevost, 315–316.
294. Prevost, 315.
295. Florence E. Babb, *After Revolution: Mapping Gender and Cultural Politics in Neoliberal Nicaragua* (Austin: University of Texas Press, 2001), 114.
296. Florence E. Babb, *After Revolution*.
297. Babb.
298. Babb.
299. Babb, 113
300. Prevost, 310.
301. Babb, 54.
302. Prevost, 310.
303. Prevost, 317.
304. Prevost, 317–318.
305. Prevost, 318.
306. Prevost, 318.
307. Prevost, 319.
308. Harold Pinter—Lecture: "Art, Truth & Politics."
309. Babb, 10.
310. Babb, 2.
311. Prevost, 318.
312. Babb, 108.
313. Puig and Wright, 90.
314. Puig and Wright, 91.
315. Kenneth E. Morris, *Unfinished Revolution*, 71.
316. Daniel Kovalik, "Weekend Perspectives: U.S. Out of Nicaragua," *Pittsburgh Post-Gazette*, November 17, 2001, http://old.post-gazette.com/forum/20011117edkov18p4.asp.
317. Daniel Kovalik.
318. Daniel Kovalik.
319. Daniel Kovalik.
320. Puig and Wright, 91.
321. Puig and Wright, 92.
322. Puig and Wright, 92.
323. Puig and Wright, 92.
324. Puig and Wright, 93.
325. Puig and Wright, 93.
326. Puig and Wright, 103, fn. 46.
327. Puig and Wright, 95–98.
328. Puig and Wright, 84.
329. Ben Norton, "An inside look at Nicaragua's Sandinista Revolution on its 41st anniversary," *Monthly Review*. July 27, 2020. https://mronline.org/2020/07/27/an-inside-look-at-nicaraguas-sandinista-revolution-on-its-41st-anniversary/
330. J. Thomas Ratchford III, "Policing in Partnership: Nicaraguan Policies with Implications for U.S. Police Forces," *Emory International Law Review* 32, no. 1 (2017). https://scholarlycommons.law.emory.edu/eilr/vol32/iss1/5/.

331. Santiago Ramirez, Inter-American Development Bank [IDB], *Violence and Crime in Nicaragua: A Country Profile,* Discussion Paper, No. IDB-DP-306, 34 (June 2013) (measuring GDP per capita; in terms of real GDP Nicaragua ranks second poorest behind Belize), cited in J. Thomas Ratchford III, "Policing in Partnership."

332. J. Thomas Ratchford III, "Policing in Partnership."

333. Ratchford.

334. U.S. House Democrats Media Release, "React to New Immigration Raids Targeting Refugee Women and Children from Lofgren, Roybal-Allard & Gutiérrez," May 12, 2016, https://wikileaks.org/dnc-emails/emailid/8731.

335. Ratchford.

336. Ratchford.

337. Stansfield Smith, "The gains of Nicaraguan women during the second Sandinista Government," *Monthly Review,* February 17, 2022. https://mronline.org/2022/02/17/the-gains-of-nicaraguan-women-during-the-second-sandinista-government/.

338. Ratchford.

339. McCune and Zeese.

340. Stansfield Smith.

341. María Mercedes Vanegas Cantarero, "Reviewing the Nicaraguan transition to a Renewable Energy System: Why is 'business-as-usual' no longer an option?" Interdisciplinary Institute for Environmental-, Social- and Human Studies Department Energy and Environmental Management, Europa-Universität Flensburg, 2018. http://www.elsevier.com/open-access/userlicense/1.0/

342. Vanegas Cantarero.

343. Tim Rogers, "The next 'revolution' for Nicaragua: energy independence," *Christian Science Monitor,* February 7, 2012, https://www.csmonitor.com/World/Americas/2012/0207/The-next-revolution-for-Nicaragua-energy-independence.

344. Tim Rogers.

345. Tim Rogers.

346. Julie Varughese, "After Daniel Ortega's Victory in Nicaragua, Biden Signs RENACER Act and OAS Votes to Condemn," *Toward Freedom,* November 14, 2021, https://towardfreedom.org/story/archives/americas/after-daniel-ortegas-victory-in-nicaragua-biden-signs-renacer-act-and-oas-votes-to-condemn/.

347. Stansfield Smith.

348. Stansfield Smith.

349. Stansfield Smith.

350. Stansfield Smith.

351. Stansfield Smith.

352. Ben Norton.

353. Ben Norton.

354. Stansfield Smith.

355. Stansfield Smith.

356. Julie Varughese.

357. Stansfield Smith.

358. Stansfield Smith.

359. Stansfield Smith.
360. Stansfield Smith.
361. Stansfield Smith.
362. Stansfield Smith.
363. Stansfield Smith.
364. Stansfield Smith; and Rohan Rice, "Hunger and food production in Nicaragua: How do we feed the people?" *People's Dispatch*, June 27, 2021, https://peoplesdispatch.org/2021/06/27/hunger-and-food-production-in-nicaragua-how-do-we-feed-the-people/.
365. Rohan Rice.
366. Michael Hudson. *Super Imperialism: The Economic Strategy of American Empire,* 3rd Edition (Dresden: ISLET-Verlag, 2021), 214–216.
367. Daniel Kovalik, "Free Trade: The Big Lie," *Pittsburgh Post-Gazette*, October 10, 2011, https://www.post-gazette.com/opinion/Op-Ed/2011/10/10/Free-trade-the-big-lie/stories/201110100139.
368. Daniel Kovalik.
369. Daniel Kovalik.
370. Daniel Kovalik.
371. Porsia Tunzi, "Nicaragua to No Longer Send Troops to School of the Americas," *National Catholic Reporter*, September 7, 2012. https://www.ncronline.org/blogs/ncr-today/nicaragua-no-longer-send-troops-school-americas.
372. James Hodge and Linda Cooper, "U.S. Continues to Train Honduran Soldiers," *National Catholic Reporter,* July 14, 2009, https://www.ncronline.org/news/world/us-continues-train-honduran-soldiers.
373. Roque Planas. "Hillary Clinton's Response to Honduran Coup Was Scrubbed From Her Paperback Memoirs," *Huffington Post*, March 12, 2016, https://www.huffpost.com/entry/hillary-clinton-honduras-coup-memoirs_n_56e34161e4b0b25c91820a08.
374. Roque Planas.
375. Greg Grandin, "Before Her Murder, Berta Cáceres Singled Out Hillary Clinton for Criticism," *The Nation*. March 10, 2016, https://www.thenation.com/article/archive/chronicle-of-a-honduran-assassination-foretold/
376. Dan Bilefsky, "Libya Taps Nicaraguan as Its Envoy at the UN," *New York Times,* March 2011, https://www.nytimes.com/2011/03/31/world/africa/31nations.html.
377. Bilefsky.
378. "Nicaraguan President Daniel Ortega at 80% Approval Rating: Poll," *Telesur*, October 19, 2017, https://www.telesurenglish.net/news/Nicaraguan-President-Daniel-Ortega-at-80-Aproval-Rating-Poll-20171019-0008.html.
379. Chris Cameron, "These Are the People Who Died in Connection with the Capitol Riot: A bipartisan Senate report found that at least seven people had lost their lives in connection with the Jan. 6 attack," *The New York Times*, January 5, 2022, https://www.nytimes.com/2022/01/05/us/politics/jan-6-capitol-deaths.html.
380. Nik Popli and Julia Zorthian, "What Happened to Jan. 6 Insurrectionists Arrested in the Year Since the Capitol Riot," *Time*, January 6, 2022, https://time.com/6133336/jan-6-capitol-riot-arrests-sentences/.

381. Charles Sykes, "Trump Should be Charged. Don't Let the House Pass the Buck," *MSNBC*, April 13, 2022, https://www.msnbc.com/opinion/msnbc-opinion/trump-should-be-charged-don-t-let-house-pass-buck-n1294380.

382. Charles Sykes.

383. Jacqueline Alemany and Scott Clement, "Slight majority say Trump should be charged with crime over Jan. 6 role, poll finds," *Washington Post*, May 3, 2022, https://www.washingtonpost.com/politics/2022/05/03/slight-majority-say-trump-should-be-charged-with-crime-over-jan-6-role-poll-finds/.

384. Frances Robles, "With Death in Streets, Nicaragua Cancels Social Security Revamp," April 22, 2018, https://www.nytimes.com/2018/04/22/world/americas/nicaragua-ortega-protests.html.

385. "U.S. House Passes NICA Act Against Nicaragua, Imperiling Social Programs and Development," *Telesur*, October 3, 2017, https://www.telesurenglish.net/news/US-House-Passes-NICA-Act-Against-Nicaragua-Imperiling-Social-Programs-and-Development-20171003-0030.html.

386. "U.S. House Passes NICA Act Against Nicaragua," *Telesur*.

387. "U.S. House Passes NICA Act Against Nicaragua," *Telesur*.

388. "U.S. House Passes NICA Act Against Nicaragua," *Telesur*.

389. Yorlis Gabriela Luna, "The Other Nicaragua, Empire and Resistance," *Council on Hemispheric Affairs* (COHA), October 2, 2019, https://www.coha.org/the-other-nicaragua-empire-and-resistance/.

390. William I. Robinson, *Faustian Bargain*, 14–15.

391. Max Blumenthal, "U.S. govt meddling machine boasts of 'laying the groundwork for insurrection' in Nicaragua," *The Grayzone*, June 19, 2018, https://thegrayzone.com/2018/06/19/ned-nicaragua-protests-us-government/. (*The Grayzone* originally broke the story about this admission by *Global Americans* and pointed out its relationship with the NED.)

392. Benjamin Waddell, "Laying the groundwork for insurrection: A closer look at the U.S. role in Nicaragua's social unrest," *Global Americans*, May 1, 2018. https://theglobalamericans.org/2018/05/laying-groundwork-insurrection-closer-look-u-s-role-nicaraguas-social-unrest/.

393. Alliance for Global Justice, 38.

394. Alliance for Global Justice, 40–41.

395. Martin Pengelly, "John Bolton says he 'helped plan coups d'etat' in other countries," *Guardian*, July 13, 2022, https://www.theguardian.com/us-news/2022/jul/13/john-bolton-planned-coups-donald-trump-january-6.

396. Alliance for Global Justice, 59.

397. Frances Robles, "With Death in the Streets."

398. Gabriela Selser, "Student Leader who Confronted Ortega returns to Nicaragua," *Associated Press*, October 7, 2019, https://apnews.com/article/a3121cb84eee433ab1d4577fefd03008.

399. Melissa Castillo, "My Contra Parents Are Marching For a New 'Old' Nicaragua: Are We, Too?", *Latino Rebels*, April 29, 2018, https://www.latinorebels.com/2018/04/29/mycontraparents/.

400. Kenneth E. Morris, *Unfinished Revolution*, 234–246.

401. Atilio Boron, "Nicaragua, la revolución y la niña en el bote," *Atilio Boron* (blog), July 17, 2018, https://atilioboron.com.ar/nicaragua-la-revolucion-y-la-nina-en-e/.

402. Ben Norton and Max Blumenthal, "DSA/Jacobin/Haymarket-sponsored 'Socialism' conference features U.S. gov–funded regime-change activists," *The Grayzone*, July 6, 2019, https://thegrayzone.com/2019/07/06/dsa-jacobin-iso-socialism-conference-us-funded-regime-change/.

403. Alliance for Global Justice, 83–84.

404. McCune and Zeese.

405. Yorlis Gabriela Luna.

406. Enrique Hernandez, "Why were there 15 days of protests without deaths from April 23rd to May 10th?" *Tortilla con Sal*, September 10, 2018, https://tortillaconsal.com/tortilla/node/4192.

407. Ibid.

408. Barbara Moore, "Letter from Nicaragua: A catastrophic well-orchestrated event is occurring," *Popular Resistance*, June 9, 2018, https://popularresistance.org/letter-from-nicaragua/.

409. John Perry and Rick Sterling, "How Virtual Crime Scenes Became a Propaganda Tool in Nicaragua, Ukraine and Syria," *Antiwar.com,* May 26, 2022, https://www.antiwar.com/blog/2022/05/26/how-virtual-crime-scenes-became-a-propaganda-tool-in-nicaragua-ukraine-and-syria/.

410. Alliance for Global Justice, 105.

411. *See, e.g.,* Perry and Sterling.

412. Yorlis Gabriela Luna.

413. Alliance for Global Justice, 88.

414. I cite the *Mision Verdad* for these details in an article I wrote at the time. The *Mision Verdad* article is now down, so I refer readers to my piece, "The Empire Its Empire on Nicaragua—Again," *Counterpunch*, April 25, 2018, https://www.counterpunch.org/2018/04/25/the-empire-turns-its-sights-on-nicaragua-again/.

415. Robert Fisk, "The search for truth in the rubble of Douma—and one doctor's doubts over the chemical attack," *Independent*, April 17, 2018, https://www.independent.co.uk/voices/syria-chemical-attack-gas-douma-robert-fisk-ghouta-damascus-a8307726.html.

416. Perry and Sterling.

417. Stephen Kinzer, *All The Shah's Men: An American Coup and the Roots of Middle East Terror*, Second Edition (Wiley, 2008).

418. Note, in particular, Wheelock speaking for the Miskitus. Interestingly, after 1990 Wheelock went on to obtain a master's degree in public administration from Harvard University, a considerable achievement for a former revolutionary. *See,* https://stephenkinzer.com/2019/05/40-years-later-grappling-with-regime-change-in-nicaragua/.

419. Jorge Capelan, "What is Happening in Nicaragua and a Challenge to 'Left Intellectuals,'" *Tortilla con Sal,* May 29, 2018, https://tortillaconsal.com/tortilla/node/3034.

420. Ben Norton, "From Nicaraguan revolutionaries to U.S. embassy informants: How Washington recruited ex-Sandinistas like Dora María Téllez and her MRS party," *The Grayzone*, November 21, 2021, https://thegrayzone.com/2021/11/05/nicaragua-us-informant-dora-maria-tellez-mrs/.

421. Yorlis Gabriela Luna.

422. "Nicaragua: Forensic Doctors Confirm Death of Bismark Martinez," *Telesur,* June 5, 2019, https://www.telesurenglish.net/news/Nicaragua-Forensic-Doctors-Confirm-Death-of-Bismark-Martinez-20190605-0010.html.

423. "Nicaragua: Forensic Doctors Confirm Death of Bismark Martinez".

424. Elizabeth Malkin and Frances Robles, "Nicaragua Clergy, Siding with Protesters, Becomes 'Terrible Enemy'of Ortega," *The New York Times,* July 22, 2018, https://www.nytimes.com/2018/07/22/world/americas/nicaragua-protests-catholic-church.html.

425. Jorge Capelan.

426. Christopher Dickey, "Pope Heckled During Mass in Nicaragua," *Washington Post,* March 5, 1983, https://www.washingtonpost.com/archive/politics/1983/03/05/pope-heckled-during-mass-in-nicaragua/493a0dd6-d77b-495a-9a17-8bedae5db27e/.

427. Lauren Smith, "Nicaragua: Imperialist snakes in holy vestments," *Tortilla con Sal,* June 13, 2018, https://tortillaconsal.com/tortilla/node/3169.

428. Carlos Alejandro, "Encuentran armas de fabricación casera dentro de iglesia en Nicaragua," *elciudadano.com,* July 9, 2018, https://www.elciudadano.com/latinoamerica/encuentran-armas-de-fabricacion-casera-dentro-de-iglesia-en-nicaragua/07/09/.

429. McCune and Zeese.

430. John Perry, "Masaya 2018—Testimony of Violent Opposition Crimes," *Tortilla con Sal,* January 5, 2022, https://www.tortillaconsal.com/tortilla/node/13702.

431. Alliance for Global Justice, 131.

432. Alliance for Global Justice, 131.

433. "Nicaragua: Forensic Doctors Confirm Death of Bismark Martinez."

434. Alliance for Global Justice.

435. Alliance for Global Justice.

436. Daniel Kovalik, "I monitored the U.S.-denounced Nicaraguan election; the people believe in the Ortega government," *El 19* Digital, November 9, 2021, https://www.el19digital.com/app/webroot/tinymce/source/2021/Noviembre/09%20NOV/kovalik/KOVALIK.pdf.

437. Kovalik, "I monitored the U.S.-denounced Nicaraguan election."

438. Anatoly Kurmanaev and María Silvia Trigo, "A Bitter Election. Accusations of Fraud. And Now Second Thoughts.", *The New York Times,* June 7, 2020, https://www.nytimes.com/2020/06/07/world/americas/bolivia-election-evo-morales.html.

439. "Daniel Ortega with High People's Approval in Nicaragua," *JPMas,* January 25, 2022, https://jpmas.com.ni/daniel-ortega-with-high-peoples-approval-in-nicaragua/.

440. "Daniel Ortega with High People's Approval in Nicaragua."

441. John Perry, "NicaNotes: Nicaragua celebrates 43 years of revolution: A clash between reality and media misrepresentation," *Alliance for Global Justice,* July 21, 2022, https://afgj.org/nicanotes-07-21-2022.

442. "70% of Nicaraguans Support President Ortega: M&R Consultants," *Telesur,* January 26, 2022, https://www.telesurenglish.net/news/70-of-Nicaraguans-Support-President-Ortega-MR-Consultants-20220126-0009.html.

443. Dennis Schwartz, "Nica Notes: Nicaragua's Finance Minister Ivan Acosta: 'We are going to have GDP growth...of between 4 and 5%, which is important!'" *Alliance for Global Justice*, June 16, 2022, https://afgj.org/nicanotes-06-16-2022?eType=EmailBlastContent&eId=89214332-c677-44f0-8922-3ee1cdffe658.

444. Dennis Schwartz.

445. Dennis Schwartz.

446. Daniel Kovalik, "No Mas! Nicaragua Quits OAS as EU Tries to Undermine Venezuela Elections," *MintPress News*, November 22, 2021, https://www.mintpressnews.com/no-mas-nicaragua-quits-oas-eu-tries-undermine-venezuela-elections/279015/.

447. Kovalik, "No Mas!"

448. Rachel Hu and Chris Garaffa, "International Solidarity Threatens Biden's Summit of the America," *Covert Action Bulletin*, May 25, 2022, https://covertactionmagazine.com/2022/05/25/covertaction-bulletin-podcast-international-solidarity-threatens-bidens-summit-of-the-americas/.

449. Ben Norton, "How USAID created Nicaragua's anti-Sandinista media apparatus, now under money laundering investigation," *The Grayzone*, June 1, 2021, https://thegrayzone.com/2021/06/01/cia-usaid-nicaragua-right-wing-media/.

450. Mike Spetalnick, "Biden signs bill calling for more sanction, pressure on Nicaragua," *Reuters*, November 10, 2021, https://www.reuters.com/world/americas/biden-signs-bill-calling-more-sanctions-pressure-nicaragua-2021-11-10/.

451. Paul Wiseman and Gabriela Selser, "Turning up heat, U.S. targets Nicaraguan sugar imports," *Associated Press*, July 21, 2022, https://apnews.com/article/united-states-global-trade-nicaragua-daniel-ortega-ff975a5e33b2ebf44c84b5d00417d636.

452. Associated Press. "U.S. Considers Expelling Nicaragua from Trade Pact Over Crackdowns," *NBC News*, February 18, 2022, https://www.nbcnews.com/news/latino/us-considers-expelling-nicaragua-trade-pact-crackdowns-rcna16885.

453. "Colombia, U.S. Announce Joint Exercises With Nuclear Sub," *The Defense Post*, March 1, 2022, https://www.thedefensepost.com/2022/03/01/colombia-us-exercises-nuclear/.

454. Comisión de la Verdad, Justicia y Paz (CVJP), Cuarto (IV) Informe: Preliminar 18 de abril de 2018 al 15 de julio de 2019 (Managua, Nicaragua), 26.

455. Gobierno de Reconciliación y Unidad Nacional (GRUN), *Plan Nacional de Lucha contra la Pobreza para el Desarrollo Humano 2022–2026* (July 27, 2021), 28-29, https://www.pndh.gob.ni/.

456. GRUN, 29.

457. Ibid., p. 27.

458. Ibid., pp. 32-33.

459. Ibid., p. 33.

460. GRUN, 49.

461. GRUN, 34-35.

462. GRUN, 49.

463. GRUN, 49.

464. GRUN, 30.
465. Edén Lenin Fisher Chavarría, *Golpe de estado blando, Nicaragua 2018: Otra victoria del FSLN* (Managua: Editoria Universitaria, 2020), 1.
466. GRUN, 48.
467. Fisher Chavarría, 1.
468. Fisher Chavarría, 43.
469. CVJP, Primer (I) Informe: Período 18 abril al 10 julio 2018 (Managua, Nicaragua).
470. CVJP, Tercer (III) Informe: Período 18 abril al 10 julio 2018 (Managua, Nicaragua, Feb. 5, 2019).
471. CVJP, Tercer (III) Informe.
472. CVJP, Cuarto (IV) Informe.
473. Fisher Chavarría, 86.
474. Canal TV 4 (+Video), "Cura es cómplice de terroristas que asesinaron a Sub Oficial," July 16, 2018, https://www.canal4.com.ni/cura-es-complice-de-terroristas-que-asesinaron-a-sub-oficial/.
475. Fisher Chavarría, 89, 279.
476. CVJP, Cuarto (IV) Informe.
477. John Perry, "A year after Nicaragua's coup, the media's regime change deceptions are still unravelling," *NicaNotes* (August 14, 2019)." Cited in the compilation book: *Nicaragua Advances despite U.S. Unconventional Warfare* (Alliance for Global Justice, July 2020), 179–180.
478. Fisher Chavarría, 373–74.
479. CVJP, Tercer (III) Informe.
480. David Gutiérrez López, "Líbranos del obispo Báez y de todo mal… Amén," November 24, 2018, https://www.visionsandinista.net/2018/11/24/libranos-del-obispo-baez-y-de-todo-malamen/.
481. Omerlo, "Cardenal Brenes confirma grabación de obispo Báez," *NicaLeaks,* October 25, 2018, http://nicaleaks.com/2018/10/25/cardenal-brenes-confirma-grabacion-de-obispo-baez/.
482. Omerlo.
483. Nan McCurdy, "The Guardian pushes more lies on Nicaragua, covering up for putschist priests," *The Grayzone,* Nov. 16, 2018, https://thegrayzone.com/2018/11/16/the-guardian-pushes-more-lies-on-nicaragua-covering-up-for-putschist-priests/.
484. Omerlo.
485. Omerlo.
486. Emiliano Chamorro Mendieta, "Obispo Aberlardo Mata sobre su reunion con Mike Pense: EE.UU. conoce muy bien la situacion de Nicaragua." 6 de junio de 2018. https://www.laprensa.com.ni/2019/06/06/politica/2556837-obispo-abelardo-mata-sobre-su-reunion-con-mike-pence-eeuu-conoce-muy-bien-la-situacion-de-nicaragua.
487. CVJP, Cuarto (IV) Informe.
488. CVJP, Cuarto (IV) Informe.
489. GRUN, 53.
490. CVJP, Cuarto (IV) Informe.
491. CVJP, Cuarto (IV) Informe.
492. GRUN, 54.

493. CVJP, Cuarto (IV) Informe.
494. CVJP, Cuarto (IV) Informe.
495. Fisher Chavarría, 350.
496. Nan McCurdy, "Amnesty," cited in *The Revolution Wont't Be Stopped: Nicaragua Advances Despite U.S. Unconventional Warfare* (Alliance for Global Justice. July 2020), 37.
497. Asamblea Nacional, Ley No. 996: "Ley de Amnistía," publicada en *La Gaceta Diario Oficial* no. 108 (Managua, Nicaragua, June 10, 2019).
498. McCurdy, "Amnesty."

INDEX

A
abortion, 164, 188
Abrams, Elliott, 102, 150
activists, 4, 192, 208, 219, 288
Afghanistan, 45, 76, 173
AFL-CIO, 150–51
Africa, 133, 142
Agrarian Reform, 94, 100, 102, 155
Agricultural Workers Confederation, 153, 180
AIDS, 54
AIFLD, 150
Airborne Division, 130
airline, 110
airplanes, 43, 44, 69, 70, 93
Alemán, Arnoldo, 155, 163, 169, 172, 174–75, 258
Alemán, Lesther, 202
Allende, Salvador, 65, 66, 160, 248
 Puerta Salvador Allende (park), 166
American allies, 34
American bankers, 32
American Left, 113
American public, 24, 113, 203
Amnesty International, 80, 278
ANC (African National Congress), 142
ancien regime, 2
anemia, 164
anti-colonial, 133
anti-imperialist, 29, 36, 83, 255
Anti-Imperialist League, 44
anti-malarial workers, 137
anti-sodomy legislation, 164
Apartheid, 142
Arce, Bayardo, 152

Argentina, 67, 68, 74, 93, 277
Arias, Costa Rican President Oscar 145
armed conflict, 130, 134
Asia, 133
assassins, 21
Assembly, 66, 88, 101, 123, 149, 152–53, 155, 164, 175, 193
Associated Press, 46, 250, 281, 287, 290
ATC, 61, 96, 153, 180, 205, 210, 225
Atlantic Ocean/coast, 17–20, 24, 27, 42, 43, 62, 109–114, 273, 280
 –Pacific canal, 17
attacks, 14, 36, 85, 106, 108–112, 117, 122–23, 129, 131, 137, 145, 173, 195, 208, 216, 222, 262

B
Barranca-Coyotepe, battle of, 33
baseball, 54
 Amateur Baseball World Series tournament, 55
 Major League Baseball (MLB), 54
 black players, 54
 Nicaraguan teams—"Youth" and "The Insurgency", 23
 also see: Clemente, Roberto
Bay of Pigs, 36, 56, 57, 276
"Bilingual-Bicultural Education in Nicaragua's Atlantic Coast Region" (article by Michael Shapiro), 109, 111, 280
Bishop, 10, 63, 120, 175, 229, 230, 239, 267, 268
blockade, 123
blood transfusions, 53, 54

293

Bogota, mayor of, 19
Bolivia, 78, 204, 242, 248
bombardment, 8, 21, 44–45, 67–72, 110, 116, 129–30, 193
Bourgeois, Philippe, 113–114
Borge Martínez, Tomás, 75, 78–81, 84, 88, 90, 102, 115, 154, 221, 256
Brazil, 12, 68, 83
breastfeeding, 101
brigadistas, 94, 101
Britain, 16, 17
   hunger-relief organization, 50
Brown University study, 106–8, 280
brutality, 13, 42, 74, 104
bulwark, 93
Bunau-Varilla, Philippe, 18, 19
Bureau of Economic Research, 135
bureaucrats, 104
Bush, Jeb, 173
Bush, U.S. President George H.W., 137, 140, 142, 145–46
Bush, U.S. President George W., 173

C
capitalism, 24, 29, 184, 263
Cardenal, Father Fernando, 93, 257
Caribbean coast, 25, 38, 40
Carlos Fonseca Northern Front, 92
Carter, Jimmy, U.S. President Administration, 82, 85, 89, 92, 141
   Carter Center, 141, 143, 147, 282, 283
Casco, Miguel Angel, 152
Castillo-Knox Treaty (1914), 35
Catholic Church, 9–10, 61, 75, 89, 163–64, 175, 214, 216, 223, 225, 229, 230, 232, 235, 239, 262, 266–69
   high school, 2
   Second Vatican Council, 88
CBS, 105, 280
cease-fire agreements, 113
Center for Constitutional Rights, 121

Center for Latin American Studies (CLAS) at University of Pittsburgh, 205, 220
Central America, 2, 4, 6, 17–18, 20–22, 25, 28, 35, 103, 129, 150, 181, 183–84, 192, 200, 226, 250, 274, 278–79, 281, 283
Central Bank, 77
Chamber of Commerce, 71, 262
Chamorro Administration, 153
Chamorro-Bryan Treaty, 35
childbirth, 101
Chile, 12, 58, 65, 66, 68, 84, 160, 197, 277
China, 19, 29, 36, 177, 247, 248
Chinandega, 69, 72, 222
Chinese guerilla forces, 37
Chamorro, Edgar, 125–26
Chamorro, Emiliano, conservative general, 38–39
Chamorro family, 144, 154, 184, 225
Chamorro, Pedro Joaquin, 53
Chamorro, Violeta Barrios de, 144–45, 153–55, 159, 169, 201, 247, 258
   government, 159–165
Chamorro-Bryan Treaty (1916), 35
Chomsky, Noam, 27, 51, 79, 93, 138, 276, 278, 279, 281
Christians, 10, 88, 232
Christmas, 78, 110–12, 280
Christmas Day, 111
church, 9, 10, 52, 162, 203, 229, 231, 289
churchwomen, 89, 90, 279
CIA, 31, 56–57, 67, 76, 93, 107–108, 110–17, 120, 125–27, 129, 132, 134–37, 144, 150, 164, 196–98, 223–24, 248, 276, 278, 281–82
Cincinnati, 1, 2
citizenship, 176
civil society groups, 61, 179, 200, 233
civilian population, 8, 36, 43, 48, 69–70
Clayton-Bulwer Treaty, 17, 18, 273

Clemente, Roberto, 6, 54–55
Clemente Night at PNC Park in Pittsburgh (2021), 55
cocaine, 105, 133–36, 196
coffee, 35, 41–42, 90–91, 94, 96, 225, 237
Cold War, 108, 200, 282
Colombia, 18–19, 36, 74, 135, 164, 191, 251, 275, 277, 290
Columbia University, 102
Commission, 68, 71–73, 75, 152, 164, 277
Communism, 26, 60, 66, 79, 89, 280
Communist, 62, 65, 89, 102, 120
Congress, iii, 13–14, 18–19, 35, 37–39, 45–46, 49, 65, 66–67, 124–125, 127, 133, 148–50, 153–54, 196, 200–201, 206, 226, 242, 250, 253, 274–75
Connection, 51, 276, 286
Conservative Party, 35, 38
constitutional rights, 63, 68, 70
Contras, 2, 3, 8, 11, 13–14, 19, 26, 45, 93–95, 103, 105–108, 110, 112–13, 115–18, 122–34, 136–38, 140, 144–46, 148, 158, 160, 164, 167, 169, 173, 175, 196, 200, 209, 225, 235–36, 254, 262–63, 280–82
coup, 25, 27, 42, 56, 57, 65, 84, 127, 160, 184, 192, 193, 199, 201, 215, 216, 223, 224, 225, 230, 235, 236, 239, 240, 241, 242, 248, 259, 261, 262, 263, 265, 266, 267, 268, 269, 270, 271, 286, 291
Creole, 110, 258
Cuba, 29, 36, 48, 56–57, 60, 76, 92, 102, 105, 108, 129, 132, 177, 189, 196, 205, 248, 256, 273, 280
Cuban Revolution, 92
custody, 181
customs, 4, 28, 46
Cyane, 20

D

Daily Worker, 44
daycare centers, 164, 271
Defense Intelligence Agency, 106
Defense Minister, 116
Delta Force, 31
democracy, 2, 11, 20, 29, 98, 107, 132, 172–74, 176, 180, 198, 200
Democracy Now!, 149
democratic coalition, 124
Democratic Party (U.S. House), 20, 182, 194, 285
Democratic Socialists of America (DSA), 102, 206, 288
Dental Association, 71
Department of Nueva Segovia, 8
dictatorship, 12, 48, 49, 56, 61, 63, 78, 82–83, 87, 90, 99, 103–104, 106–107, 182, 208, 211–12, 253, 255–57, 266
diplomacy, 27, 84
"Dollar diplomacy", 28
domestic, 66, 132, 161, 188, 198, 250

E

earthquake, 6, 49–51, 53–55, 87, 269
Eastern Bloc, 102, 141–42
economics, 17–18, 26–28, 31, 47, 50, 58, 62, 81–83, 88, 103–104, 116, 118, 130–31, 138, 140, 142, 144–45, 160–61, 163, 165, 168, 180, 184, 187, 190, 196–97, 203, 218, 222, 225, 235–36, 246, 250, 253–54, 259–61, 263, 269–71
education, 4, 62, 93, 96–97, 99, 110, 139, 163, 165, 181, 184, 186, 196, 220, 245, 258–60, 262, 264
El Salvador, 2, 12, 21, 89, 106, 108–109, 128–30, 132, 182, 196, 211, 279
Salvadoran jail, 129
Salvadoran revolutionaries, 108
electoral law, 175
electric power, 7
elite, 81–83, 153, 184, 225, 253, 272

embargo, 133, 145–46
Emotional Rescue (Rolling Stones album), 1
Empire, 21, 142, 159, 190, 238, 242, 249, 274, 282, 286–88
Empire Strikes Back period, 142
entrepreneur, 96
epidemic, 134–35
Estelí, 64, 70–72, 93, 207–208, 222, 230, 240, 268
ethnocide, 110
Europe, 16, 43, 53, 84, 149
eyewitness, 69

F

Face the Nation, 105, 280
family code, 164
Farabundo Martí National Liberation Front (FMLN), 89, 129, 132
fascism, 58, 65, 67, 93, 107, 125, 239
Faustian Bargain, 140–43, 197, 282–83, 287
FDN, 106–107, 125–26
feminist, 168, 183
firemen, 71
Fonseca Amador, Carlos, 63–64, 75, 94, 101–2, 156, 163, 179, 256, 258
    Northern Front, 92
Fonseca Terán, Carlos, 156, 179, 186
foreign aid, 160, 191
foreign intervention, 158, 223
foreign leaders, 31
Foreign Minister, 88, 123, 193
foreign policy, 12, 13, 23, 31, 57, 62, 68, 98, 133, 193, 197–98, 253
foreigners, 20
freedom, 2, 11, 20–21, 29, 61, 64, 83, 87, 170, 173–74
FSLN (Sandinista National Liberation Front), 12, 42, 48, 57, 59–63, 75, 77–78, 83–88, 92, 96, 99–103, 108, 110, 115–16, 124, 141, 143, 145–48, 151–56, 159, 163–64, 167–69, 171–77, 179, 182, 186, 190, 204, 213, 221, 226–27, 236, 238–39, 241, 245–46, 256–57, 266, 276, 283, 291

G

Gangsters of Capitalism, 77, 274–75, 278
gender, 8, 167–68, 189, 284
genocide, 31, 56, 70, 275
Giant of the North, 139
Global South, 28, 45, 191
Gloria Quintania Cooperative, 94
God, 11, 88, 162, 249, 268
Golden Glove Award, 54
government, 2–4, 6, 10, 12, 14, 18, 20–27, 31–34, 36, 38–40, 42, 45–47, 50, 56–57, 60–63, 65–66, 68, 70, 80, 83, 88–98, 101–103, 105, 107–110, 113–14, 117–18, 121–27, 132, 134, 143–50, 153, 160–65, 169, 171, 174, 176, 180, 183–242, 245, 250, 257–270, 285, 287, 289
Government of National Reconstruction, 80, 98, 257
Great Britain, 16, 273
Greece, 12
Grenada, 6, 20, 32, 219
Greytown, 20
Guardian, 67, 277, 282, 287, 291
Guatemala, 12, 39, 56, 57, 64, 106, 109, 114, 120, 182, 196–97, 225, 276
guerrilla movement, 148
Guevara, Che, 105, 280
guns, 16–17, 19, 21, 23, 25, 27, 29, 31, 33, 35, 37, 39, 41, 43, 45, 47
Guzzetti, Admiral Cesar Augusto, 67

H

Haiti, 12, 29, 53, 191
harassment, 52, 227
Harkin Amendment, 63
Havana conference, 43
Hay-Bunau-Varilla Treaty of 1903, 19

Hay-Pauncefote Treaty of 1901, 18
healthcare, 4, 163, 186, 259, 262
helicopter, 70
Hemisphere, 11–12, 16, 22, 58, 74, 245, 248
history, 13, 19, 22, 27, 41, 43, 49, 56, 57, 63, 77–78, 80, 85, 87–88, 101–102, 107, 123, 139, 143, 147, 153, 162, 167, 173, 177, 191, 242, 246, 257, 264, 271, 273–76, 279, 280, 282
Hollywood movie, 20
homicides, 182
homosexuality, 164
Honduras, 4, 21, 29, 39, 40, 56, 90, 92–93, 105–106, 113, 117, 120, 129, 182, 191–93, 196, 211, 225, 249, 254, 256, 286
human rights, 20, 61, 63, 65, 66–68, 75, 82, 83, 99, 107–109, 116, 122, 132, 149, 196, 200, 218, 223, 276
Human Rights Watch, America's Watch division, 108
humanitarian, 6, 14, 54, 69, 116, 119, 121, 128, 196
humanitarian aid, 119

I

imperialism, 22, 24, 32, 115
inauguration, 6, 55, 57, 178, 247, 257
Indian Pragmatism, 113
indigenous, 10, 42, 48, 109, 114, 184, 189, 192, 209, 258–59
Indonesia, 12
infrastructure, 7, 11, 184, 219, 247, 254, 258, 260, 262, 264, 269
insurrection, 49, 51, 53, 55, 57, 59, 61, 63, 65, 67, 69, 71, 73, 75, 77, 79, 81, 83, 85, 194
Inter-American Commission on Human Rights (IACHR), 68–70, 72, 74–76, 277
International Banking House of Brown Brothers, 29

International Court of Justice (ICJ), 36, 123–28, 130, 132, 164, 281
International Democratic Institute, 150
international law, 123, 127, 141
International Monetary Fund (IMF), 159, 160, 202, 262
International Republican Institute, 150
InterPress, 113
interventions, 14, 19, 20, 21, 28, 253, 254
invaders, 22, 46
invasion, 20–21, 23–24, 26, 28, 31, 40, 44, 56, 134, 141–42, 194, 211, 234, 248
invasions, 21, 31
Iran, 58, 105, 127, 133–34, 137, 150, 197, 223–24, 248, 280, 282
Iraq, 45, 76, 133–34, 282
Israel, 83, 133

J

Jaguar Smile, 97, 278–79
Japan, 22, 24, 35, 248
Jesuits Massacre, 90
journalists, 71, 264
July 16 Central Park, 9
juveniles, 181

K

Kennedy, John F., U.S. President, 57
King, Martin Luther, Jr., 54
Kissinger, Henry, 65–68
de Klerk, F. W., 142
Korea, 45, 132

L

La Modela prison, 76
La Pedrada, 21
La Prensa, 53, 144, 173, 225
labor, 50, 62, 82, 93, 149, 151, 159, 161, 184, 197

Latin America, 10, 12, 17, 21–22, 43, 45, 56–57, 62, 76, 79, 85, 100, 122, 133, 148–49, 177, 186, 222, 230, 246, 248, 273–75
Latin American Studies Association (LASA), 103, 130–31, 281
Law Regulating Relations Between Mothers, Fathers and Children, 100
lawyers, 16–17, 19, 21, 23, 25, 27, 29, 31, 33, 35, 37, 39, 41, 43, 45, 47
leftist movements, 85
Letelier, Orlando, 66–67
Legal Aid Service, 52
legislation, 62, 65, 83, 109, 125, 127, 135, 136, 164, 181, 196
legitimacy, 33, 81, 181, 183
Leninist model, 88
Leon University, 52
Liberal Party, 22, 38, 46, 91, 169, 173–75
liberalism, 174
liberation, 41, 48, 57, 82, 89, 99, 102, 117, 142–43, 247, 266, 279
Liberation Theology, 88–89, 230
Libya, 8, 45, 193, 286
life-threatening diseases, 101
Lincoln, Abraham, 21, 116
Linder, Ben, 3, 4, 6, 169, 273
Literacy Award, 98
Lombardo, Guy, 47
L.A. Times, 54
los muchachos, 87

M
mainstream, 43, 113, 156, 194, 202, 209, 216–18, 236, 241, 264
Managua, iii, 4, 6, 8, 23, 32, 43, 47–50, 53, 55, 64, 75–76, 78, 82, 87, 90, 92, 109, 115, 121–22, 129, 161, 163, 166, 170, 174, 208, 215–17, 220, 222, 225, 228, 239–40, 242, 250, 256, 264, 267, 268–69, 290–92

Mandela, Nelson, 142, 170
mano duro, 182
martyrs, 62, 72, 127
Marxism-Leninism, 120
media, 12, 25–26, 43, 51, 55, 93, 154, 157–58, 194, 196–97, 199–200, 203, 207–208, 210–12, 214, 216–18, 235–36, 253, 266, 268, 271, 289, 290–91
Medical Society, 71
memories
 author's, of Nicaragua, 65
 and beliefs of American people, 113
Mexico, 21, 29, 38–39, 74, 110, 119–20, 191, 248, 277
Middle East, 58, 134, 224, 228, 282, 288
militant, 84, 115, 171, 183, 227
military, 12, 18–20, 28, 33, 36–38, 42, 47, 49, 52, 56, 58, 60, 63, 65, 67, 72–74, 83–84, 100, 103–104, 107–108, 112–14, 122–28, 130–33, 138–41, 144, 145, 147, 153, 158, 171, 173, 177, 180, 182, 191, 193, 231, 249, 250, 253–57, 276
mining, 24–25, 27, 40, 128, 137, 146, 164
Miskitu (var. Miskito) peoples, 42, 109–114
 allegations against Sandinistas re treatment of, 109–110, 113
 Coast, 112, 131, 164
 language, 110, 258
money, 16–17, 19, 21, 23, 25, 27, 29, 31, 33, 35, 37, 39, 41, 43, 45, 47
monopoly, 26, 225
Monroe Doctrine, 12, 16–17, 22, 251, 273
Monroe, James, U.S. President, 16–17
motherland, 64, 255
MRS (Sandinista Renovation Movement), 148–56, 203, 215, 225–29, 242, 262, 288

murder, 2, 14, 52, 63, 74, 78, 89, 90, 135, 192, 219, 227, 231, 266, 270
"My Personal Revenge" (Tomás Borge poem), 80–81

N
North American Congress on Latin America (NACLA), 149
Nation, The (magazine), 4
National Assembly, 153, 164
National Bank of Nicaragua, 27
national defense, 138
National Guard, 3, 38, 40, 45–51, 64, 68, 70–84, 87, 90, 92–93, 106, 114, 118, 124–25, 129, 220, 253, 256, 257, 266
national independence, 108, 248
National Palace, 84, 87, 228
National Security Council leaked document, 103
nationalist, 23, 91
NATO, 36, 42, 193, 251
Nazi Germany, 134
NBER, 135, 282
National Endowment for Democracy (NED), 149, 150, 197–201, 225, 287
neoliberalism, 11, 36, 58, 156, 158–159, 160, 167–68, 176, 182, 184, 190, 213, 249, 254, 257, 258–61, 263
New Confessions of an Economic Hitman, The (book by John Perkins), 31
New England Journal of Medicine, 98
New World Order, 142
New York Times, The, 43–44, 51, 129, 130, 137, 195, 229, 242, 274, 277, 281, 282, 286, 289
U.S. paper of record, 51
NGOs, 26, 144, 149, 223, 225, 266, 271
"Nicaragua" song by Bruce Cockburn, 64–65

"Nicaragua: The Threat of a Good Example" (1985 Oxfam report), 50
Nicaraguans, 3, 11, 15, 20, 22, 27, 31–32, 41, 44–45, 48, 51, 53, 55, 63, 68, 77, 80, 85, 87, 93–94, 96, 98–99, 105–106, 120–21, 137–42, 145–47, 158, 161–62, 172–73, 184, 186–87, 200, 211–13, 221, 228, 230, 236, 240–42, 245, 250, 258–61, 267–68, 289
Niquinohomo, 35
Nobel Peace Prize, 145
Nobel Prize for Literature, 12, 165
North American troops, 91
Nueva Segovia, 10, 39–43
nurses, 13

O
occupation, 21, 38, 40–41, 45–46, 83, 255
Occupational Conversion Plan, 162
Ocotal, 4, 7–11, 41, 208, 261
OMs (mass organizations), 179–80
Operation Mop-up, 72
operation PBSUCCESS, 56
Oxfam, 50–52, 96–98, 112, 137–38, 276

P
Pacific Ocean/coast, 17–19, 273
Panama, 18–19, 23–24, 26–27, 32, 35–36, 74, 137, 141–42, 273–74, 282
Canal, 18–19, 23, 35–36, 74, 273–74; rejection of treaty by Colombia, 18
pan-American, 43
Paraguay, 2, 12, 68, 211
peace, 4, 13, 38–39, 43, 46–48, 96, 105, 113–15, 144–45, 171, 175, 193, 200, 211, 215, 231, 234, 236, 239, 242, 255, 264, 270–71
Peasant Workers Union, 96

Pennsylvania, 24
Petro, Gustavo, 19
Pew Research, 136
Philippines, 12, 29, 31, 275
Pinochet, Augusto, 58, 65–68, 277
Pinter, Harold, 12–14, 165
Pirates, 6, 54
Pirates baseball, 6
Pittsburgh, 6, 24, 54–55, 205, 213, 219, 220, 284, 286
Plaza of the Revolution, 87
poverty, 7, 8, 40, 50, 53, 82, 138, 161–62, 165, 176, 184, 186–88, 241, 245, 257, 260, 264
Prevost, 160–61, 163, 168, 279, 283–84
priests, 71, 75, 88–89, 231–32, 291
prisoners, 73, 75–78, 80, 125, 256, 271
propaganda, 42, 62, 107, 110–11, 163–64, 196, 211, 213, 225, 267, 288
proxies, 35
Puerto Rico, 54
Pulitzer Prize, 22

R
radical, 2, 89, 231
Radio Havana, 92
railroad, 32
Rape, 99
Reagan, Ronald, U.S. President Administration, vii, 2, 4, 79, 89, 93, 102, 105, 107, 109–10, 112, 114, 122, 127, 131–37, 196, 282
Red Cross, 71, 74, 80, 90, 93, 265
regime, 24, 27, 32, 33, 39, 50, 55, 57, 74, 76, 83, 94, 99, 107, 127, 132, 183, 192, 197, 199, 202, 205, 209, 222–24, 226, 232, 249, 253, 255, 288, 291
rehydration centers, 101
reign of terror, 25
religions, 62

Renovation Movement, Sandinista. *See* MRS
repression, 49, 51, 53, 55, 57, 59, 61, 63, 65, 67, 69, 71, 73, 75, 77, 79, 81, 83, 85
Reproductive rights, 99
Republican Administration, 26
resistance, 22, 31–32, 36–37, 40, 45, 72–73, 118, 142, 159, 162, 165, 253, 255–56, 287
restorative justice, 181
Rio Coco, 110, 111
rocket, 69
Rolling Stones, 1
Roman Catholic, 2, 9, 89, 225, 233, 262, 267
Roosevelt, Teddy, 18–19, 22, 24
Russia, 42, 132, 177, 248
Russian Revolution, 26

S
San Jacinto, battle of, 21
San Carlos, 111
San Jose Mercury News, 134
San Juan del Norte, 20
sanctions, 14, 66, 67, 123, 246, 250, 253, 271, 290
Sandinistas, v, vii, 1–3, 6, 9–12, 15, 23, 25, 36, 40–45, 47–48, 50–51, 53, 57–58, 60–63, 68, 72–89, 92, 93, 94, 96–100, 102–16, 119, 121–33, 137, 139–42, 144, 146–50, 152–68, 171–74, 176, 178–80, 182–90, 196, 198–200, 203–9, 211, 213, 215–20, 223–42, 249–72, 276, 278–81, 283–85, 288, 290
revolution, 1, 2, 4, 6, 22–23, 25–26, 32–34, 38, 41–42, 50, 51, 53, 57–58, 60–64, 75, 77, 79, 80, 81, 83–88, 89–90, 92–97, 99–101, 103–109, 115–17, 129, 133, 135, 140, 146–48, 153–57, 159, 163–65, 167–72, 177, 179, 180, 182, 184–85, 202–205, 209–210,

220, 223–24, 226–29, 231, 236, 239, 240–42, 244, 253–55, 257–58, 261, 263, 266, 268, 276, 278–80, 283–85, 287–89, 292;
  triumph of, 44, 87, 89, 91, 93, 95, 97, 99, 101, 103
Sandinista National Liberation Front. *See* FSLN
Sandinista Renovation Movement. *See* MRS
Sandino, Augusto C., 8
  campaign, 36
  rebellion, 40, 43, 273, 275
school, 1–2, 4, 13, 29, 46, 52, 81, 90, 92, 96, 118, 183, 186, 257–58, 286
School of the Americas (SOA), U.S. Army, 74, 83, 191
security forces, 38, 76, 79, 129, 171, 223, 236
segregation, 54
self-defense, 33–34, 48, 130, 235
Serbia, 45
settlements, 112
Shadow Wars, 134, 282
slavery, 20, 21
small-scale community, 52
Social Democrats USA, 150
social justice, 137
social movements, 179
social security, 62, 161, 198, 201, 202, 206–207, 262–63, 269
socialism, 89, 101, 142, 154, 203, 288
socioeconomic, 179, 255, 264
soil, 64, 108, 277
soldaderas, 142
solidarity, 4, 15, 43, 57, 62, 149, 193, 200, 212, 249, 290
Solidarity Center, 150
Somalia, 45
Somoza, Anastasio, 1
  air force, 72
  National Guard, 1, 50, 75, 106, 236, 266
South Africa, 142

South America, 17, 58
sovereignty, 64
Soviet, 26, 60, 62, 102, 106, 108, 120, 128, 133–34, 142, 156
Soviet encroachment, 26
Soviet Union, 60, 62, 102, 108, 120, 133–34, 142, 156
Spain, 16, 22, 29, 231, 248
Special Commission, 75
Star Wars, 142, 282
State Department, 28, 58, 60, 62–63, 65, 67, 129, 138–39, 151, 173, 226, 281
State of Siege, 70
State Security officials, 126
strong hand, 182
SUV, 170

T

Telesur, 53, 196, 228, 235, 245, 276, 286–87, 289
Terceristas, 84, 86
terrorism, 8, 11, 44, 45, 69–71, 76, 118, 126, 173, 216, 224, 228, 236, 238, 242, 262, 265, 288
terrorists, 173, 228, 265
  military campaigns, 145
Third World Fascism, 51, 276
Tipitapa, 76, 207
trades unions, 52
Tripoli, 8
Truman, Harry, U.S. President, 56
Turkey, 12

U

Ukraine, 42, 223, 245, 288
Under Fire (film), 1
UNESCO, 98, 204
UNHCR, 113
unions, 94, 99, 144, 149, 151, 179, 184, 197, 209, 210, 262, 266
United Nations High Commissioner of Human Rights, 113
United Press International, 46

United States, 2, 12–13, 16, 19,
　21–23, 25, 33, 35, 38–40, 42, 44,
　45–46, 47, 53–54, 66–67, 87, 92,
　103, 105, 118, 122–31, 133, 136,
　141–42, 158–60, 162, 165, 169,
　172–73, 185–86, 190, 19–94,
　200, 224, 226–27, 246, 248, 251,
　253–55, 266, 271, 273–74, 276,
　279, 281–82
　ambassador, 77, 139, 224
　Army
　　School of the Americas, 74, 83,
　　　191
　banks, 27, 32
　Customs and Immigration, 119
　corporations, 25
　Department of State, Office of the
　　Historian, 16, 18, 28
　Embassy, 13, 226, 288
　federal court, 121
　financial policy, 28, 40
　forces, 33, 38–39, 45
　foreign policy, 16
　House of Representatives,
　　Democrats in, 182, 285
　imperialiam, 17, 28, 43
　intervention and war, 4
　investments, 82
　Marines, 8, 10, 26, 28–29, 31, 35,
　　36, 38, 43, 77, 90; as defenders
　　of U.S. Capital, 16–48
　Navy, 8, 20
　Navy SEALS, 31
　Organization of American States, 68
　press, 113, 124, 132
　Secretary of State, 22, 65, 121
　Special Forces, 31
　State Department, 16, 27, 51,
　　56–59, 106, 129, 149, 27–74,
　　276, 280
UPI, 122, 123, 281
Uruguay, 12, 68
USAID, 162, 199–201, 225, 249, 290
USSR, 79, 120, 133, 142
USW, 150

V

Vampire, 52–53
Venezuela, 177, 185, 189, 196,
　204–205, 222–23, 248, 251, 290
veteran, 4, 64
Veterans Peace Convoy, 119, 121–22,
　170
Vice President, 6, 148
Vietnam, 4, 45, 76, 108, 119, 132,
　142, 177, 282
violence, 8, 19–20, 38, 40, 42, 52,
　81, 85, 117, 135, 163–64, 174,
　181–83, 188, 192, 194, 197,
　199, 204, 207–209, 211, 213–16,
　218–19, 221–22, 224–25,
　228–30, 234–35, 239–40, 267,
　269

W

Walker (film), 20
Walker, William, 20–21, 219, 274
Wall Street, 29, 35, 82, 277
war, 4, 6, 8, 11, 14, 40, 43–45, 48,
　59, 64, 67–69, 74, 76, 80, 89,
　93, 96, 101, 103–104, 107–108,
　110, 114, 116, 122–23, 127–30,
　132–39, 146–48, 150, 163–64,
　171–73, 177, 180, 191, 193, 195,
　199, 230, 253, 254, 257, 262–63,
　282
warships, 18, 20
Washington, 20, 22, 25, 27, 32, 48,
　51, 56–58, 67, 83, 102, 122, 137,
　192, 195, 206, 222, 225, 227,
　230, 248, 273, 276, 277, 281,
　287–89
weapons, 30, 66, 87, 125, 127, 135,
　205, 222–23, 232
West, 65, 103, 134, 156, 158–59, 172,
　226, 254, 264
Western press, 172
White House, 105, 132, 268
Willson, S. Brian, viii, 4–6, 48,
　144–46, 199
Wisconsin, 146

Washington Office on Latin America
 (WOLA), 122–123
women, 9, 30, 43, 47, 52, 61–62, 73,
 87, 94–96, 99–101, 105–106,
 118, 155, 164, 168, 172, 179–80,
 183, 186–89, 225, 257, 259–60,
 265, 269, 285
World War II, 12, 134

Y
Yankee, 9, 35, 40, 141
Yankee troops, 9

Z
Zelaya, José Santos, 22–27, 91
Zelaya, Manuel, 191-92
Zeledón, 32–35